MYSTERIES OF THE HOPEWELL

Astronomers, Geometers, and Magicians of the Eastern Woodlands

SERIES ON OHIO HISTORY AND CULTURE

John H. White and Robert J. White, Sr., *The Island Queen: Cincinnati's Excursion Steamer*

H. Roger Grant, *Ohio's Railway Age in Postcards*

Frances McGovern, *Written on the Hills: The Making of the Akron Landscape*

Keith McClellan, *The Sunday Game: At the Dawn of Professional Football*

Steve Love and David Giffels, *Wheels of Fortune: The Story of Rubber in Akron*

Alfred Winslow Jones, *Life, Liberty, and Property: A Story of Conflict and a Measurement of Conflicting Rights*

David Brendan Hopes, *A Childhood in the Milky Way: Becoming a Poet in Ohio*

John Keim, *Legends by the Lake: The Greatest Games, Players, and Coaches of the Cleveland Browns*

Richard B. Schwartz, *The Biggest City in America: A Fifties Boyhood*

Tom Rumer, *Unearthing the Land: The Story of Ohio's Scioto Marsh*

Ian Adams, Barney Taxel, and Steve Love, *Stan Hywet Hall and Gardens*

William F. Romain, *Mysteries of the Hopewell: Astronomers, Geometers, and Magicians of the Eastern Woodlands*

MYSTERIES OF THE HOPEWELL

Astronomers, Geometers, and Magicians of the Eastern Woodlands

WILLIAM F. ROMAIN

The University of Akron Press  Akron, Ohio

Manufactured in the United States of America

First Edition 2000

04 03 02 01 00   5 4 3 2 1

LIBRARY OF CONGRESS CATALOGING-IN-PUBLICATION DATA
Romain, William F., 1948–
    Mysteries of the Hopewell : astronomers, geometers, and
magicians of the eastern woodlands / William F. Romain.—1st ed.
        p.   cm. — (Ohio history and culture)
    Includes bibliographical referencs and index.
    ISBN 1-884836-61-5 (cloth : alk. paper)
        1. Hopewell culture.   2. Indian astronomy—Ohio.   3. Indians of
North America—Ohio—Mathematics.   4. Ohio—Antiquities.
    I. Title.   II. Series.
    E99.H69 R65   2000
    977.1'01–dc21
                                                        00-055959

The paper used in this publication meets the minimum requirements
of American National Standard for Information Sciences—Perma-
nence of Paper for Printed Library Materials, ANSI Z39.48-1984.
♾

This book is dedicated to my mother, Frances Spania-Rothenberg, who, always and in every possible way, supported and encouraged me in my quest to know the past and to my wife, Evie Romain, who always brought a smile to my face.

CONTENTS

PREFACE

Arguments against new ideas generally pass through three distinct stages,
from "It's not true", to "Well, it may be true, but it's not important", to "It's
true and it's important, but it's not new—we knew it all along."
        —John D. Barrow, astronomer

It is the theory that decides what we can observe.
        —Albert Einstein

Looking back on it, now, it all seems quite remarkable. Understandably, then, there will be people who doubt what follows. Nevertheless, I must tell of my findings that show, beyond any reasonable doubt, that the Native Americans who lived here—in eastern North America some two thousand years ago—were accomplished in astronomy, geometry, measuring, and counting.

Having said this, I think it is virtually certain that a handful of archaeologists will object that I have ventured too deeply into the realm of speculation, while those who are more intuitively inclined will not be happy with my emphasis on certain technical aspects of astronomy, geometry, and mathematics. And, too, no one will be happy with my reliance, in some instances, on maps and data that are more than a hundred years old.

My response is that I have tried to take the middle ground. Too often archaeologists forget that one of our objectives is the reconstruction of past lifeways. To the extent that it is possible, this includes the reconstruction of belief systems, religions, and ideology. Deductive reasoning, inference, and analogy are often the tools we use to accomplish this objective. The difficult part is to recognize when we are entering the realm of speculation—and if we do, then to state that what we are offering is opinion rather than fact. In this book, I have tried to do just that. That is, I have tried to identify and separate speculation and opinion from fact. I will leave it to the reader to judge how successful I have been.

For those who are inclined to an intuitive view of the world, part 2 of this book should make the journey worthwhile. I should point out, however, that the opinions I express in part 2 are not based in any personal belief in mysticism, sacred power, a personal God, or gods, but in the idea that, because the human brain is basically structured the same among all humankind, many of the ways in which we perceive and react to the world around us are likewise the same (see, for example, D'Aquili, Laughlin, and McManus 1979; Laughlin and D'Aquili 1974).

Now, of course, I recognize that there are many wonderful examples of diversity that exist among us. And clearly, we do have differences both individually and culturally. However, my belief is that underneath it all, below the superficial trappings of whatever culture we are born into, we are fundamentally more alike than we are different. Our physical drives and needs, even our hopes and dreams and fears, are pretty much the same across humanity.

Admittedly, some may consider this to be a naive or simplistic point of view. But if what I have just proposed is true, even to the slightest extent, then surely this gives us something of an intuitive ability to understand and relate to the thought processes of humankind across time.

Finally, to those who might protest my occasional use of maps and data generated by nineteenth century surveyors and explorers, like Ephraim G. Squier and Edwin H. Davis, I have to agree that I am also unhappy with this situation. However, because so many of the ancient

Hopewell sites have been destroyed, it sometimes happens that these old maps and data are all we have left. Now we could lament this loss, throw up our hands in despair, and make no effort to unravel the mysteries of the Hopewell. Or we can make the most out of what we have. For better or worse, I have chosen the latter path. Let it be known, however, that in all instances I have used the most accurate and complete data currently available. Along these lines too, I note for the record that the data presented in this book supercedes and, in a few instances, corrects some of my earlier published efforts.

In the pages to follow, I hope to bring some new ideas to the world of Hopewell archaeology. Perhaps some of these ideas will find general acceptance. Others may not. This is the way of science, and I accept that. In the meantime, though, I would like to leave the reader with the following thought.

The Hopewell preceded us by two thousand years. In evolutionary terms, two thousand years is not a very long time. Moreover, from everything the physical anthropologists can tell us, there is no reason to think that the people of two thousand years ago were any less intelligent or clever than we are today. Indeed, we can assume that the Hopewell were our cognitive equals.

If we accept the idea that the Hopewell were our cognitive equals, then it becomes easier to accept the idea that the Hopewell, too, might have developed their own systems of astronomy, geometry, measuring, and counting. After all, such matters are not the exclusive domain of Western culture. And certainly, many of the universal truths that are found in these mathematically based subjects are accessible to people of intelligence everywhere.

In the chapters to follow, I will explore these subjects with the idea in mind that, although there are certainly some differences in the ways of thinking between Western peoples and the Native Americans of two thousand years ago, there are nevertheless sufficient similarities in how we all look at the world that we will recognize in the Hopewell many of the more important facets of consciousness that we all have in common.

MYSTERIES OF THE HOPEWELL

Astronomers, Geometers, and Magicians of the Eastern Woodlands

INTRODUCTION

The question of questions for mankind—the problem which underlies all others, and which is more deeply interesting than any other—is the ascertainment of the place which Man occupies in nature and of his relations to the universe of things.

—Thomas Huxley

They're all dead now. But sometimes, in the early morning, when the fog is still hovering there in the valley and the ground is wet with dew, one can almost make out the ancient encampments of the Hopewell there in the shifting, changing mist. Other times it happens at night, when shadows from the fire flicker and dart about like wandering ghosts from some ancient, forgotten burial ground.

Spirits of the Old Ones who lived here? Powerful warriors or medicine men who once knew this land as their home? No—surely such images are tricks of the brain, illusions of the mind's eye. . . .

Still, this is the land of the Hopewell—Native Americans whose powers of mind and spirit reached deep into unexplored realms. Indeed, the Hopewell were a special people who, to a greater extent than any of the peoples in eastern North America who preceded them, unlocked the secrets of geometry, developed a sophisticated system of measurement, and even came to understand the great cycles of the sun and moon. These were tremendous accomplishments of the mind and spirit that have almost been forgotten, almost lost in the shadows of time.

Sometimes, especially in some of the earlier literature, one finds the Hopewell referred to as the "Mound Builders." The term "Mound Builder," however, can also be used to refer to the earlier Adena Indians as well as the later Mississippian Indians—all of whom also built mounds. And so, throughout this book we will refer to the people who we are concerned with as the Hopewell.

In chronological terms, it has been about fifteen hundred years since the Hopewell people lived. Their time on this earth was brief, from sometime around 100 B.C. to about A.D. 400 or 500. From what we can tell, the Hopewell lived in small, scattered hamlets that surrounded their great ceremonial centers (Pacheco 1996; Dancey 1992). Most likely, each hamlet was made up of one or maybe a few extended families.

The Hopewell were hunters and gatherers. But they were also agriculturalists. In fact, to a greater extent than any other people in eastern North America, the Hopewell were responsible for accelerating the change from food gathering to food producing economies (Smith 1992). The foods the Hopewell grew were not the same as what we eat. Their cultivated foods included marsh elder, maygrass, goosefoot, knotweed, and sunflower—mostly seed crops, although gourds and some small amounts of corn were also grown.

The Hopewell were farmers. But that does not mean they were parochial or provincial. Quite the contrary. The Hopewell were wide-ranging in their contacts, with a resource network that reached for hundreds of miles in all directions—north to Lake Superior, south to the Florida Gulf Coast, east to the Carolinas, and west to the Rocky Mountains. From these distant places, the Hopewell imported huge quantities of precious materials that included copper, silver, mica, obsidian, quartz, and even alligator and shark teeth. The Hopewell then fashioned these materials into some of the finest examples of craftsmanship ever seen—beautiful creations that include delicate musical panpipes, effigy smoking pipes, copper breastplates, rings and bracelets, pearl-covered blankets, ornate headdresses, and other rare works of art.

We know that the Hopewell were accomplished in agriculture

and fine craftsmanship. Only now, though, are we beginning to appreciate the full extent of their accomplishments in other areas, such as plane geometry, measurement, arithmetic, and observational astronomy.

Such were the golden days of the Hopewell. As happens with all things, however, the Hopewell disappeared. Like fireflies in the night, their individual points of consciousness burned bright for a moment, only to merge again with the transcendental. Most likely, we will never know the life histories of those individual points of light. But from what the Hopewell left behind, it may be possible to gain some sense of their worldview or their vision of the universe. Indeed, that is my purpose here.

In the pages to follow, we will probe the boundaries of the Hopewell worldview. We will bring to life ancient symbols that held deep truths for their creators, and in so doing, touch a way of life that is now forever lost. In the pages to follow, we will travel to a time and place where things were explained by myth and where the otherworld was as close as the imagination.

For our own part, we have come close to answering the big questions—the origin of life, the nature of consciousness, the creation of the universe. Quantum physics, relativity, and biochemistry have given us a deep understanding of the world around us. Self-organizing complex adaptive systems, superstring theories, neurochemical driven consciousness—these are some of the ideas that make up much of today's worldview. So why then, the skeptic might ask, should we study the worldview of an ancient people long dead? What possible value or relevance can there be to such a study?

One answer is that such inquiries provide us with a point of reference. Like all people, including those who have gone before us, we have a fundamental need as a species, I think, to know how we fit into the scheme of things. Studies of ancient people like the Hopewell, therefore, help us to better define our place in the universe.

Additionally though, there is a more immediate and more pressing reason to study the worldview of a long-ago people. Hopewell culture as we know it came to an end sometime around A.D. 500. In Ohio, the building of the great geometric earthworks stopped. The vast Hopewell trade network fell apart. The manufacture of exotic goods ceased. With the collapse of these components the golden days of the Hopewell were over.

But why did the Hopewell way of life end? Did they suffer a plague, or a succession of droughts, or floods? Did warfare or internal conflict lead to their demise? Or did the Hopewell overexploit the finite resources of their valley homelands? If we can learn what happened to the Hopewell, then maybe we can avoid a similar fate. Maybe it's not too late. Or is it? Anthropologist Loren Eiseley once observed that, "Modern man, the world eater, respects no space and no thing green or furred as sacred. The march of the machines has entered his blood" (Eiseley 1970:70). In our rush toward civilization, we have eroded the ozone layer, destroyed the rain forests, and polluted our rivers and streams. Worse yet, we continue to overpopulate what is really a very small planet with billions of our own species.

Perhaps our greatest evil, though, has been to cause the extinction of thousands of plant and animal species. And it is not just a matter of having destroyed some obscure little plant that might hold a cure for cancer or AIDS. Equally significant is that we have forever lessened the genetic diversity and potential of our world. Extinct life-forms have no opportunity for growth. Now their possibilities are zero.

And how do we justify such behavior toward living beings that share this world with us? Language researcher Susan Savage-Rumbaugh and author Roger Lewin explain, "Man's ability to exploit the planet, to take its resources as he needs, and to usurp entire forests and all living creatures therein, rests upon the unwritten assumption that the chasm between himself and all other creatures is impassable" (Savage-Rumbaugh and Lewin 1994:20). Contrast this view with the traditional beliefs of Native Americans who tell us of an ancient time when animals and humans could talk to each other—a distant time when animals and humans shared the same language, feelings, and thought processes. Perhaps we will one day appreciate the attitude of the Native

Americans, as we become more cognizant that self-reflective awareness and consciousness are not unique or possessed only by human beings.

Perhaps, too, by studying the Hopewell, we can bring back something that will benefit our world. Maybe we can bring back something that will help ensure our survival.

Having said all this, we can learn much about the Hopewell from a study of their sacred or religious structures. For reasons I will discuss, it often happens that people will symbolically encode many of their beliefs into their sacred architecture. In the case of the Hopewell, their sacred structures take the form of huge, geometrically shaped enclosures, various kinds of platform mounds, burial mounds, charnel houses, and walled passageways or avenues.

This is not to say that the Hopewell were the only people who built such structures. Indeed, the tradition of earthwork and mound building has its origins deep in the Archaic period of eastern North America, at such places as Poverty Point and Watson Brake. But it was the Ohio Hopewell who, at least in the Middle Woodland period, brought the tradition of earthwork building to unprecedented heights of accomplishment.

Sadly, most of the structures that were built by the Hopewell have long since been erased by time or overrun by our own civilization. But enough remains to tell us that, in their pristine form, the earthworks were built in the shapes of tremendous circles, squares, and octagons. Like the ancient Greeks who built their temples to Pythagorean proportions, or the stonemasons of the Renaissance who built their cathedrals to Vitruvian proportions, the Hopewell had a deep fascination with geometry. And, too, like their contemporaries in the Western world, the Hopewell built their sacred structures to tremendous size.

The Hopewell thought big. They thought big thoughts about a big universe, and their architecture reflects this grandeur. Most often, the Hopewell earthworks enclose dozens upon dozens of acres. Each figure is made up of walls that, even when rediscovered some two hundred years ago, were anywhere from six to twenty feet in height, and twenty to fifty feet in width at their base. Some idea of the tremendous

size of these earthworks is given by the photos shown in figures 1.1 and
1.2. These are the famous Newark Earthworks. Located near Newark,
Ohio, these earthworks were built by the Hopewell people. And while
most of the geometric enclosures are not quite as big as these; some are
even bigger, such as the Liberty Large Circle and the Marietta Large
Square.

FIG. 1.1. Aerial view of the Newark Octagon and Observatory Circle. *Photo by the author.*

FIG. I.2. Aerial view of the Newark Fairground Circle. *Photo by the author.*

In the territory that was Hopewell, millions of tons of earth and hundreds of miles of embankments were moved and shaped by generations of people—united across time, in a common goal and a shared vision. Throughout the ages, there have been only a few forces sufficient to command such efforts. War is one such force, while religion, with its promise of eternal life, is another.

For the Hopewell, the driving force behind their monumental architecture appears to have been religion. The essence of their religion or worldview was shamanistic. In this shamanistic worldview, time and space could be traversed by telepathy, it was possible to communicate with all that is, and everything was interrelated and connected in a universal field of magic.

Most likely, shamanistic beliefs were carried to North America by the very first visitors who crossed the Bering Strait. What distinguished the Hopewell from their predecessors, however, was that through their shamanic journeys, the Hopewell came to know something very special about the fabric of the universe. What they discovered was that this fabric can be described in the language of plane geometry, arithmetic, measurement, and observational astronomy. Using this knowledge, the Hopewell built tremendous symbols of their universe in the shape of the geometric enclosures. They then tied these symbols into the great solar and lunar cycles of time through a unique alignment system.

The real magic, however, took place inside the symbols. For as I will show, it was within these earthen symbols that the Hopewell engaged in the most important of their ceremonies, ceremonies that were concerned with the deepest of all mysteries, including passage from this world to the next, death and rebirth, world renewal, and creation.

Part One

PHYSICAL PARAMETERS

Chapter 1

THE ENCHANTED VALLEY

We saw the Great Spirit's work in almost everything: sun, moon, trees, wind, and mountains. Sometimes we approached him through these things. Was that so bad?

—Walking Buffalo, *Every Part of This Earth Is Sacred*

For most living creatures, certain places are special. Deep in our primate memory, we can recall a time when we cautiously made our way to a favorite pond or stream. There, life-giving water awaited us. Or maybe it was at the end of a day in the forest when we scurried about, looking for a hiding place to sleep, secure in some enclosed and protected space.

These were special places, and as we developed as a species, our special places became sacred. Indeed, as our experience and explorations continued, we found physical settings that evoked all kinds of feelings—peace and serenity, pleasure and power, or a merging with nature. We learned that certain places like the caves at Altamira, or the peaks of Mount Shasta and Sinai, or the rivers of the Ganges and Amazon could bring us closer to the transcendental. We declared these places magical or sacred and built either on them or near them—churches, temples, and shrines.

There are many kinds of sacred space and many reasons for

declaring a space sacred. Some places are sacred because they inspire us to great thoughts or transcendental feelings in their beauty or majesty. Yet other places manifest the spirit world in the unusual rock formations, plants, or animals that are found there, thus triggering in us a sense of mystery that can only be explained by the divine. J. Donald Hughes summed it up in the following way: "Sacred space is where human beings find a manifestation of divine power, where they experience a sense of connectedness to the universe. There, in some special way, spirit is present to them" (Hughes quoted in Suzuki and Knudtson 1992:152).

The first step then, was to mark those places that were sacred. Where sacred space revealed itself, we built incredible structures like Stonehenge, the Pyramids, Machu Picchu, and countless other marvels. In essence, these structures identified and celebrated those places where the material world and the spirit world overlapped or merged into one another. In such places, priests, medicine men, and magicians were able to transcend the boundaries of the material world and normal consciousness and enter the world of spirit. As explained by Nigel Pennick, "where the boundaries between the material and non-material, the living and the dead, past, present, and future, are thin or confused, are the places where shamanism, the oracular arts and sacred rites are best performed"(Pennick 1989:106).

The Hopewell, too, had their sacred places where they made contact with the spirit world. And it was in those places that they built their ceremonial centers, geometric earthworks, and burial mounds. By looking at how such man-made features relate to the surrounding land, we can surmise that the Hopewell found the sacred manifested in many of the same places that humanity has found special since the beginning. Such places include the locus of intersecting physiographic areas and biotic zones, near certain rivers, at or near river confluences, near special outcroppings of rock, and on certain hilltops. As we will see, there is something special in the immediate area of each and every Hopewell earthwork, something special that suggests the sacred, or the transcendental.

INTERSECTING PHYSIOGRAPHIC
AND BIOTIC ZONES

Sometimes it happens that an entire large-scale area is special. Shangri-la and the Garden of Eden come to mind. But closer to home, the Grand Canyon, the Niagara Gorge, and the Shenandoah Valley are also areas that evoke feelings of specialness. I mention these places in particular because what they have in common is that they are valleys of one sort or another. We like valleys. We enjoy their scenic views and cherish their promise of serenity. Perhaps the feeling goes back again to a primate sense of protectedness in space that is enclosed, whether by mountains, walls, or other kinds of boundaries. So, too, it might have been for at least one group of Hopewell people who centered their culture in the Ross County-Scioto River Valley.

If the leaders of some ancient Indian tribe were to choose a home for their people, then surely the Ross County-Scioto River Valley must have seemed like paradise (see figure 1.1). Generations later, the white man, too, would center himself in this valley—in the first Ohio capital city of Chillicothe. And for both the red man and the white man, there were good reasons for doing so.

To begin with, the entire valley is blessed with a temperate climate and an abundance of sunshine, punctuated at just the right time by fairly predictable rains. For those who enjoy crunching the hard data, the valley averages three to five miles in width and is about fifty miles in length from Chillicothe to Portsmouth. The average annual temperature at Chillicothe is about fifty-four degrees Fahrenheit, with a mean January temperature of about thirty-two degrees Fahrenheit. The growing season is roughly 173 days in length, and the annual growing season precipitation averages about fifteen inches (Maslowski and Seeman 1992:11).

The centerpiece of this little valley, however, is the powerful Scioto River which reaches 180 miles from north of Columbus, south to the Ohio River. Along the banks of this river are some of the most productive and fertile soils in the country. So much so, in fact, that at one

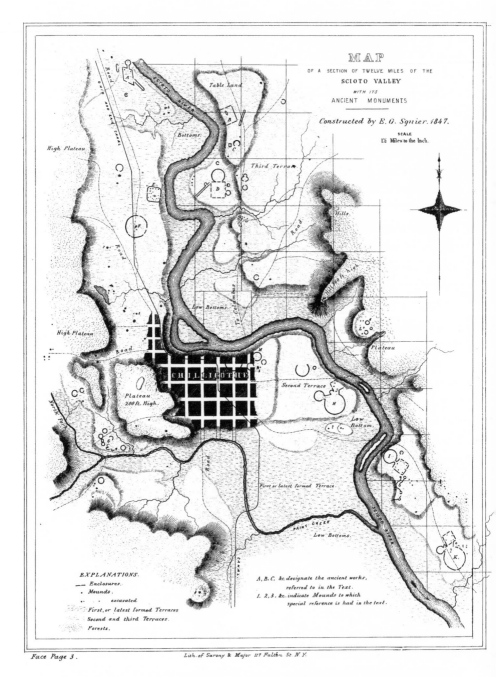

FIG. I.I. *Squier and Davis's (1848:plate 2) map of the Ross County, Scioto River Valley area.*

time the lower Scioto River Valley was nicknamed Little Egypt, recalling the fertility of the Nile Valley.

Flanking the Scioto River to the east and west, starting around Chillicothe and proceeding southward to the Ohio River, are gentle mountains with thousands of acres of forest. These mountains and forests, in turn, feed a shower of tributaries with names like Sunfish, Beaver, Walnut, Deer, Salt, and Brush Creeks. For the Hopewell, the Scioto River and its tributaries provided an abundance of food and fresh water, as well as easy access to more distant places.

Certainly, the entire length of the Scioto Valley is idyllic enough. And given its picturesque setting and interrelated network of earthworks and mounds, it might just as easily have been named the "enchanted valley." What made this river valley really special, though, was its diversity of microenvironments.

For reasons I will explain, this diversity was especially apparent in the immediate Chillicothe area. And so it is here, in the Chillicothe area of the Scioto River Valley, that we find evidence of a Hopewell presence. To be sure, there were other important Hopewell centers such as those at Marietta, Moundsville, Portsmouth, and Newark. And, too, there were other groups of Hopewell scattered across most of eastern North America—in Illinois, Indiana, Kentucky, Tennessee, and even Kansas. But it is here, in the Chillicothe area of Ohio, where we find the majority of the geometric earthworks that are the focus of this investigation.

Within a four-mile radius of downtown Chillicothe, for example, we find the geometrically shaped earthworks of Dunlap, Cedar Bank, Hopeton, Mound City, Shriver, High Bank, and the Works East. If we increase the radius of our compass by just a few more miles but still remain within the boundaries of Ross County, we can include the Anderson, Hopewell, Seip, Baum, Liberty, and Frankfort Earthworks.

In technical terms, the uniqueness of the Chillicothe area comes from its special location at the intersection of several major physiographic and biotic zones. More specifically, the Chillicothe area is situated: (1) at the border between the Mississippian and Devonian bedrock systems; (2) at the edge of the farthest extent of the Illinoisan and Wisconsin glaciations; (3) at the boundary between the Central Lowland and Appalachian Plateau provinces; (4) near the boundaries of the Till Plains, Glaciated Appalachian Plateau, and Unglaciated Appalachian Plateau physiographic regions; (5) near the juncture of three major soil types; and (6) at the intersection of three major forest types (Romain 1993; see also Maslowski and Seeman 1992; Shane 1971; Prufer and Shane 1970).

Of course, to the Native Americans who lived in the Chillicothe area these formal classification schemes of Western science would have mattered little. What was important was the real-life, synergistic effect of these physiographic and biotic zones. Here, the action of recurring glaciations on the underlying bedrock resulted in a tremendous diversity of topography and soil types. These differing soil types and topographies, in turn, affect the kinds of plants that will grow in each microenvironment. Thus, in the Chillicothe area, there is a wide variety of forest types, including a cottonwood/willow shoreline forest, a floodplain swamp forest, a white oak/sugar maple mesophytic forest, and an upland mixed oak forest (Maslowski and Seeman 1992:11). Different animals, of course, prefer different environments. White-tailed deer, black bears, bobcats, raccoons, turkey vultures, and timber rattlesnakes, for example, prefer the upland mixed oak forests, while minks, beavers, wood ducks, and snapping turtles prefer shoreline forests.

From the upland forests of the surrounding mountains to the prairie openings and floodplains of the Scioto, thousands of different plant and animal species are found in their own little niches. In an environment like this, if a particular resource fails or is depleted, then one can, in theory, draw upon another. This diversity helped ensure the survival of all who settled in the valley.

These are some of the factors that no doubt made the Scioto River Valley and the Chillicothe area in particular seem like a bit of paradise. Thus the Scioto Hopewell centered themselves in this enchanted valley, and probably considered the mountains and the river sacred, and called the valley home.

RIVERS OF LIFE

Water is a peculiar thing. In its liquid form, it flows and saturates and engulfs. But it can also appear as a mist, a vapor, or a fog. So, too, water seeps and gushes from the earth and falls from the sky. In either case, the changeable form of water creates entire worlds of fishes, plants without air, and strange life-forms with gills and webbed feet.

But these things are not what make water really special. What makes water really special is its life-giving essence. Water is crucial to all creatures and all life. At the microscopic level, water maintains cell equilibrium and makes possible the transfer of nutrients. Indeed, water makes organic life wet and messy. But without it, there would be no living matter as we know it—no plants, no animals, no human beings.

As a people, we have long recognized the life-giving essence of water, and in that recognition we have made certain springs, rivers, and lakes sacred. Ritual bathing, baptisms, and anointings recall our ancient association of water with life. Perhaps the Mascouten Indian quoted by Skinner said it best: "When the Great Spirit created mankind he dipped his finger in water and put it in their mouths. Therefore, water is life. It has perpetual motion; it is the blood in our bodies. It is the life in our hearts. Our hearts are only wind and water moving" (Skinner 1924:217).

As I will explain in a later chapter, there are good reasons to suspect that the Hopewell, too, recognized the life-giving essence of water, even to the extent of incorporating its symbolism into the ceremonial function of their geometric earthworks and their burial mounds. For now, though, suffice it to say that virtually all of the major geometric enclosures are located in close proximity to water.

Table 1 provides the exact distances that separate some of the major geometric enclosures from the nearest river or stream. As can be seen, the average of these distances is a mere 1,270 feet, or less than one quarter of a mile. As to whether or not these distances are reflective of the distances that separated the enclosures from the water some two thousand years ago, the following observations can be made.

Geologically, the Scioto River is a mature stream. As such, it has a

Table 1. Distances from geometric earthworks to nearest major water source

Geometric Earthwork	Distance to Water Source (in feet)	Water Source
Anderson	2,300	N Fork Paint Creek
Baum	2,200	Paint Creek
Cedar Bank	400	Scioto River
Circleville	700	Hargus Creek
Dunlap	600	Scioto River
Frankfort	1,200	N Fork Paint Creek
High Bank	1,000	Scioto River
Hopeton	1,700	Scioto River
Hopewell	900	N Fork Paint Creek
Liberty	5,000	Walnut Creek
Marietta	1,400	Muskingum River
Milford	1,600	E Fork Little Miami River
Mound City	200	Scioto River
Newark Octagon	400	Raccoon Creek
Seal	600	Scioto River
Seip	300	Paint Creek
Shriver	3,100	Scioto River
Turner	1,000	Little Miami River
Works East	0	Scioto River

tendency to meander across the bottom lands. Accordingly, the Scioto River and its tributaries may have changed course or meandered by a few feet here and there in relation to the earthworks. However, since these changes may just as easily have brought the Scioto closer as farther away from the Hopewell sites, we can surmise that the distances noted in table 1 are probably, on average, fairly representative of the distances from the water to the enclosures during Hopewell times. Given this, it is apparent that the Hopewell intended to locate their geometric enclosures close to flowing water. Quite literally, the geometric enclosures are all within a stone's throw of nearby rivers and streams.

RIVER CONFLUENCES

If the life-giving quality of water is apparent in the flow of a nearby river or stream, then surely its essence must be multiplied where two rivers or streams come together. Such locations are also convenient as meeting places where people can get together. For these reasons and perhaps others, we often find that many of the geometric earthworks are also located close to major river confluences.

The magnificent Newark Earthworks, for example, are located in a pretty little valley where Raccoon Creek and the north and south forks of the Licking River come together, while the Circleville Earthwork is located only seven hundred feet southeast of the confluence of Hargus Creek and the Scioto River.

Continuing down the Scioto, just past downtown Chillicothe is the High Bank Earthwork. This unique structure is three quarters of a mile northeast of the confluence of Paint Creek and the Scioto River. The importance of this confluence is that Paint Creek leads directly to a number of major earthwork sites including Hopewell, Seip, Baum, Anderson, and Frankfort.

At the far end of the Scioto, at the confluence of the Scioto and Ohio Rivers, are the Portsmouth Earthworks. The importance of this confluence is that it marks the most direct approach by water to the Hopewell heartland from the south. That the significance of this gateway location was well recognized by the Hopewell is suggested by the fact that when first surveyed, the Portsmouth Earthworks extended along at least seven miles of the Ohio River, on both sides of the confluence, and included about twenty miles of embankment walls (Squier and Davis 1848:77–78).

Located just a few miles northeast of Cincinnati are the Turner Earthworks. Turner was a major Hopewell site, nestled in one of the most peaceful little valleys I have ever seen. Notably, the Turner Earthworks are located just one-half mile southwest of the confluence of the Little Miami River and its east fork. Both the Little Miami and its east fork are major waterways that penetrate deep into Ohio territory.

Last, we find that the Marietta Earthworks are located at the confluence of the Muskingum and Ohio Rivers. What probably made Marietta important to the Hopewell was that this confluence marks the most direct approach by water, via the Muskingum River, from the Ohio River to the Newark and Flint Ridge areas. Flint Ridge, in turn, was the source of a gem quality flint that was highly prized by Indians throughout the eastern Woodlands.

From this quick tour, we see that riverbanks and river confluences were preferred locations for many of the geometric enclosures. In fact, as table 1 shows, at least nineteen major Hopewell earthworks are located in close proximity to water.

RIVER TERRACES AND SPECIAL SOILS

The observation that the geometric enclosures are located along rivers has two very interesting associated findings. First is that most of the enclosures along the Scioto River and its tributaries are located on a specific river terrace level. Second is that almost all of the enclosures along the Scioto River and its tributaries are located in zones of a very specific soil type.

After the last glaciation, the Scioto and other southern Ohio rivers eroded their way down through layers of glacial outwash. In this way, a series of very flat and increasingly lower river terraces were formed. Figure 1.2 shows an idealized representation of these formations. As can be seen, there are three major terrace levels in Ross County and surrounding areas. These levels are usually referred to simply as the lower, middle, and upper terraces.

Surprisingly enough, in every place where these terrace levels exist, it also happens that almost every major geometric enclosure is located on the middle terrace level. The Hopewell could have built their geometric earthworks on the lower or the upper terrace levels, or even in the sur-

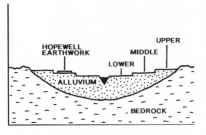

FIG. 1.2. Profile view of the Scioto River Valley showing the three major river terraces. *Drawing by the author.*

Table 2. Locations of selected Hopewell geometric enclosures

Site	USGS Quadrangle	Geographical Coordinates
Anderson	Chillicothe West	39°21'52"N x 83°03'35"W
Baum	Bourneville	39°15'27"N x 83°09'14"W
Circleville	Circleville	39°36'04"N x 82°56'35"W
Dunlap	Andersonville	39°24'41"N x 83°00'04"W
Frankfort	Frankfort	39°24'14"N x 83°10'58"W
High Bank	Chillicothe West	39°17'53"N x 82°55'04"W
Hopeton	Kingston	39°23'07"N x 83°58'42"W
Hopewell	Chillicothe West	39°21'41"N x 83°05'23"W
Liberty	Chillicothe East	39°15'27"N x 82°52'40"W
Marietta Large Square	Marietta	39°25'30"N x 81°27'36"W
Milford	Madeira	39°10'17"N x 84°16'35"W
Mound City	Andersonville	39°22'35"N x 83°00'16"W
Newark Fairground Circle	Newark	40°02'28"N x 82°25'53"W
Newark Observatory Circle	Newark	39°03'08"N x 82°26'56"W
Newark Octagon	Newark	40°03'18"N x 82°26'39"W
Portsmouth Circle	Portsmouth	38°44'05"N x 82°56'17"W
Seal	Wakefield	38°59'34"N x 83°01'31"W
Seip	Morgantown	39°14'15"N x 83°13'12"W
Shriver	Chillicothe West	39°22'01"N x 83°00'21"W
Tremper	Tremper	38°48'05"N x 83°00'37"W
Turner	Madeira	39°08'45"N x 84°18'39"W
Works East	Chillicothe East	39°19'26"N x 83°55'44"W

rounding higher upland or tableland areas. But instead, they chose to build on the middle terrace. A look at the relevant USGS 7.5 minute series topographic maps (see table 2) shows this to be the case for the Baum, Dunlap, Frankfort, High Bank, Hopeton, Liberty, Mound City, Seal, Seip, and Shriver Earthworks.

As to the reason for this preference for building on the middle terrace, my guess is that the middle terrace, as compared to other areas, offered a good compromise. That is, the middle terrace provided flat, level land that was close to water but was also sufficiently elevated above its parent river so as to avoid most low-level flooding.

More to the point, flood level studies of the Scioto River (cited in

NPS 1979:19) tell us that the lowest river terrace will completely flood about once in every ten years. Partial flooding will occur even more often. On the other hand, the middle terrace level is completely flooded only about once in every fifty to one hundred years. Surely, the Hopewell would not want to see their earthen enclosures washed away by floodwaters.

The second observation, alluded to above, is that several different kinds of soils are found on the middle terrace level. Interestingly enough, however, almost all of the geometrically shaped enclosures (in Ross County, at least) are located in areas predominantly made up of one soil. This soil is known as Fox.

My discovery of this peculiar fact came about in the following way. First, I located and plotted all of the known major Hopewell geometric enclosures found in Ross County onto soil survey maps developed for the area by the U.S. Department of Agriculture Soil Conservation Service and the Ohio Department of Natural Resources (Petro, Shumate, and Tabb 1967; ODNR 1962). These very detailed maps show the various soils, as well as slope and erosion information for each mapping unit. Essentially, each map is an aerial photograph that covers either four or six square miles. Soil, slope, and erosion data, as determined by extensive and detailed ground survey and on-site testing by the Soil Conservation Service, is then printed on to the aerial photos. Using these maps, it was a simple matter to determine what specific soils are found within each enclosure. Figure 1.3 presents a composite assemblage of the soil map sections I used for this analysis, while table 3 summarizes the data. More to the point, table 3 shows that out of twelve Ross County geometric enclosures examined, at least ten are located in areas predominantly made up of Fox series soils.

This finding takes on special significance when we consider that Fox soils make up only about 28 percent of the total acreage of the floodplains and outwash terraces of the Scioto and its tributaries (Petro, Shumate, and Tabb 1967:3). Many other soils are also found on the river terraces, including such soils as Warsaw, Sleeth, Casco, Rodman, Warners, and Willette. But again, the geometric enclosures are not located

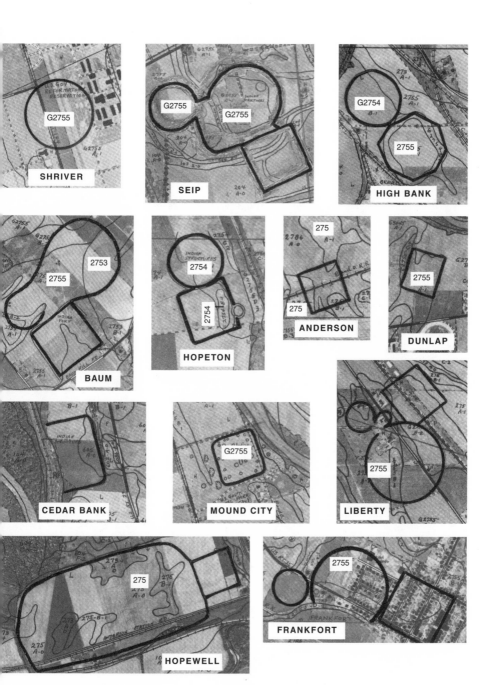

FIG. 1.3. Soil map sections for Hopewell sites in Ross County, Ohio. Fox series soils are identified by the numbers 275, 2751, 2753, 2754, G2754, 2755, and G2755. *Hopewell earthworks drawn in by the author; soil maps from ODNR 1962.*

Table 3. Site-soil associations for Ross County geometric enclosures

Site	Soil	Percent of Site	Slope (in percent)
Anderson	Westland silt clay loam	70	0–2
	Fox loam	15	2–6
	Fox silt loam	10	2–6
	Fox silt loam	5	0–2
Baum	Fox loam	55	0–2
	Fox sandy loam	20	0–2
	Mentor very fine sandy loam	15	0–2
	Fox gravelly loam	10	2–6
Cedar Bank	Kendallville silt loam	60	2–6
	Kendallville silt loam	40	0–2
Dunlap	Fox loam	100	0–2
Frankfort	Fox loam	60	0–2
	Fox loam	40	2–6
High Bank	Fox loam	50	0–2
	Fox sandy loam	40	2–6
	Fox loam	10	2–6
Hopeton	Ockley silt loam	50	0–2
	Fox sandy loam	40	0–2
	Fox sandy loam	10	2–6
Hopewell	Fox silt loam	90	0–2
	Fox silt loam	<10	2–6
	Thackery silt loam	<10	0–2
Liberty	Fox loam	50	0–2
	Fox gravelly loam	40	2–6
	Fox loam	10	2–6
Mound City	Fox gravelly loam	100	0–2
Seip	Fox gravelly loam	60	0–2
	Wea silt loam	25	0–2
	Wea silt loam	5	2–6
	Eel silt loam	5	0–2
	Ross silt loam	5	2–6
Shriver	Fox gravelly loam	100	0–2

on these other soils. They are, instead, almost exclusively located on Fox series soils. In fact, the deliberate selection of Fox soils becomes even more apparent when we consider that Fox soils comprise only about 5 percent of the total acreage for Ross County (Petro, Shumate, and Tabb 1967:table 6).

Initially, I was puzzled over what made Fox soils so special. I had walked over miles and miles of river terrace earth, but nothing about the soils I encountered really stood out. What I needed was more data. More to the point, I needed engineering data.

As it happens, in today's world, engineering studies are usually done prior to most major construction projects like the building of shopping centers and commercial buildings. Moreover, such studies usually include detailed soil analyses.

Reviewing the available engineering and soil data for Ross County soils, I found that, as compared to other soils, Fox soils are very friable (Petro, Shumate, and Tabb 1967:87). This means that Fox soils are made up of an ideal combination of silt, clay, and sand which is loose but not too sandy. In other words, Fox soils are easy to work with and easy to build with. In contrast, upland soils are more clay-based, more subject to clodding, and more difficult to work and build with.

Here, then, was a possible answer as to why the Hopewell preferred Fox soils for the location of their enclosures. Certainly, the matter of friability would have been very important to the Hopewell, whose digging, scraping, and building tools were made of easily broken materials such as shell, bone, antler, and wood. Quite simply, Fox soils provided the Hopewell with the perfect building material.

INDIAN TRAILS

In science, it is often pointed out that "correlation does not necessarily imply causation," and certainly this is true. In the case of the Hopewell enclosures, however, there is an interesting correlation that I will leave to the reader to evaluate.

Earlier in this chapter, it was noted that the geometric enclosures are often located along rivers. Also located along these same rivers, though, are Indian trails that may have been in use for thousands of years. In many instances, these Indian trails pass directly through, or right next to, major Hopewell earthworks.

For example, one of the most important of the Indian trails was the Scioto Trail, or Warrior's Path. As explained by historian Frank Wilcox, this trail "was the Great Highway of the Shawnee from the neutral hunting ground of Kentucky to the fishing grounds of Sandusky Bay and Lake Erie; his use of it for predatory raids upon the early settlements of Kentucky and the flatboatmen of the Ohio gave it its name" (Wilcox 1933:69).

Actually, the Warrior's Path originated deep in the Southeast, in Cherokee country, passed across the Cumberland Gap, and then into Kentucky and northward to Ohio. From Portsmouth, the trail proceeded up along "the second bottom" of the Scioto River, north through Chillicothe, Circleville, Columbus, and finally to the Upper Sandusky, near Lake Erie.

Today, very little of the original trail can be seen because, as Wilcox (1933:69) explains, most of the Ohio section is covered by State Route 23. By using historic maps of the trail, in conjunction with modern topographic maps that show the exact location of State Route 23, however, it is possible to reconstruct the trail's likely location. Doing this, we find that the Scioto Trail passed either directly through or, quite literally, to within a few dozen feet of the Portsmouth, Seal, Liberty, High Bank, and Mound City enclosures. Major branches of the trail likewise passed immediately adjacent to the Cedar Bank and Circleville Earthworks.

At Chillicothe, a secondary trail branched off from the Warrior's Path and paralleled the north fork of Paint Creek. Notably, this trail too passed directly through or immediately next to several Hopewell sites— including Anderson, Hopewell, and Frankfort—while yet another secondary trail passed to within a few dozen feet of the Seip enclosure.

All together, at least eleven of the Scioto River Valley enclosures are located on major Indian trails. My own opinion is that these trails probably predate the Hopewell earthworks. If this is the case, then certainly these trails could have been used to facilitate the sort of pilgrimages or journeys that authorities like Bradley T. Lepper (1995) and Roger G. Kennedy (1994) believe were made to these sacred places.

SPECIAL OUTCROPPINGS OF ROCK

On a fateful day in prehistory, maybe two million years ago, one of our brighter ancestors picked up a rock, pondered its use for a moment, and sent it crashing into the world of toolmaking and tool using. Since that time and probably before, we have been fascinated by the color and feel of all kinds of rocks. From rocks and stones, we fashioned lethal points for our spears and arrows. Later, we built castles and monuments from stone. Where we found crystalline rocks or minerals, we discovered in those sparkling forms ways to tell the future. From the beginning, though, we almost always associated special rocks with the divine. Unusual rocks were gifts from the earth or gifts from the gods.

So, too, it might have been for the Hopewell, for we find quartz crystals, meteoric rocks, mica sheets, lumps of galena, and strange fossil rocks accompanying Hopewell burials to the otherworld. Moreover, we find several very important geometric enclosures located near significant outcroppings of some very special rocks.

FLINT AND THE NEWARK EARTHWORKS

The Newark Earthworks, for example, are located only nine miles from one of the most important resources the Hopewell had—namely, Flint Ridge flint. At first, nine miles may not seem especially close. But the valley that the Newark Earthworks are located in is the nearest valley of sufficient size to accommodate the tremendous earthworks that are located there.

For thousands of years, the quarries at Flint Ridge have provided a very unique, high quality flint that was chipped and flaked by the Hopewell into some of the most stunning examples of craftsmanship ever seen.

Beautiful, ceremonial spear points—bigger than a man's open hand—were made from this flint, as were thousands upon thousands of smaller, more utilitarian points and blades. Flint Ridge flint was traded across most of eastern North America and ultimately, it was one of the most important resources that the Hopewell had. No wonder they honored the area by building the tremendous earthworks we know as Newark.

PIPESTONE AND THE TREMPER EARTHWORK

Like Newark, the Tremper Earthwork is also located close to an important mineral resource. In this case, however, the mineral is Ohio pipestone.

As its name implies, pipestone has long been used to make smoking pipes. What makes this stone so suitable for pipe making is that it is fairly soft and easy to carve. Hence, it is a fairly easy job to hollow out pipe bowls and stems.

The Hopewell are well known for their beautifully carved effigy pipes. By far, the vast majority of the these pipes were made from Ohio pipestone. If the rituals of more recent Native Americans are any clue, then the Hopewell most likely used these pipes to offer prayers to the spirit world.

In any event, Ohio pipestone is found in a formation that extends across Scioto County, with outcroppings located in the eastern cliffs of Feurt Hill, along the Scioto River, directly across from Tremper (Mills 1916:265). Notably, Feurt Hill is pitted with evidence of ancient quarries where countless generations of Indians have dug to remove the pipestone.

That the association between Tremper and the nearby occurrence of pipestone was recognized and considered significant by the Hopewell is revealed by the fact that, of the 145 smoking pipes recovered from Tremper, the vast majority were made from the pipestone found across the river (Mills 1916:265). This cache, by the way, was the second largest collection of Hopewell pipes ever found, surpassed in quantity only by those found at Mound City. Given this, it seems entirely likely that Tremper was located where it is so as to honor, or mark the special nature of, the pipestone-bearing earth at that location.

RED OCHER AND THE SEIP EARTHWORK

Another inorganic substance that was used by the Hopewell was red ocher. Quite often, Hopewell artifacts and even human burials are found to have been painted or sprinkled with red ocher (Morgan 1941; Magrath 1940; Mills 1922:454; Baby and Langlois 1979:18; Whitman 1977; Seeman 1988). Interestingly enough, we also find that the Seip Earthwork—a major Hopewell burial ground and geometric enclosure—is located very near to outcroppings of this substance.

Red ocher is actually an iron oxide-based compound that, when pulverized, heated, and mixed with water, makes a very good paint. Because of this, red ocher has been used as a paint for thousands of years. Additionally, because of its color, red ocher has also been used for thousands of years as a magic symbol for blood.

As a substitute for blood, red ocher is used to impart symbolic life to the dead. By sprinkling or painting red ocher onto the bones of the dead—including perhaps the Hopewell—a hope is expressed that the deceased might again be charged with the essence of life, even if this only happens in the otherworld.

Relevant to us here is the Seip Earthwork's location on the bank of Paint Creek. As it happens, the name Paint Creek is derived from the occurrence of red ocher outcroppings that are found along its cliffs (Atwater 1820:148). That the association between the Seip Earthwork and these deposits of red ocher was recognized and considered significant by the Hopewell is suggested by the discovery of a very peculiar mound within the Seip enclosure. Squier and Davis (1848:58) describe this mound as comprised of a clayey loam. However, Atwater (1820:148) very specifically notes that this "very singular mound [is] five feet high, thirty feet in diameter, and composed entirely of a red ochre, which answers very well as a paint."

SALT AND THE MCKITTRICK EARTHWORKS

Located about twenty-five miles southeast of Chillicothe in Jackson County, Ohio, the McKittrick Earthworks are comprised of two square enclosures (Long 1981). As compared to other geometric enclosures, the McKittrick Earthworks are small. The large square is only 150 by 150 feet, while the small square is only about fifteen feet across. What may have made the McKittrick enclosures special, though, was their location—less than one-half mile from the Old Scioto Salt Licks.

Today, we take salt for granted as we sprinkle it on our food and pour it by the ton on our roads. In the primitive wilderness that was Ohio, however, salt was not so easy to come by. In those early days, salt was a valuable and appreciated luxury.

Given this, it is of considerable interest to learn that, for hundreds of years, the brine water that issues from the salt springs near the McKittrick Earthworks has been boiled down by both the Indians and the white man to make salt. Some indication of just how rich the springs are is given by the observation that commercial salt-making at the Scioto Licks, in the years 1806 to 1808, supported twenty salt furnaces. Each of these furnaces made between fifty and seventy bushels of salt per week (Williams 1900:87). As Williams also explains, "it is known that the Shawanese owned and occupied Jackson County when it was discovered by the whites. It appears, however, that all the Ohio tribes were allowed to visit the salt springs and to make salt. [The salt springs] . . . were visited by hundreds, and sometimes, thousands of Indians during the summer months" (Williams 1900:31). We may never know for certain, but it seems possible that the Hopewell also valued this salt. If so, then that could explain why the McKittrick Earthworks are located where they are: to mark the sacred nature of the earth. In this case, it was where salt is found.

CONCLUSION

From the foregoing, I think it is reasonable to conclude that the Hopewell found the sacred manifested all around—in the rivers and streams that gave them life-sustaining water, in the land that provided the plants and animals that were used for food, and in the special rocks that provided the materials for their weapons, tools, and ceremonial needs.

Spirit was all around. But in some places, spirit revealed itself more strongly. In those places, the earth revealed its abundance—in the form of water, salt, ocher, flint, or pipestone—in a very visible and accessible form. And so it was in these places that the Hopewell honored the earth and marked these special places with their sacred enclosures. As I will show, however, identifying and marking these special places was only the beginning.

Chapter 2

SACRED GEOMETRY

Geometry existed before the Creation. It is co-eternal with the mind of God
. . . Geometry provided God with a model for the Creation . . . Geometry is
God Himself.

—Johannes Kepler

. . . our brains lack the capacity to take in the universe as a whole; we have to
structure it in order to put little bits of it into our heads.

—Ian Stewart and Martin Golubitsky

Fearful Symmetry: Is God a Geometer?

It was a god-awful climb as I struggled up the last few hundred feet to the small temple. At 14,170 feet above sea level, my lungs burned as they grabbed at every stray molecule of oxygen.

I was in Nepal, along the Tibetan border, on my way to Base Camp I, Mount Everest. Chomolungma—"Goddess Mother of the World"—that is what the Sherpas call the mountain. And scattered along its way, in the shadow of the mountain, are a number of small Buddhist temples, safe havens for a tired traveler.

After several years of working as a business executive in New York City, I needed this change of scenery to restore my connectedness to the real world. As a matter of fact, after this little trip, I would leave New York and pursue an advanced degree in anthropology.

Such matters were far away, however, as I climbed the last few dozen feet of trail and came into the open. Like others of its kind, this temple boasted a rectangular courtyard and several small square buildings—welcome order after days of travel through a jumble of rock, ice, and sky. Years later, in journeys to other sacred places, I would again find these same geometric patterns.

In fact, the predilection, desire, or even compulsion to build sacred or religious structures in symmetrical geometric patterns seems universal. From the shrines of Tibet to the temples of India and cathedrals of Europe, humankind has for thousands of years defined its sacred spaces and built its sacred structures in geometric shapes. The logic of this behavior perhaps can be explained by the magical premise attributed to the mythical father of alchemy, Hermes Trismegistus, the Thrice Great Hermes: "That which is in the lesser world (the microcosm) reflects that of the greater world (the macrocosm)." In other words, sacred structures are designed to replicate, on a smaller scale, our vision of the universe, which is geometric in nature. Through our interactions with these microcosmic shrines, temples, and churches, we then strive to bring our consciousness into harmony with the macrocosmic universe through prayer, meditation, contemplation, and other mind-altering techniques.

Echoing the thoughts of philosophers throughout the ages, Nigel Pennick (1980:7) has pointed out that "Geometry exists everywhere in nature: its order underlies the structure of all things from molecules to galaxies, from the smallest virus to the largest whale." While this statement is undoubtedly true in a very deep sense, the interesting paradox is that this underlying geometry is not especially self-evident. Nor is this underlying geometry the simple Euclidean geometry that we learned in high school. As explained by mathematician Benoit Mandelbrot:

> Clouds are not spheres, mountains are not cones, coastlines are not circles, and bark is not smooth, nor does lightning travel in a straight line. More generally . . . many patterns of Nature are so irregular and frag-

mented, that, compared with . . . standard geometry, Nature exhibits not simply a higher degree but an altogether different level of complexity. (Mandelbrot 1977:1)

More than a century ago, the same sort of realization led artist Eugène Delacroix to note that, "It would be worthy to investigate whether straight lines exist only in our brains" (quoted in Shlain 1991:33).

Indeed, where we find straight lines or absolutely regular curvature in the world around us, we usually interpret these findings as evidence of human activity. Irregularity and variation of shape characterize natural forms, whereas perfect geometric shapes are usually more representative of the human mind and the human hand. Except for snowflakes, beehives, rock crystals, and a few other such things, strict Euclidean geometric patterns are mostly something that we superimpose on the universe. The real world is much more fuzzy.

In fact, it took the genius of Albert Einstein to finally break the two-thousand-year-old Euclidean worldview that we imposed on the universe. In the words of Henry Margenau,

> The central recognition of the theory of relativity is that geometry . . . is a construct of the intellect. Only when this discovery is accepted can the mind feel free to tamper with the time-honored notions of time and space, to survey the range of possibilities available for defining them, and to select that formulation which agrees with observation. (quoted in Capra 1991:162–63)

Thought of in another way, we simplify the universe and make things comprehensible by isolating patterns and superimposing simple geometric forms and models on the phenomena around us. For the most part, this way of looking at the world usually works pretty well. Essentially, geometry is our way of expressing the hope that the world functions in accordance with rational laws that we can understand. Geometry implies that there is order in a universe that might otherwise appear random and chaotic. Having imposed our geometric models on the universe, we then shape and design our sacred structures as microcosms of the geometric order that we believe to be evident all around us. In this way, we bring our sacred structures into a reflected harmony with the cosmos. And again, through our interaction with these structures, we strive to bring our consciousness into harmony with the universe.

As already noted, our Euclidean models of the universe may not be very realistic. According to recent thought such as expressed by Riemann, Einstein, Minkowski, and others, the space-time continuum is probably something very different from the two-, three-, or even four-dimensional models that have served us so well in the past. Models of the universe now involve such things as wrinkles in time, ten-dimensional hyperspace, and quantum inseparability. In this century, our understanding of the universe has expanded exponentially—far beyond, perhaps, even the wildest dreams of the ancient geometers and shamans. What has always been appealing about Euclidean models of the universe, however, is that the geometric forms used in these models—such as circles and squares—are capable of virtually limitless expansion or subdivision, much like the idea behind fractal geometry.

Euclidean geometric shapes can be expanded to encompass the heavens or subdivided into infinity. In either case, though, expanded or contracted geometric forms still maintain their essence. No matter how big, or how small, a square is still a square, and a circle is still a circle. This characteristic makes geometric figures ideally suited as cosmic symbols, so that even the smallest circle can be used as a model for the entire earth, or even the tiniest square can be used as a symbol for the entire heavens, and so on. As we will see later, the Hopewell used this characteristic of geometric shapes to good advantage in their representations of the earth and heavens in the form of their circular and square enclosures.

Continuing with our model of how a sacred structure takes form, we find that once a place has been recognized as special, the next step is to define it by assigning a shape to it. Shape, in turn, is defined by boundaries. Whether they are walls, fences, or ditches, boundaries identify the special space within, separating it from the ordinary or undefined space outside. By enclosing a region of space with a boundary, we make the space inside distinct from the surrounding environment. Boundary closure, therefore, is really the first tangible step in building a sacred structure. And again, as we have noted, for the Ohio Hopewell, the boundaries of their special places were defined by earthen walls, mostly in the shape of circles, squares, and octagons.

FUZZY GEOMETRY

With regard to these Hopewellian circles, squares, and octagons and the accuracy of their construction, it happens that no one has ever drawn a perfect circle, or a perfect square, or a perfect octagon. As mathematician Bart Kosko explains, "Zoom in close enough and you will see imperfections in the drawing or printing or engraving or assembly of subatomic particles. Maybe God or superaliens can draw perfect circles and squares right down to the last quark and farther. And maybe they can't" (Kosko 1993:45). The point is that perfect geometric shapes exist only in the world of imagination.

Having said this, we find that some of the Hopewell enclosures are closer to being ideal geometric figures, while others are more "fuzzy," meaning that they are something less than perfect. Among the more perfect shapes are the Newark Observatory Circle and Octagon, the Newark Square, the High Bank Circle, and the Baum Square.

According to Thomas (1894:464), for example, field survey of the Newark Observatory Circle shows that this earthwork, which is more than 1,000 feet in diameter, is to within four feet of being a perfect circle. So, too, the High Bank Circle, which is also more than 1,000 feet in diameter is to within five feet of being a perfect circle (Thomas 1894:478). Looking at the Newark Square, we find that the corners of that earthwork vary by less than 1° of arc from being true right angles (Thomas 1894:466). Similarly, the corners of the Baum Square also vary by less than 1° from being perfect right angles (Thomas 1894:483). Likewise, the Seal and Hopewell squares are near perfect figures. And, in the case of the Newark Octagon, the intersecting diagonals of that earthwork are to within ten minutes and two minutes of arc respectively, from being perfect right angles (Thomas 1894:465).

So how did the Hopewell achieve such accuracy? Unfortunately, we may never know the exact techniques they used. But engineering feats such as near perfect circles and squares are possible using nothing more complicated than a length of cord. To make a circle, for example, one end of a cord is held in place while the other end is used to trace a circle around the center point.

To make a square, we again use a cord. But this time, the cord is knotted so that it has thirteen sections comprised of twelve evenly spaced knots. Known as the Druids' Cord, this simple device enables one to lay out very accurate 3, 4, 5 right triangles. Right triangles, of course, give us right angles, such as those found among the Hopewell earthworks. Hence, it is possible to lay out tremendous squares, with great precision, simply by using the Druids' Cord to establish the corners of the squares.

As already mentioned, some of the Hopewell enclosures are less than perfect. The Hopeton Circle, for example, has a north-south diameter of 960 feet, while its east-west diameter is 1,018 feet (Thomas 1894:474). So, too, the Hopeton Square is not perfect. Nor are the Dunlap and Anderson squares perfect.

The geometry of the Hopewellian earthworks was fuzzy. But as we will see in a later chapter, it may be that the important thing for the Hopewell was the symbolic meaning of their circles, squares, and octagons, rather than absolute and consistent perfection in geometric execution on the ground.

Given all this, what I have done in this chapter is use the best available data to reconstruct symmetrical geometric shapes for each site. In other words, if, for example, the north-south diameter of the Hopeton Circle is 960 feet, and its east-west diameter is 1,018 feet, then I used one of those lengths to establish the diameter of a more symmetrical circle and used that for illustration purposes. Similarly, if the northwest to southeast width of the Baum Square is given by Thomas (1894:483) as 1,112 feet, and the northeast to southwest width is 1,124 feet, then what I did was use one of these actual measured distances to construct a more symmetrical square—having in this instance equal sides of 1,124 feet.

The important point is that, although the illustrations that follow are sometimes more symmetrical in their shape than their real-life counterparts, the size of each earthwork illustration is nevertheless tied to or established by an actual, on-the-ground measurement.

My first task was to identify those Hopewell sites in Ohio evidencing geometric symmetry. This was done by reference to Squier and Davis's magnum opus, *Ancient Monuments of the Mississippi Valley* (1848).

Ephraim G. Squier was editor of the *Chillicothe Gazette*, while his colleague, Edwin H. Davis, was a Chillicothe area physician. Together, Squier and Davis—with the help of John Locke, James McBride, Charles Whittlesey, and others—surveyed and mapped hundreds of ancient earthworks throughout the eastern United States. In 1848, their findings were published as volume one of the Smithsonian Institution's *Contributions to Knowledge* series.

To appreciate fully the magnitude of their accomplishment, we need to journey back to the early 1840s, as Squier and Davis set out to explore an ancient earthwork. After traveling for hours or even days in a horse-drawn cart, our intrepid explorers finally reach the end of the road. Using machetes, they hack their way through the dense underbrush. Step by step, they cut their way toward the sacred place, their progress slowed by tangles of "wait-a-minute" bushes. Wait-a-minute bushes are known to travelers in such areas as the webs of stickers, thorns, and branches that do their best to scratch your hands, claw your face, and trip you on your way.

Stopping for a few moments to wipe the sweat that burns into their eyes, our explorers are soon greeted by swarms of buzzing, biting mosquitoes that guard the earthworks. Add a few dozen pounds of antique surveying equipment to a picnic lunch and you will have some idea of what these early surveyors must have gone through. Understandably, there may be occasional errors in their work. But, quite simply, no one has yet equaled Squier and Davis's achievement.

To return to the matter at hand, from the resulting list of geometrically shaped earthworks, I selected for analysis those sites that were comprised of two or more geometric components, or otherwise seemed related to nearby sites.

The next step, as discussed earlier, was to redraw these sites in such a way as to reduce them to their most essential geometric shapes, while at the same time standardizing their scale. In this instance, all figures were redrawn to a scale of one inch equals five hundred feet. (For publication purposes, this scale may be further reduced, and figures may appear at different scales.) Where measurement data had to be taken directly from Squier and Davis's figures, an engineer's scale was used, with distances being measured from the crest of each embankment wall to the opposite crest. Where possible, use of Squier and Davis's data was superseded by the use of more recent and more accurate information such as provided by Thomas (1894), Anderson (1980), and others. For reasons discussed elsewhere (Romain 1992), I consider Thomas's and Anderson's work to be accurate to within 1 or 2 percent of measured distances. In fact, recent ground surveys (see, for example, Hively and Horn 1982:table 1) have shown that the maps and figures by Thomas (and Middleton) of Newark and High Bank are accurate to within fifteen minutes of arc and less than two feet in linear distance. Nevertheless, I make no claim that the dimensions for each and every earthwork given here are precise, especially with regard to Squier and Davis's maps. Again, because most of the earthworks have been so extensively destroyed, we will probably never know their exact size. The data I used are simply the best that are currently available.

The resultant set of drawings were then examined for geometric relationships between component parts and between sites. Recurrent patterns were grouped together and are presented here, generally from the simplest to the more complex. For comparative purposes, reduced images of the original illustrations of the earthworks made by Squier and Davis, Thomas, and others accompany each of the idealized figures.

INTRASITE RELATIONSHIPS

The first set of relationships to be looked at are intrasite relationships found between component parts of individual earthwork complexes. The simplest of these concepts is expressed in the relationship between the Newark Fairground Circle and Square.

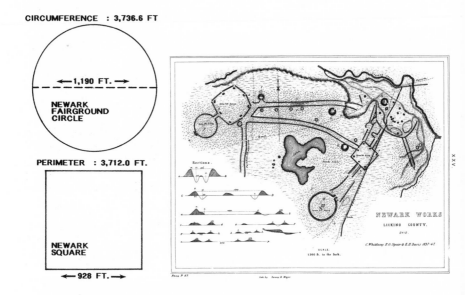

FIG. 2.1. Schematic plan of the Newark Fairground Circle and Square earthworks. Note how the circumference of the Fairground Circle is almost the same length as the perimeter of the Newark Square. *Drawing by the author; inset figure from Squier and Davis 1848:plate 25.*

As shown by figure 2.1, according to Thomas (1894:462,466), the Fairground Circle has a northeast-southwest diameter of about 1,190 feet, while the Newark Square has sides that are about 928 feet in length. These dimensions are from midline to opposite midline of the embankments.

Given Thomas's data, it turns out that the perimeters of these two figures are almost equal to each other. More specifically, the circumference of the Fairground Circle is 3,736.6 feet, while the perimeter of the Newark Square is 3,712.0 feet, for a difference of only 24.6 feet. In terms of percentages, therefore, the circumference of the Fairground Circle and the perimeter of the Newark Square differ from each other by less than 1 percent (3712.0/3736.6 = 0.99357).

Among geometers, the practice of constructing a square and circle that have equal perimeters or equal areas is known as "squaring the circle." It has been suggested that ancient efforts to square the circle are found in the Great Pyramid (Tompkins 1971), Stonehenge (Gaunt 1979), and perhaps even in the Bible (Michell 1988).

As far as I can tell, the squared-circle relationship of the Newark Fairground Circle and Square is the only Hopewell example of its kind. We will run into this situation again, wherein only one example of a particular phenomenon is known. In such instances, we must be careful about assigning too much weight or significance to a single example of any phenomena, as contrasted to a series or pattern of such occurrences. Indeed, it is preferable to have several examples of the same phenomenon if we intend to argue that the phenomenon in question is not random.

However, when it comes to large-scale, man-made structures, often the most notable examples of such structures are one-of-a-kind creations. Structures like the Statue of Liberty, the Verrazano Bridge, and the Empire State Building immediately come to mind.

In view of the geometric relationships that we will discuss below, it seems likely that the Newark Fairground Circle and Square were intentionally designed to have equal perimeters. If this is the case, then what we see at Newark is a tremendous Hopewell example of squaring the circle. Indeed, along with Stonehenge and the Great Pyramid, the Newark complex stands as one of the world's largest examples of this particular geometric exercise.

INCOMMENSURATE RATIOS

The next concept to be discussed is found in the relationship between the Hopeton Circle and Hopeton Square. According to Thomas (1894:474), the north-south diameter of the Hopeton Circle is 960 feet. Correspondingly, the longest and straightest side of the Hopeton Square is 957 feet (Thomas 1894:474). As shown by figure 2.2, the north-south diameter of the Hopeton Circle is virtually the same length as one side of the Hopeton Square.

What is especially fascinating about this geometric construction is that a visual representation of two ratios that are each dependent upon

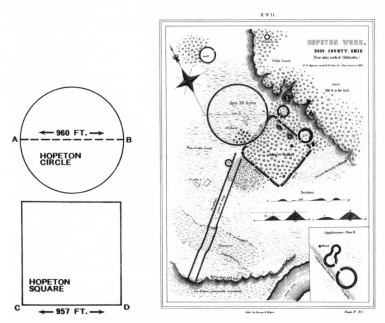

FIG. 2.2. Schematic plan of the Hopeton Earthwork. Note how the diameter of the Hopeton Circle (line A-B) is virtually the same length as any one side of the Hopeton Square (e.g., line C-D). *Drawing by the author; inset figure from Squier and Davis 1848:plate 17.*

incommensurate numbers is expressed without recourse to numbers or mathematics.

What I mean is this: If we take a circle and square and give a value of 1 to both the diameter of the circle and any side of the square, then the circumference of the circle and the diagonal of the square will both be incommensurable or irrational numbers. In the case of the circle, this value is 3.1415 . . . , or pi. In the case of the diagonal of the square, this number is 1.4142. . . . In other words, the ratio of the circumference of the circle to the diameter of the circle is 3.14159 to 1, whereas the ratio of the diagonal of the square to any one side of the square is 1.4142 to 1. By making the diameter of the Hopeton Circle and the sides of the Hopeton Square the same length, a visual expression and comparison of the above two ratios or incommensurable numbers becomes apparent.

Before we proceed too much further, allow me to clarify something. I am not proposing that, when the Hopewell set out to build an earthwork like the Hopeton Circle and Square, they said, "Gee, let's make a visual representation of the relationship between two incommensurate ratios." Nor at Newark did they say: "Let's make a visual representation of a squared circle." Such expressions are our own culturally based interpretations of geometric relationships and visual phenomena. The Hopewell may simply have said—at Newark, for example—something like "Let's make a circle and square that have the same perimeters." Or at Hopeton, "Let's make a circle that has the same diameter as a square."

In the pages that follow, we will use terms such as nested squares, doubled squares, equilateral triangles, and truncated squares. However, this is not to say that the Hopewell referred to these things in the same way. What may have been important to the Hopewell was the visual expression of such ideas, rather than defining these relationships in some sort of mathematically oriented terminology. In other words, you do not need to be able to define what an incommensurate ratio is in order to make a circle and square that have components that are of equal length. The same thing holds true for the rest of the figures we will look at.

NESTED SQUARES

The next four earthworks seem to demonstrate one underlying concept, namely, that of nested squares. That is to say, the four square earthworks that we discuss in the next few paragraphs all fit into their corresponding circles. For example, according to Marshall (1987:fig. 7), the diameter of the Circleville Outer Circle is 1,188 feet and the Circleville Inner Circle is 1,056 feet, while at least two sides of the Circleville Square are 841.5 feet in length. The length of 841.5 feet gives us a diagonal for the Circleville Square of 1,190 feet. As Figure 2.3 shows, this means that the diameter of the Circleville Large Circle is virtually the same length as the diagonal of the Circleville Square—to within two feet. Also of interest is how the Circleville Square fits into the Large

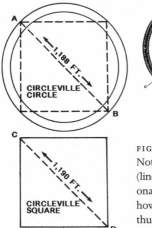

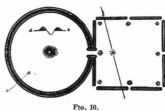

Fig. 10.

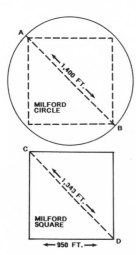

FIG. 2.3. Schematic plan of the Circleville Earthwork. Note how the diameter of the Circleville Large Circle (line A-B) is almost exactly the same length as the diagonal of the Circleville Square (line C-D). Also note how the Circleville Square fits into the Large Circle, thus dividing the circle into quadrants. *Drawing by the author; inset figure from Squier and Davis 1848:fig. 10.*

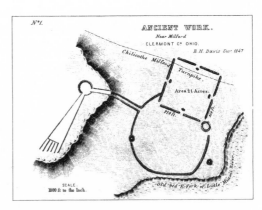

FIG. 2.4. Schematic plan of the Milford Earthwork. Note how the diameter of the Milford Circle (line A-B) is almost the same length as the diagonal of the Milford Square (line C-D). Also note how the Milford Square fits into the Milford Circle, thus dividing the circle into quadrants. *Drawing by the author; inset figure from Squier and Davis 1848:plate 34, no. 1.*

Circle, thus dividing the Large Circle into quadrants. Thought of in another way, if we draw a circle around the Circleville Square, then the resulting circle will be equal in size to the Circleville Large Circle. Conversely, if we inscribe a square within the Circleville Large Circle, then the resulting square will be equal in size to the Circleville Square. As we will see, this same proportional relationship is also found in the Milford, Works East, and Frankfort enclosures.

For the Milford, Works East, and Frankfort enclosures, it was necessary to use measurement data derived directly from Squier and Davis's figures. Unfortunately, because these three earthworks are almost entirely obliterated, it is not possible to confirm Squier and Davis's measurements.

According to Squier and Davis's figure (1848:plate 34, no. 1), the Milford Large Circle has an east-west diameter of about 1,400 feet; while the Milford Square has sides that are each 950 feet in length. As figure 2.4 shows, these dimensions result in a square that closely fits within the perimeter of the Milford Circle.

Similarly, at the Works East Earthwork, according to Squier and Davis's figure (1848:plate 21, no. 3), the Works East Large Circle has a diameter of 1,480 feet, while the Works East Square has a corresponding and equal diagonal of 1,480 feet. Again, as shown by Figure 2.5, the Works East Square neatly fits within the Large Circle and divides the Large Circle into quadrants. And the Works East Small Circle is close to one-half the size of the Works East Large Circle.

The Frankfort Earthwork is shown in figure 2.6. As can be seen, the dimensions of this earthwork are almost exactly the same as the Works East. Also like Works East, what we find at Frankfort is that, as per Squier and Davis's figure (1848:plate 21, no. 4), the diameter of the Frankfort Large Circle and the diagonal of the Frankfort Square are almost the same. Again, too, the Frankfort Square fits neatly within the Frankfort Large Circle and divides the Large Circle into quadrants. And the Frankfort Small Circle is almost exactly one-half the size of the Large Circle.

In a way, what seems expressed in the earthworks just discussed is

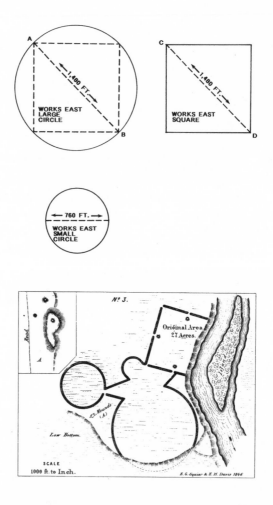

FIG. 2.5. Schematic plan of the Works East Earthwork of Chillicothe. Note how the diameter of the Works East Large Circle (line A-B) is the same length as the diagonal of the Works East Square (line C-D). Also note how the Works East Square precisely fits into the Works East Large Circle, thus dividing the circle into quadrants. *Drawing by the author; inset figure from Squier and Davis 1848:plate 21, no. 3.*

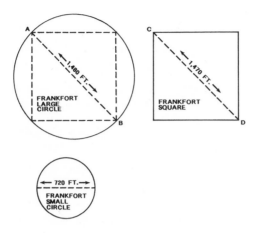

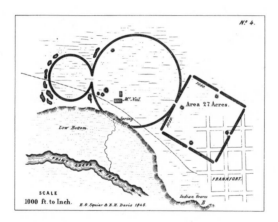

FIG. 2.6. Schematic plan of the Frankfort Earthwork. Note how the diameter of the Frankfort Large Circle (line A-B) is almost the same length as the diagonal of the Frankfort Square (line C-D). Also note how the Frankfort Square fits into the Frankfort Large Circle, thus dividing the circle into quadrants. *Drawing by the author; inset figure from Squier and Davis 1848:plate 21, no.4.*

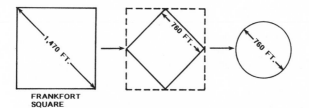

FRANKFORT
SQUARE

FIG. 2.7. Reminiscent of ad quadratum geometry, this illustration shows how the Frankfort Small and Works East Small circles can be created from a square that has the dimensions of the Frankfort and Works East Squares. *Drawing by the author.*

reminiscent of ad quadratum geometry. In Western mathematics, the procedure of creating new figures from a series of geometric progressions based on a square is known as ad quadratum geometry. As shown by figure 2.7, for example, a second square can be constructed within the Frankfort Square by joining the midpoints of the sides of the Frankfort Square. If any one side of this new square is used as the diameter for a new circle, then the new circle will be found to have the same diameter as the Frankfort Small Circle. The same geometric progression can also be demonstrated for the Works East.

CIRCLE AND SQUARE RELATIONSHIPS

From the different spatial relationships evident in the earthworks, it appears that the Hopewell may have recognized the four fundamental relationships between a circle and square. Figure 2.8 shows these relationships. They are: (1) square containing a circle, wherein the circle contained in a square has a diameter equal to any side of that square; (2) square contained in a circle, wherein the circle containing the square has a diameter equal to the square's diagonal; (3) square and circle with equal perimeters; and (4) square and circle with near equal areas. Interestingly enough, each of these four relationships is evident in one or more of the earthwork complexes.

The square containing a circle relationship, for example, is expressed in the Hopeton Earthwork, while the square contained in a circle relationship is evident in the Circleville, Milford, Works East, and

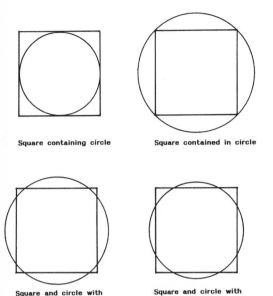

Square containing circle   Square contained in circle

Square and circle with   Square and circle with
equal perimeters   equal areas

FIG. 2.8. The four funda-
mental relationships between
a circle and square. *Drawing
by the author.*

Frankfort Earthworks. The square and circle with equal perimeters relationship is found in the Newark Square and Fairground Circle earthworks, whereas the square and circle with near equal areas relationship
is evident in the Marietta Large Square and Liberty Large Circle earthworks. Clearly, the Hopewell had a great interest in exploring the geometric and spatial relationships between circles and squares, and they
were fairly sophisticated in their understanding of those relationships.
In fact, interconnected relationships between circles and squares may
have been at the very heart of the Hopewells' belief system and worldview.

INSCRIBED TRIANGLES

The next group of four earthworks seem related to each other in
that they can be explained by inscribed equilateral triangles. In this
sense, the design of these earthworks is reminiscent of ad triangulum
geometry. Simply stated, ad triangulum geometry refers to the creation

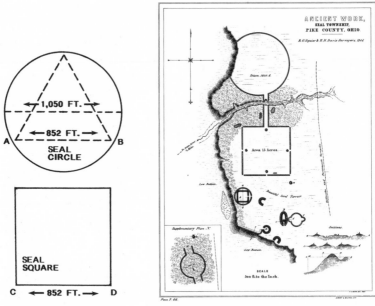

FIG. 2.9. Schematic plan of the Seal Earthwork. Note how any one side of the Seal Square (e.g., line C-D) is very close to the length of any one side of an equilateral triangle inscribed within the Seal Circle (e.g., line A-B). *Drawing by the author; inset figure from Squier and Davis 1848:Plate 24.*

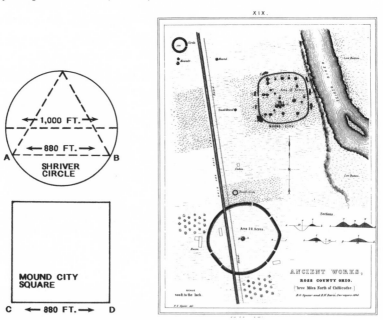

FIG. 2.10. Schematic plan of the Shriver Circle and Mound City Square. Note how any one side of the Mound City Square (e.g., line C-D) is the same length as any one side of an equilateral triangle inscribed within the Shriver Circle (e.g., line A-B). *Drawing by the author; inset figure from Squier and Davis 1848:plate 19.*

of geometric figures based on the shape of a triangle. For example, according to Squier and Davis (1848:plate 24), the Seal Circle has a diameter of 1,050 feet, while, according to Thomas (1894:491), the Seal Square has sides that are 854 feet in length east and west, and 852 feet north and south. As shown by figure 2.9, if we divide the circumference of the Seal Circle into three equal segments and then connect the end points of these segments, we find that an equilateral triangle is thereby formed within the Seal Circle. Notably, any one side of this inscribed triangle is very close in length to any one side of the Seal Square.

As shown by figure 2.10, the same geometric construct that is found at the Seal Earthwork also seems expressed between the Mound City and Shriver Earthworks, wherein any one side of an equilateral triangle inscribed within the Shriver Earthwork is very close in length to any one side of the idealized Mound City Square. For this analysis, I used Marshall's data (1987:fig. 6) for Mound City, which shows a north-south width of about 880 feet, and Squier and Davis's figure (1848:plate 19) for Shriver, which shows a north-south diameter of about 1,000 feet.

Like the Mound City, Shriver, and Seal Earthworks, at Baum it happens that, if an equilateral triangle is inscribed within the Baum Large Circle, then any one side of this triangle will be very close in length to any one side of the Baum Square. This correspondence is shown in figure 2.11. Also noteworthy is that the Baum Small Circle is almost one-half the size of the Baum Large Circle. For Baum, I used Squier and Davis's data (1848:plate 21, no. 1) for the circular enclosures, which shows northwest to southeast diameters for the large and small circles of 1,320 feet and 760 feet, respectively; and Thomas's data (1894: 484) for the square, which shows a northwest to southeast width of 1,124 feet. Unfortunately, Thomas does not provide data for the circular features at Baum.

There are several ways of making a circle and square with the same proportions as expressed in the Seal, Mound City, Shriver, and Baum Earthworks. One such procedure is demonstrated in figure 2.12. First, a circle of any diameter is constructed. Next, a second circle having the same diameter as the first is drawn using any point on the cir-

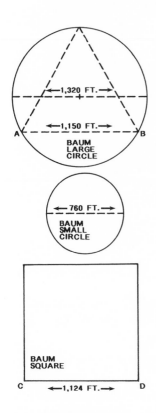

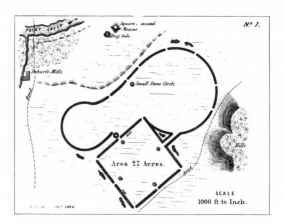

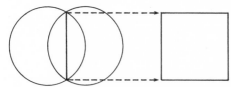

FIG. 2.11. Schematic plan of the Baum Earthwork. Note how any one side of the Baum Square (e.g., line C-D) is almost equal to the length of any one side of an equilateral triangle inscribed within the Baum Large Circle (e.g., line A-B). *Drawing by the author; inset figure from Squier and Davis 1848:plate 21, no. 1.*

FIG. 2.12. This illustration shows how a circle and square having the same proportions as the Seal, Mound City, Shriver, and Baum earthworks can be constructed. *Drawing by the author.*

cumference of the first circle as the center of the second circle. The two overlapping circles will form a vesica piscis. The long axis of this vesica piscis is then used as one side of the new square. The first circle and the new square will then have the same proportions as found in the earthworks just discussed. From a symbolic point of view, what is especially appealing about this construction is that the square has a direct relationship to the first circle. In effect, the square is created from the first circle.

For the next two earthworks, that is, Liberty and Seip, it was necessary to use Squier and Davis's data for the circular enclosures and
Thomas's data for the squares. Again, Thomas does not provide data for
the circular features at these sites. Specifically, Squier and Davis (1848:
plate 20) show the diameters of the Liberty Large and Small circles to
be 1,700 and 800 feet in diameter, respectively, and the diameters of the
Seip Large and Small circles (1848: plate 21, no. 2) to be 1,530 feet and 750
feet, respectively. Thomas (1894:482, 488) gives the north-south diagonal
of the Liberty Square as 1,566 feet, and the northeast-southwest diagonal of the Seip Square as 1,607.5 feet.

Given these dimensions, a slightly modified version of the equilat-

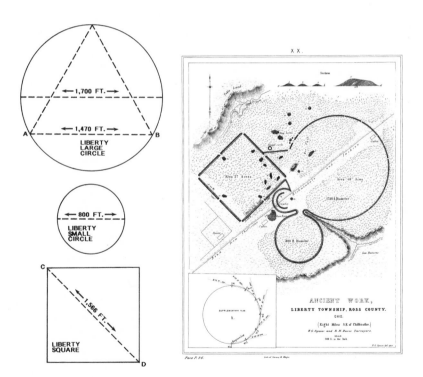

FIG. 2.13. Schematic plan of the Liberty Earthwork. Note how the diagonal of the
Liberty Square (line C-D) is approximately equal to the length of any one side of an
equilateral triangle inscribed within the Liberty Large Circle (e.g., line A-B). *Drawing
by the author; inset figure from Squier and Davis 1848:plate 20.*

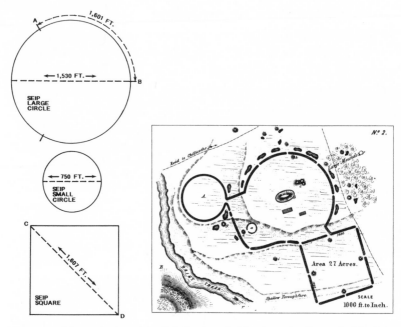

FIG. 2.14. Schematic plan of the Seip Earthwork. Note how the diagonal of the Seip Square (line C-D) is virtually equal to one-third of the circumference of the Seip Large Circle (arc A- B). *Drawing by the author; inset figure from Squier and Davis 1848:plate 21, no. 2.*

eral triangle concept just discussed is evident at Liberty. In this case, any one side of an equilateral triangle inscribed within the Liberty Large Circle is found to be close to the length of the diagonal of the Liberty Square. This correspondence is shown in figure 2.13.

At the Seip Earthwork, yet another variation of the ad triangulum concept is evident. In this case, however, as shown by figure 2.14, the diagonal of the Seip Square is very close in length to one-third the circumference of the Seip Large Circle.

TRUNCATED SQUARES

The last intrasite concept to be discussed is found at the High Bank and Newark Earthworks. Fortunately, for both High Bank and

Newark, we have the very accurate data of Thomas (1894) to work with. In this regard, Thomas (1894:478–79) notes that the High Bank Circle approximates a circle having a diameter of 1,052 feet, while the east-west diagonal of the High Bank Octagon is 1,250 feet. Further, Thomas (1894:464–65) notes that the Newark Observatory Circle best approximates a circle having a diameter of 1,054 feet, while the east-west width of the Newark Octagon is 1,720 feet.

High Bank and Newark are unique in that, although they are separated from each other by about fifty-seven miles, both sites include octagons and circles in their designs. Moreover, both sites demonstrate similar geometric relationships between their respective circles and octagons. At High Bank, for example, the apothem of the octagon—shown in figure 2.15 as line C-D—is equal in length to line A-B, which is

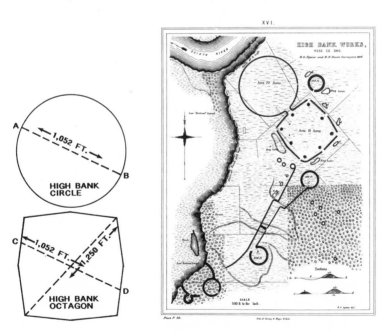

FIG. 2.15. Schematic plan of the High Bank Earthwork. Note how the apothem of the octagon (e.g., line C-D) is equal in length to the diameter of the High Bank Circle (line A-B). Note, too, that the High Bank Circle is virtually equal in size to the Newark Observatory Circle, which is illustrated in Figure 2.16. *Drawing by the author; inset figure from Squier and Davis 1848:plate 26.*

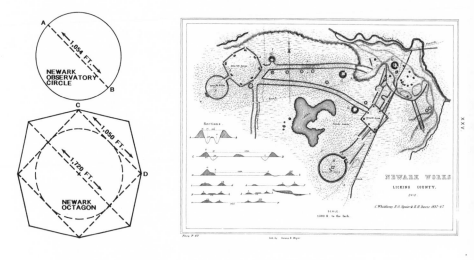

FIG. 2.16. Schematic plan of the Newark Observatory Circle and Octagon. Note how a line extending between the octagon's alternate vertices (e.g., line C-D) is equal in length to the diameter of the Observatory Circle (line A-B). *Drawing by the author; inset figure from Squier and Davis 1848:plate 25.*

the diameter of the High Bank Circle. Similarly, at Newark, we find that a line extending between the octagon's alternate vertices—shown in figure 2.16 as line C-D—is almost equal in length to line A-B, which is the diameter of the Observatory Circle. (The correspondences just noted for High Bank and Newark were first pointed out by Ray Hively and Robert Horn [1984:S92; 1982:S8].)

In addition to the similarities just noted, there are some further correspondences between High Bank and Newark. As pointed out by Squier and Davis (1848:71), the High Bank Circle and the Newark Observatory Circle are almost exactly the same size, that is, about 1,053 feet in diameter. Moreover, the length of the High Bank apothem and the length of a line extending between alternate vertices of the Newark Octagon are also both about 1,053 feet. At both High Bank and Newark, therefore, we find that the length of 1,053 feet determines the size of the earthwork complexes. Clearly, there was something very special about this particular unit of length. In fact, in the next chapter I will show how this special unit of length is directly related to what may be a basic Hopewell unit of length.

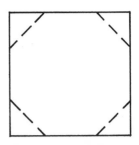

Returning to the matter of geometry, however, we find that octagons can be related to squares if they are thought of as truncated squares. By truncated, I mean that the corners of the square are each progressively cut back so that an octagon is formed (see figure 2.17). At High Bank and Newark, we again find the ever-present circle and square, except that at these two sites, certain squares have been truncated so as to form octagons. By this interpretation, the square and the octagon can be considered as interchangeable symbols in their relationship to their opposite figure, the circle.

FIG. 2.17. This illustration shows how an octagon is created from a truncated square. *Drawing by the author.*

INTERSITE RELATIONSHIPS

In the preceding section, it was shown how various components within specific sites relate to each other. It also happens, however, that a series of geometric relationships can be established between sites.

We cannot say with certainty that the Hopewell recognized the intersite relationships that will be discussed in the next few pages. Indeed, it may be that the following relationships are simply the unintended result of a common unit of measurement being used to design each individual earthwork. Nevertheless, the following relationships are noted, along with the thought that, given their expertise in geometry, as well as their demonstrated interest in establishing geometric relationships between very closely situated circle and square earthworks, perhaps the Hopewell likewise recognized and intentionally designed some of the following intersite relationships.

In figure 2.18, for example, we see how the dimensions of the Marietta Large Square can be defined or established by the diagonals of the combined Frankfort, Marietta Small, and Works East squares to an

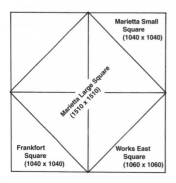

FIG. 2.18. Schematic plan showing how the Marietta Large Square can be defined by the diagonals of the Frankfort, Marietta Small, and Works East Small squares to within about 3 percent. *Drawing by the author.*

accuracy of about 3 percent. (Dimensions of the Marietta squares are based on Squier and Davis's figure [1848:plate 26]; and it is duly noted that Squier and Davis's figure shows one side of the Marietta Large Square to be made up of two embankments that are somewhat tangent to each other, thus giving rise to the possible argument that the figure actually has five sides.)

Essentially though, figure 2.18 provides a geometric solution to the following problem: Given a square with sides that are of a given unit length, how can a second square be constructed that has twice the area as the first square? Using only rational numbers, the problem cannot be solved by arithmetic. By using the geometric solution shown in figure 2.18, however, the problem is solved and the square is doubled. For instance, again with reference to figure 2.18, to make a square that has twice the area of either the Frankfort, Marietta Small, or Works East Small squares, the diagonal of any of these small squares is used as one side of the new square. In figure 2.18, therefore, each side of the Marietta Large Square is equal in length to any one of the diagonals of the small squares, and the Marietta Large Square is approximately double the area of any one of the small squares.

In fact, figure 2.18 provides a visual expression of what we know as the Pythagorean theorem. In mathematical terms, this relationship is expressed by the formula $a^2 + b^2 = c^2$. Clearly, the Hopewell would not recognize our algebraic expression of the Pythagorean theorem. However, it is intriguing to think that maybe they recognized its geometric equivalent, as found in the interrelated construction of the above squares.

In any event, if we now take the Marietta Large Square and perpendicularly bisect its sides, the figure that results will be made up of four smaller squares, technically known as Sierpinski fractals. A circle

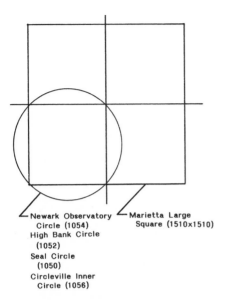

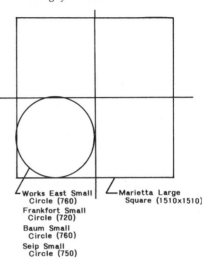

FIG. 2.20. Schematic plan showing how the Works East, Frankfort, Baum, and Seip Small circles can be defined by drawing a circle inside any of the four constructed squares within the Marietta Large Square. *Drawing by the author.*

Newark Observatory Circle (1054)
High Bank Circle (1052)
Seal Circle (1050)
Circleville Inner Circle (1056)

Marietta Large Square (1510x1510)

FIG. 2.19. Schematic plan showing how the Newark Observatory, Circleville Inner, High Bank, and Seal Circles can be defined by circumscribing any of the four constructed squares within the Marietta Large Square. *Drawing by the author.*

Works East Small Circle (760)
Frankfort Small Circle (720)
Baum Small Circle (760)
Seip Small Circle (750)

Marietta Large Square (1510x1510)

drawn around any one of these four squares will, interestingly enough, be equal in size to the diameters of the Newark Observatory, High Bank, Circleville Inner, and Seal circles. This correspondence is shown by figure 2.19.

Next we see how a circle drawn inside any one of the same four squares is equal in size to the Works East Small, Frankfort Small, Baum Small, and Seip Small circles. This correspondence is shown by figure 2.20. It is one way to account for the peculiar size of the four small circles just noted.

Figure 2.21 is simply a further iteration of the small circle concept just discussed. However, if we take figure 2.21 and draw a circle such

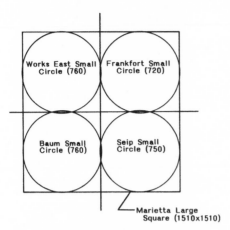

FIG. 2.22. Schematic plan showing
how eight circular Hopewell earthworks are geometrically interrelated.
Drawing by the author.

Works East Small Circle (760)

Frankfort Small Circle (720)

Baum Small Circle (760)

Seip Small Circle (750)

Marietta Large Square (1510x1510)

FIG. 2.21. Further iteration of figure 2.20 showing how the Works East, Frankfort, Baum, and Seip Small Circles fit within the constructed squares inside the Marietta Large Square. *Drawing by the author.*

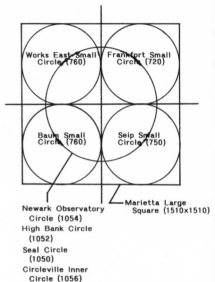

Works East Small Circle (760)

Frankfort Small Circle (720)

Baum Small Circle (760)

Seip Small Circle (750)

Newark Observatory Circle (1054)
High Bank Circle (1052)
Seal Circle (1050)
Circleville Inner Circle (1056)

Marietta Large Square (1510x1510)

that its circumference intersects the centers of the four small circles, then the resultant circle will be equal in size to the Circleville Inner, Newark Observatory, Seal, and High Bank circles. This observation is shown in figure 2.22. In figure 2.22, therefore, we can account for the size of eight circular enclosures as well as the Marietta Large Square.

Lastly, figure 2.23 shows one way of accounting for the peculiar size of the Hopeton and Shriver circles as well as a number of other circular earthworks—again, by reference to the Marietta Large Square and its diagonal. That is, in figure 2.23, we see how the size of either the Shriver and Hopeton circles, or any of the four illustrated smaller circles, is a function of how the two different sized circles fit together inside the Marietta Large Square.

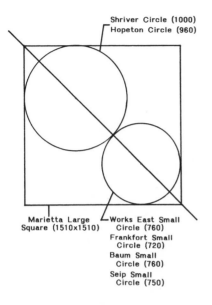

Shriver Circle (1000)
Hopeton Circle (960)

Marietta Large Square (1510x1510)
Works East Small Circle (760)
Frankfort Small Circle (720)
Baum Small Circle (760)
Seip Small Circle (750)

FIG. 2.23. Schematic plan showing how the Hopeton and Shriver circles can be defined by their relationship to each other and the Marietta Large Square. *Drawing by the author.*

ICOSATWISTS

Whether by design, or by coincidence, or as a function of using a common unit of measurement, the extent to which the Hopewellian earthworks are interrelated is shown by figures 2.24–2.26. Figure 2.24 shows how the Newark Octagon neatly nests within both the Marietta Large Square and the Liberty Large Circle. So, too, the Marietta Small, Works East, and Frankfort squares all fit within the Newark Octagon, while the Circleville Inner, Newark Observatory, High Bank, and Seal circles all fit within the four squares just mentioned.

Interestingly enough, in connection with figure 2.24, the area of the Liberty Large Circle and the area of the Marietta Large Square are equal to each other to within 1 percent. More specifically, the area of the Liberty Large Circle is 2,268,650 square feet, while the area of the Marietta Large Square is 2,280,100 square feet. Hence, 2,268,650/2,280,100 = 0.9949. (These calculations are based on the constructed figures used as illustrations in this chapter.)

Continuing our analysis, figure 2.25 shows how the High Bank Octagon defines the size difference between the Marietta Small, Works

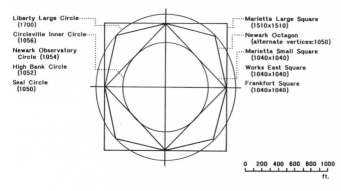

Liberty Large Circle (1700)
Circleville Inner Circle (1056)
Newark Observatory Circle (1054)
High Bank Circle (1052)
Seal Circle (1050)

Marietta Large Square (1510x1510)
Newark Octagon (alternate vertices:1050)
Marietta Small Square (1040x1040)
Works East Square (1040x1040)
Frankfort Square (1040x1040)

0 200 400 600 800 1000
ft.

FIG. 2.24. Idealized Hopewell geometric earthworks drawn to scale. Note how the size and shape of various earthworks are directly related to the configuration of other earthworks. *Drawing by the author.*

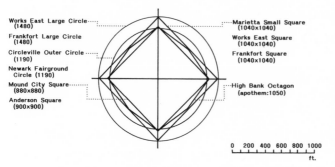

Works East Large Circle (1480)
Frankfort Large Circle (1480)
Circleville Outer Circle (1190)
Newark Fairground Circle (1190)
Mound City Square (880x880)
Anderson Square (900x900)

Marietta Small Square (1040x1040)
Works East Square (1040x1040)
Frankfort Square (1040x1040)
High Bank Octagon (apothem:1050)

0 200 400 600 800 1000
ft.

FIG. 2.25. Scale drawing showing the geometrically interrelated nature of several more Hopewell earthworks. *Drawing by the author.*

East, and Frankfort squares, and the Mound City and Anderson squares. Figure 2.25 also shows how the Works East and Frankfort Large circles are defined by the inscribed Marietta Small, Works East, and Frankfort squares. And figure 2.25 shows how the size of the Circleville Outer and Newark Fairground circles are defined by the inscribed High Bank Octagon, and Mound City and Anderson squares.

In figure 2.26, we see how all the above earthworks nest together in one interrelated design.

One of the interesting things about figures 2.24–2.26 is that they are modified forms of a class of figures known as icosatwists. An icosatwist is a figure made up of progressively smaller squares that are rotated within yet other squares (see, for example, Blackwell 1984:54). The angular changes of the squares can vary from 2° to 45°. In figures

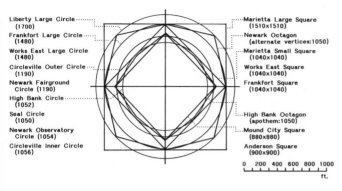

Liberty Large Circle (1700)
Frankfort Large Circle (1480)
Works East Large Circle (1480)
Circleville Outer Circle (1190)
Newark Fairground Circle (1190)
High Bank Circle (1052)
Seal Circle (1050)
Newark Observatory Circle (1054)
Circleville Inner Circle (1056)

Marietta Large Square (1510x1510)
Newark Octagon (alternate vertices:1050)
Marietta Small Square (1040x1040)
Works East Square (1040x1040)
Frankfort Square (1040x1040)
High Bank Octagon (apothem:1050)
Mound City Square (880x880)
Anderson Square (900x900)

0 200 400 600 800 1000
ft.

FIG. 2.26. Composite scale drawing of the Hopewell earthworks shown in figures 2.24 and 2.25. *Drawing by the author.*

2.24–2.26, the squares have been rotated 45°. From the way the earthworks fit together, one has to wonder if the Hopewell recognized and even intentionally incorporated the idea of the icosatwist in their earthwork constructions.

FURTHER OBSERVATIONS

From what we have seen, I don't think there is much doubt that the Hopewell were intrigued by the variety of possible relationships between a circle and square. Over and over again, the idea that seems expressed is that, for every circular enclosure, a corresponding square or octagon can be related to the circle by geometric means. Indeed, the Hopewell found more than a dozen ways to reconcile the geometrically opposite figures of the circle and square. No doubt, the ancient Hopewell would have agreed with Dan Pedoe, who explained that "The secret of proportions seems not to lie in single shapes, but in the relationship between them" (1976:108).

A COUPLE OF FINAL THOUGHTS

In our world, Plato, Pythagoras, and Euclid will long be remembered for their contributions to geometry. Regrettably, it has been more than a thousand years since the names of the Hopewell geometers have been called out. Still, their earthworks tell us that, thousands of years ago, the native peoples of this continent, too, were making significant discoveries in the realm of geometry. From squaring the circle and doubling the square to geometric expressions of incommensurate ratios, ad quadratum and ad triangulum progressions, truncation, and icosatwists, the Hopewell developed a system of geometry that was quite remarkable.

What is also extraordinary is that, to a greater extent than any other people I know of, the Hopewell used the primal element of earth to express the geometric truths they discovered. As a result, a certain visual effect is created. When we look at the Hopewell structures, it seems as though the earth itself shaped and molded the lines that form the geometric enclosures. Like malleable clay, or molten magma from deep within the earth, the geometric forms of the Hopewell seem to rise up and take shape out of the primal essence of the earth in a bold expression of the fundamental symbols of the universe.

Chapter 3

MEASURING AND COUNTING

Man is the measure of all things, of being things that they exist, and of nonentities that they do not exist.

— Protagoras (c. 481–411 B.C.)

By translating the actual into the numerical we have found the secret to the structure and workings of the Universe.

— John D. Barrow, *Pi in the Sky*

It was the perfect day for a flight. The sun was bright, the air was crisp, and there was just the hint of a breeze out of the southwest. Poised at the end of the runway, the little airplane strained at its brakes. I made a last minute check of the instruments, set the flaps, and eased the throttle forward. Faster and faster the propeller whirled. Finally, when the engine reached twenty-two hundred revolutions per minute, I released the brakes. Slowly at first, then with increasing speed, we started down the runway. Human flesh and metal machine balanced for a few precious moments between heaven and earth, balanced on the edge of flight.

As we reached rotation speed, I increased back pressure on the control column, and ever so gently, we were airborne. Within seconds, the houses and people became smaller and smaller as we climbed higher and higher into the cool currents of air. Soon we were winging our way up, over, and around the Newark Earthworks.

Ever since I was a boy, I had dreams of flight. To be part of the sky. To see the world through the eyes of a bird as it circled overhead.

In the same way, I wanted to see the earthworks from a different perspective. I wanted to see the earthworks not as a flatland drawing on a piece of paper, nor as an isolated embankment here and there covered by trees and houses, but as geometric forms with substance and in their entirety. I wanted to see the earthworks from the upperworld. Guided by these thoughts, my wife, Evie, and I were now circling the Newark Octagon at a thousand feet above the ground.

With my left hand, I aimed a camera out of the open pilot's side window and looked into the viewfinder. From this height, the octagon looked like a miniature model. On the ground, the earthwork seems enormous. And indeed it is. To walk across its width takes seven or eight minutes. But from the view we now had, the earthwork seemed small—like the figure that a child might make in the mud or sand.

It was then I realized that to build the great earthworks, like Newark, or Marietta, or a dozen others, the Hopewell probably began with a small model or drawing or design plan for each enclosure. Using this small figure, the proportions of each earthwork component could be worked out well in advance of moving even a basketful of earth. Equally important, a scale model or design plan would have provided the earthwork designers with a clear and certain way of explaining to the laborers and actual builders of each earthwork what the desired shape, size, and orientation of each structure was to be.

We have no surviving remnants of any such models or plans, but surely they existed, if only in the form of stick-drawn figures scratched on the ground. On the other hand, remnants of what may be prehistoric drafting templates and tools have been found. Consider, for example, Warren K. Moorehead's description of a group of artifacts he discovered in one of the burial mounds at the Hopewell site: "one mass of ten little copper circles . . . *forty* pieces of copper, squares, circles . . .

eleven pieces showing semi-circles, straight edges, squares, etc., one small cross with two arms" (Moorehead 1922:110; emphasis added).

Could it be that Moorehead discovered the Hopewell equivalent of an engineer's drafting kit? Certainly there are other possible explanations for these objects. Still, it is intriguing to speculate that maybe these little copper figures were used to design some ancient earthwork.

In any event, for the Hopewell to translate smaller models or figures into full-sized earthworks, three things would have been needed. First, a basic unit of measurement would have been necessary in order to express the idea of "how big." This unit of measurement would have to be capable of expansion by multiples of itself and, conversely, capable of being made smaller by lesser multiples. Second, an agreed-upon standard of measure would have been useful. And third, some method of counting would have been needed.

My search for the basic Hopewell unit of length had begun. However, I was not the first to venture into this little-known territory. Early on, Squier and Davis (1848:49) offered the thought that some standard unit of measure was used by the Mound Builders. Unfortunately, they did not offer an opinion as to what this unit of length might be.

In 1884, Colonel Charles A. Whittlesey of Cleveland, Ohio, proposed that the Mound Builders used a unit of length equal to about thirty inches. He noted that this length closely corresponds to the length of an average pace, as well as the length of an arm. However, Whittlesey's conclusions were based on site maps that were later found to be inaccurate. And so, his findings were not generally accepted.

There the subject rested until the mid-1970s, when James A. Marshall (1980) proposed that the Hopewell used a unit of measure equal to 187 feet. As it turns out, Marshall's 187-foot unit of length is directly related to what I will soon demonstrate to be a lesser multiple of the Hopewell large unit of measure. Briefly explained, the Hopewell used a large unit of measure equal to 1,053 feet, as well as lesser multiples of that figure to include 1,053 feet / 2 = 526.5 feet, and 526.5 feet / 2 = 263.25 feet. Both the large Hopewell units and the above-noted lesser multiples show up repeatedly in the earthworks. Given this, if we take a square and make the diagonal of that square 263.25 feet (which is one of the above-noted lesser multiples), then by operation of the Pythagorean Theorem ($a^2 + b^2 = c^2$), we find that each side of that square will be 186.145 feet. This figure is very close to Marshall's 187-foot figure and explains why Marshall would occasionally find, in a square earthwork having just the right overall dimensions, a very close match between multiples of his 187-foot unit and the sides of that square. As I will show, however, it is the 1,053-foot unit of length and its first generation lesser multiples that were consistently used by the Hopewell throughout their earthworks.

The next investigators on the scene were Raymond Hively and Robert Horn. Both gentlemen are professors at Earlham College in Richmond, Indiana, where Hively teaches physics and Horn teaches philosophy. What brought these two individuals together was their interest in the earthworks.

Based on their field surveys of Newark and High Bank, Hively and Horn (1982:S1) concluded that the geometric designs of these two earthwork complexes were based on a single unit of length. As they explain it, this unit of length is equal to about 321.3 meters for the Newark Earthworks and about 320.6 meters for High Bank (Hively and Horn 1982:S8, 1984:S92). The average of these two lengths is approximately 321 meters. Hence, 321 meters, or 1,053 feet, was considered by Hively and Horn (1984:S99) to be the fundamental Hopewell unit of length.

For the record, it is worth emphasizing that the 1,053-foot unit of length that Hively and Horn discovered was found as a result of their on-the-ground physical surveys of two widely separated earthworks, and not from analyses of old maps or drawings.

Hively and Horn made a tremendously important discovery. For reasons unknown to me, however, they did not pursue their work beyond Newark and High Bank. This is unfortunate because, as it turns out, the 1,053-foot unit of length is found not just in the designs of Newark and High Bank, but also in the designs of many more earthworks. Moreover, it appears that the 1,053-foot unit of length is a multiple of a more fundamental unit of length that is equal to 2.106

feet. I am jumping ahead in the story, though. Let me start at the beginning.

Once a place has been designated as special and once a shape has been given to that place, the next step is to establish the physical size of the shape. Indeed, size must be decided upon before a shape can be brought into the physical world. Until a shape is given a particular size, it exists only in our imagination. Size, in turn, is best defined by units of measurement.

Simply stated, a "unit of measurement is a precisely defined quantity in terms of which the magnitude of all other quantities of the same kind can be stated" (*American Heritage Dictionary* New College Edition 1976:812). Thus, a unit of measurement might be a pound or a kilogram, or a foot or yard, or some other such quantity. We don't know what names the Hopewell gave to their units of measurement. For lack of a better term, we will simply refer to their fundamental measure of length as the basic Hopewell unit of length. As already mentioned, it appears that this unit of length was equal to 2.106 feet, or 25.272 inches.

Like a character in *Alice in Wonderland*, though, we begin our search for the small with a look at the very large. What we find is that very large multiples of the basic Hopewell unit of length are found in different components or parts of the earthworks. More specifically, we find that the length of 1,053 feet is repeated in dozens of instances—in almost every major geometrically shaped Hopewell earthwork in Ohio. In table 4, we see that each of twenty-four earthworks listed in some way incorporates the 1,053-foot unit of length, to within plus or minus 2.0 percent or less. Also shown in table 4 are the references I used to determine the dimensions of each earthwork. (With the exception of Fort Ancient, which will be discussed later in this chapter, these references are the same as the ones I used in chapter 2 relevant to the geometry of the earthworks; hence, they are not repeated again in the narrative of this chapter.)

Also, I would like to clarify one other point before proceeding too

Table 4. Geometric earthworks that incorporate the 1,053-foot unit of length

Earthwork	Reference Used to Establish Size
Baum Small Circle	Squier and Davis 1848:pl. 21, no. 1
Baum Square	Thomas 1894:483
Circleville Inner Circle	Marshall 1987:fig. 7
Circleville Outer Circle	Marshall 1987:fig. 7
Fort Ancient	Romain 2000
Frankfort Large Circle	Squier and Davis 1848:pl. 21, no. 4
Frankfort Small Circle	Squier and Davis 1848:pl. 21, no. 4
Frankfort Square	Squier and Davis 1848:pl. 21, no. 4
High Bank Circle	Thomas 1894:478-79
High Bank Octagon	Thomas 1894:478-79
Liberty Large Circle	Squier and Davis 1848:pl.20
Liberty Square	Thomas 1894:482
Marietta Large Square	Squier and Davis 1848:pl.26
Marietta Small Square	Squier and Davis 1848:pl.26
Newark Fairground Circle	Thomas 1894:462
Newark Observatory Circle	Thomas 1894:464
Newark Octagon	Thomas 1894:464
Seal Circle	Squier and Davis 1848:pl. 24
Seip Large Circle	Squier and Davis 1848:pl. 21, no. 2
Seip Small Circle	Squier and Davis 1848:pl. 21, no. 2
Shriver Circle	Squier and Davis 1848:pl. 19
Works East Large Circle	Squier and Davis 1848:pl. 21, no. 3
Works East Small Circle	Squier and Davis 1848:pl. 21, no. 3
Works East Square	Squier and Davis 1848:pl. 21, no. 3

much further. That is, when I say "to within plus or minus 2.0 percent or less," what I mean throughout this chapter is that sometimes the unit of length we will find in an earthwork is exactly 1,053 feet, while other times it falls somewhere within a range of 1,032 feet to 1,074 feet, which is the same as saying 1,053 feet plus or minus 2.0 percent. More often, the range is even less than this, and is typically on the order of 1.0 to 1.5 percent.

Given this, I would suggest that a variation of 1 to 2 percent in the on-the-ground expression of the ideal 1,053-foot unit of length is rather minimal. Indeed, even in our modern world, a 1 or 2 percent tolerance is often acceptable in the actual layout of many different kinds of construction specifications, like road widths, excavation depths, building heights, and so on.

In any event, in addition to the list provided in table 4, I also looked at how the 1,053-foot unit of length is manifested in each earthwork, and broke that information down into several classifications. Generally, these classifications proceed from the simple to the more complex.

FIRST ORDER

First-order enclosures are the simplest. What defines a first-order earthwork is that either its sides or its diameter is equal to 1,053 feet. Hence, in these earthworks, the 1,053-foot unit of length finds its most straightforward expression. Earthworks in this category are shown in figure 3.1. Square earthworks in this category include the Marietta Small Square, the Works East Square, and the Frankfort Square. In each of these earthworks, the sides of the square enclosures are 1,053 feet in length, to within plus or minus 1.2 percent.

Circular enclosures of the first order include the Seal, High Bank, Newark Observatory, and Circleville Inner circles. In each of these earthworks, the diameters of the circles are 1,053 feet in length, to within plus or minus 1.5 percent.

The Newark Octagon and the High Bank Octagon are also first-order figures. In the case of the Newark Octagon, a line extending between alternate vertices of the Octagon is equal to 1,053 feet, to within plus or minus 1 percent. In the High Bank Octagon, a line extending between opposite midpoints between vertices is equal to 1,053 feet, to within plus or minus 1 percent.

Again, what defines first-order enclosures is that their size is based on the very simplest expression of the 1,053-foot unit of length. As figure 3.1 shows, there are nine such earthworks.

FIRST–ORDER EARTHWORKS

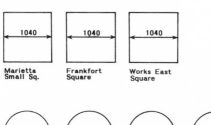

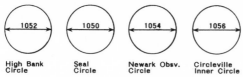

FIG. 3.1. First-order earth-works. This illustration shows how the 1,053-foot unit of length (±1.5%) is found in the dimensions of at least nine Hopewell earthworks. This is the simplest expression of the 1,053-foot unit of length. *Drawing by the author.*

SECOND ORDER

Second-order enclosures are also fairly simple. These enclosures, however, have some component or feature that is equal in length to a multiple of the 1,053-foot unit of length. The most basic of these enclosures is the Marietta Large Square. As figure 3.2 shows, the diagonal of the Marietta Large Square is equal to two times the 1,053-foot unit of length, to within plus or minus 1.5 percent. Similarly, the circumference of the Shriver Circle is equal to three times the 1,053-foot unit of length, to within plus or minus 1.0 percent. Lastly, the circumference of the Liberty Large Circle is equal to five times the 1,053-foot unit of length, to within plus or minus 1.5 percent. In this group, then, we have three enclosures that are based on the 1,053-foot unit of length.

THIRD ORDER

Third-order enclosures are a bit more complicated. The dimensions of these earthworks are still a function of the 1,053-foot unit of

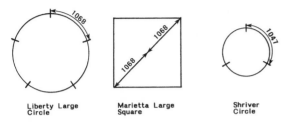

SECOND-ORDER EARTHWORKS

Liberty Large
Circle

Marietta Large
Square

Shriver
Circle

FIG. 3.2. Second-order earthworks. In this illustration, each earthwork has some feature or component that is equal in length to a multiple of the 1,053-foot unit of length (±1.5%). Hence, these earthworks, too, are based on the 1,053-foot unit of length. *Drawing by the author.*

length; however, one intermediate design step is needed to generate the particular size of these enclosures. For example, the Works East Small, Frankfort Small, Baum Small, and Seip Small circle earthworks each have a diameter of between 720 and 760 feet. Each of these circular earthworks can be constructed by inscribing a circle inside of a square that has a diagonal of 1,053 feet, plus or minus 1.5 percent. Again, the circle that results will be equal in size to the Works East Small, Frankfort Small, Baum Small, and Seip Small circles.

Similarly, the Seip Large Circle, which has a diameter of 1,530 feet, can be constructed by inscribing a circle inside of a square that has a diagonal of two times the 1,053-foot unit of length, plus or minus 1.5 percent.

Lastly, the Frankfort and Works East Large circles, which both have diameters of 1,480 feet, can be constructed by drawing a circle around a square that has sides of 1,053 feet, plus or minus 1.5 percent.

As figure 3.3 shows, in this group there are a total of seven enclosures that are based on the 1,053-foot unit of length.

FOURTH ORDER

Fourth-order enclosures are the most complicated. The dimensions of these earthworks are also a function of the 1,053-foot unit of

THIRD-ORDER EARTHWORKS

Frankfort   Baum   Seip   Works East
Small Circle   Small Circle   Small Circle   Small Circle

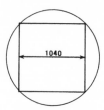

Seip Large Circle

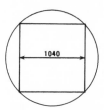

Works East Large Circle   Frankfort Large Circle

FIG. 3.3. Third-order earthworks. These earthworks are also based on the 1,053-foot unit of length. However, one intermediate design step is necessary to generate the particular size of these earthworks. *Drawing by the author.*

length. However, two or more intermediate design steps are necessary to generate these enclosures from the 1,053-foot unit. Two earthworks fall into this category. They are the Circleville Outer Circle, which has a diameter of 1,188 feet, and the Newark Fairground Circle, which has a diameter of 1,190 feet. Although separated from each other by about forty miles, these two earthworks are almost identical in size. Moreover, both earthworks can be constructed by the following procedure.

First, a circle is constructed with a circumference equal to five times the 1,053-foot unit of length, plus or minus 2.0 percent. This circle, by the way, will be almost the same size as the Liberty Large Circle. Next, a square is inscribed within the circle just constructed. The result-

FOURTH–ORDER EARTHWORKS

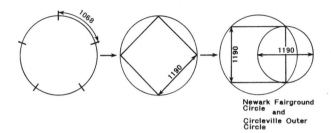

Newark Fairground
Circle and
Circleville Outer
Circle

FIG. 3.4. Fourth-order earthworks. These earthworks (i.e., Newark Fairground and Circleville Outer Circles) are also based on the 1,053-foot unit of length (±2%). However, two intermediate design steps are necessary to generate the particular size of these earthworks. *Drawing by the author.*

ing square will have sides that are each equal to about 1,190 feet. Any one side of this square is then used as the diameter for a new circle. The resultant circle will have the same diameter as the Circleville Outer Circle and Newark Fairground Circle. The procedure just described is shown in figure 3.4.

In this group, then, we have two more enclosures that are based on the 1,053-foot unit of length.

FIFTH ORDER

Fifth-order enclosures are unique in that they incorporate lesser multiples of the 1,053-foot unit of length. There are three such earthworks: the Baum Square, the Liberty Square, and Fort Ancient.

Looking first to the two square enclosures, we find that the diagonal of the Baum Square is 1,589 feet, while the diagonal of the Liberty Square is 1,566 feet. In both instances, the diagonals of these squares are equal to three times one-half of the 1,053-foot unit of length, to within plus or minus 1.0 percent. Hence, the size of these two earthworks is based on a lesser multiple of the 1,053-foot unit of length. This lesser multiple is equal to 526.5 feet.

In other words, if we divide the 1,053-foot unit by two, the result is

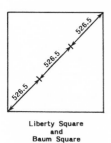

FIFTH-ORDER EARTHWORKS

Liberty Square
and
Baum Square

FIG. 3.5. Fifth-order
earthworks. In these
two earthworks (i.e.,
Liberty Square and
Baum Square), the diag-
onals of the squares are
equal to three times the
1,053-foot unit of length
(±1%). Drawing by the
author.

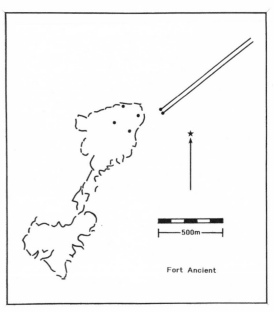

Fort Ancient

FIG. 3.6. Plan of the Fort Ancient Earthwork showing
the location of the four mounds that form a square. Figure also shows the parallel walls that are in alignment
with the winter solstice sunset. Drawing by the author,
after Connolly 1997: fig. 10.1.

526.5 feet. If we now multiply 526.5 feet by three, the result is 1,579.5,
which is equal to the length of the diagonals of the Baum and Liberty
squares to within 1.0 percent. Both of these earthworks are illustrated
in figure 3.5.

The third enclosure we wish to consider here is the Fort Ancient
site, located in Warren County, Ohio. Although Fort Ancient is not
a geometrically shaped earthwork in the same sense as the lowland
earthworks, the site is, nevertheless, a Hopewell enclosure which was
likely used for ceremonial purposes. Of interest to us here are the four
earthen mounds located within the northern section of the enclosure.
These mounds are situated so that they form a square (see figures 3.6
and 3.7). Moreover, the distances between these four mounds are all very
close to the 526.5-foot half unit of length. The measured distance, for

example, between the southeast and northeast mounds is 520.5 feet; between the northeast and northwest mounds, the distance is 512.1 feet; and between the northwest and southwest mounds, the distance is 525.12 feet. Because the view between the southwest and southeast mounds is obstructed by a glass window in the Fort Ancient museum, which precludes laser measurements, the distance between these two mounds was calculated using the measured distance between the southeast and northwest mounds (729.7 feet), the distance between the northwest and southwest mounds, and the measured angles between these three mounds. The calculated distance between the southwest and southeast mounds is 513.96 feet.

In this case, measured angles and distances were determined by a field survey that I made in April 1998, using a Nikon C-100 total station. This piece of equipment uses a built-in laser for measuring distances electronically. Distances were measured from the apex of each mound to the apex of each target mound.

FIG. 3.7. Photo of one of the four mounds that form a square at Fort Ancient. *Photo by the author.*

The four mounds that we are talking about at Fort Ancient were restored to their estimated original size by the Civilian Conservation Corps in the 1930s. However, adding earth to the original mounds would not likely have significantly affected the center to center distances as measured from the mound apexes. The situation is further clarified by archaeologists Patricia S. Essenpreis and David J. Duszynski, who conducted extensive research and excavations at the site:

> Research proceeded by first ascertaining whether reconstruction work undertaken after Fort Ancient became Ohio's first state park in 1891 had caused significant changes in the locations of the gaps or the interior mounds. . . . Much of the survey work was carried out by civil engineer, James A. Marshall in 1983–1984. Comparison of his work with the earlier surveys demonstrated that the existing mounds and gateways are in fact still located in their original position. (Essenpreis and Duszynski 1989:3)

In turn, the accuracy of Essenpreis, Duszynski, and Marshall's work is corroborated by archaeologist Robert P. Connolly's extensive field work and ground surveys at the site (1996:95, fig. 4.3).

The point here is that, like the earthworks at Newark and High Bank, which were physically surveyed by modern-day investigators, at Fort Ancient we again have hard physical evidence—evidence that we can photograph and measure—showing that the Hopewell laid out various architectural features using the 1,053-foot unit of length, or lesser multiples thereof. Notably, the distances between the above-mentioned four mounds vary from the 526.5-foot half-unit length by an average of less than 2 percent.

From the foregoing, we see how at least twenty-one of the Hopewell enclosures are based on the 1,053-foot unit of length to within plus or minus 1.5 percent. Two more earthworks, for a total of twenty-three, can be added to this list if we increase our parameters to plus or minus 2.0 percent. If we add Fort Ancient, we then have a total of twenty-four earthworks that incorporate the 1,053-foot unit of length.

On the other hand, common sense tells us that the 1,053-foot unit of length was probably not the most fundamental or basic unit of measure. For one thing, this unit of length would have been very awkward to use simply because of its large size. One can hardly imagine the Hopewell people walking around with measuring devices that were 1,053 feet in length. Clearly, a smaller unit of length would have been more practical. As already mentioned, my best estimate is that this smaller unit of length is equal to 2.106 feet, or 25.272 inches. The 1,053 foot unit of length, in turn, is equal to 500 x 2.106 feet.

My figure of 2.106 feet as the basic Hopewell unit of length is derived from the formulae provided by O'Brien and Christiansen:

> Any dimension X is the product of some unit of measure (U) multiplied by some number (Y) of them: i.e., X = UxY. This being the case if one knows X then the unit can be found by the division of Y into X: i.e., X/Y = U. Thus in theory one collects measurements from a structure, divides them by a series of whole numbers . . . and isolates the common values that emerge. The largest common value is then the unit sought or an integral multiple of it. (O'Brien and Christiansen 1986:140)

I quote O'Brien and Christiansen directly, because it is important to understand exactly how the 2.106-foot unit of length is derived (that is, 1,053/500 = 2.106) and through this understanding further recognize that the value of 2.106 feet is not some overly precise number that I arbitrarily pulled out of the air; rather it is a derived value that, like the 1,053-foot unit, also has a range. By derived, I mean that the 2.106-foot figure was calculated from the 1,053-foot unit of length, hence its apparent precision. By range, I mean that 2.106 feet is an ideal length that finds actual physical expression in a somewhat less precise fashion, in that it varies by about plus or minus 10 percent from 2.106 feet. In this regard, it might be helpful to consider the following analogous situation.

If someone in the future were to try to figure out what our basic unit of measurement is, and if that person were to try to do this by measuring the center-to-center distances of the beams in the walls of our houses, most likely he or she would find that the distance is an ideal, or average, or derived length of 16.000 inches, plus or minus 10 percent. In our world, carpenters may try to place their beams on 16-inch centers, but the reality is that there is a range to what is actually done. Some center-to-center distances may be 16.5 inches, some may be 15.75 inches, and so on.

In the same way, we might look at a large Hopewell unit like the 1,053-foot length, and derive by calculation the smaller ideal unit of 2.106 feet. But when we look at the actual use of that smaller unit, we find it is manifested in a range that can be expressed either by saying "about 2 feet," or alternatively, "2.106 feet, plus or minus 10 percent."

Let me also point out that my use of this sort of derived unit of length with an associated plus or minus value has precedence in other studies. A useful example of this precedent is found in Sherrod and Rolingson's recent work, *Surveyors of the Ancient Mississippi Valley.*

In the next section, I will show how the 2.106-foot unit of length is manifested in smaller Hopewell structures known as charnel houses.

THE BASIC HOPEWELL UNIT OF MEASUREMENT

Like sentinels of the night, the Hopewell mounds have kept a long and faithful vigil over the remaining physical essence of the Hopewell. Found within and underneath some of these mounds are the remains of Hopewell charnel houses.

A charnel house is a houselike structure where the dead are prepared for final disposition. In the case of the Hopewell, such preparations often included dismemberment, cremation, and sprinkling with red ocher. Notably, charnel houses are usually found in association with the large earthwork enclosures. As archaeologist Mark Seeman explains:

> These structures are generally identified by the presence of ovate post mold patterns or burned areas underlying burial mounds. They show considerable variation in size, but most appear to have been burned to the ground once their usefulness had ended, and subsequently were covered with earthen mounds. Numerous excavations have demonstrated that these buildings served as centers for the processing of the dead. (Seeman 1979:40)

Charnel houses, like other similar structures of their day, were built by first setting a series of upright wooden posts into the ground at regular intervals. These posts provided the support for whatever covering was used for the walls—hides, thatching, or interwoven branches. Eventually, when the walls and their supporting posts had either burned down or rotted away, a series of dark stains were left in the earth where the bases of the support poles had been. In many cases, these dark stains or post molds can still be seen today when properly excavated. Of importance to us here is that the distances that separate these post molds, or postholes, can be measured. Moreover, it turns out that the distances between a large number of these postholes are equal to either the basic Hopewell unit of length or multiples thereof.

MOUND CITY

During the mid-1960s, the undisturbed areas under Mounds 10 and 13 at Mound City were excavated by University of Chicago archaeologist James Brown and Ohio Historical Society archaeologist Raymond Baby (Brown 1979; Brown and Baby 1966). Underneath each of these mounds, Brown and Baby found the posthole patterns and cultural remains of a charnel house. The floor plans of these two structures are shown in figures 3.8 and 3.9. Superimposed on these floor plans are lines that I have drawn, with tick marks at intervals of 2.106 feet, or as close to that length as the scale in the drawings will allow. As figures 3.8 and 3.9 show, these tick marks closely coincide with the locations of the postholes. Indeed, the impression here is that the walls of these two structures were built by setting wooden posts into the ground at intervals equal to the basic Hopewell unit of length of 2.106 feet.

This is not to say that the Hopewell laid out their postholes to tolerances of hundreds or thousandths of an inch; rather, they apparently used some standard of measure that was equal to 2.106 feet, plus or minus about 10 percent. As noted earlier, the 2.106-foot length is an ideal value. Also, not every individual posthole is laid out to an interval of 2.106 feet. Nor, in retrospect, can we expect this to be the case. What we are talking about here is a preponderance of postholes.

Clearly, though, from what we see in figures 3.8 and 3.9, in these instances, the Hopewell set their postholes at very regular intervals. The spacing between the postholes is consistent and is repeated throughout both structures. The conclusion, therefore, that the interval separating the postholes is equal to the proposed basic Hopewell unit of

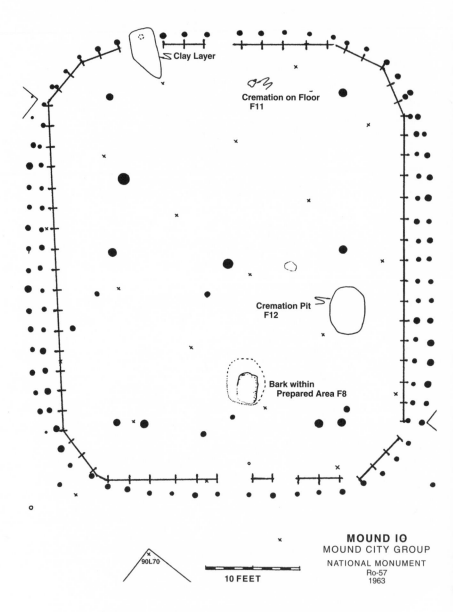

Clay Layer

Cremation on Floor
F11

Cremation Pit
F12

Bark within
Prepared Area F8

MOUND 10
MOUND CITY GROUP
NATIONAL MONUMENT
Ro-57
1963

90L70

10 FEET

FIG. 3.8. Posthole pattern of the charnel house structure found at the base of Mound 10, Mound City, with superimposed tick marks at intervals equal to the basic Hopewell unit of length of 2.106 feet. *Posthole plan from Brown 1979: fig. 27.1. Reprinted by permission of Kent State University Press.*

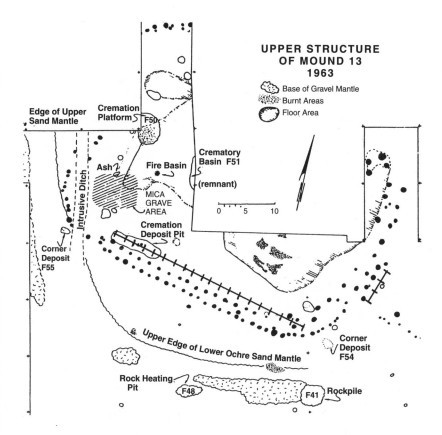

FIG. 3.9. Posthole pattern of the charnel house structure found at the base of Mound 13, Mound City, with superimposed tick marks at intervals equal to the basic Hopewell unit of length of 2.106 feet. *Posthole plan from Brown 1979: fig. 27.2. Reprinted by permission of Kent State University Press.*

length is simply a matter of mechanical comparison. In fact, if we count the number of times that tick marks correspond to the postholes, we find that the basic Hopewell unit of length is repeated no less than 106 times in the two figures just presented.

Because of the large number of fairly intact mounds found within Mound City, many of its charnel houses have been accurately mapped. Two more charnel houses that demonstrate use of the basic Hopewell unit of length are found under Mounds 6 and 20.

Excavated in 1969 and 1970 by Raymond Baby, Martha Potter, and

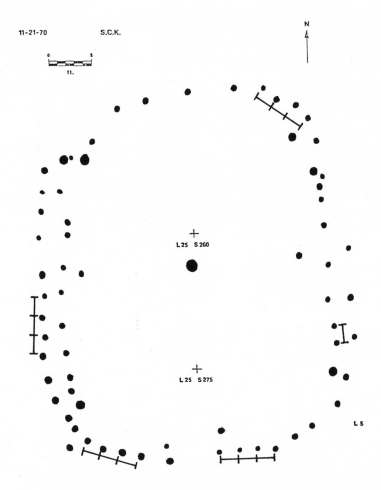

FIG. 3.10. Posthole pattern of the charnel house structure found at the base of Mound 6, Mound City, with superimposed tick marks at intervals equal to the basic Hopewell unit of length of 2.106 feet. *Posthole plan from Baby, Potter, and Koleszar 1971: N.P. Reprinted by permission of Kent State University Press.*

Stephen Koleszar (1971) of the Ohio Historical Society, the Mound 6 and Mound 20 charnel houses are shown in figures 3.10 and 3.11. In both of these figures, I again superimposed lines with tick marks at intervals equal to the basic Hopewell unit of length of 2.106 feet, or as close to that length as the scale in the drawing will allow. As can be seen, these tick marks closely match the distance that separates many of the postholes. Again, the impression here is that the basic Hopewell unit of length was used to lay out these posthole intervals.

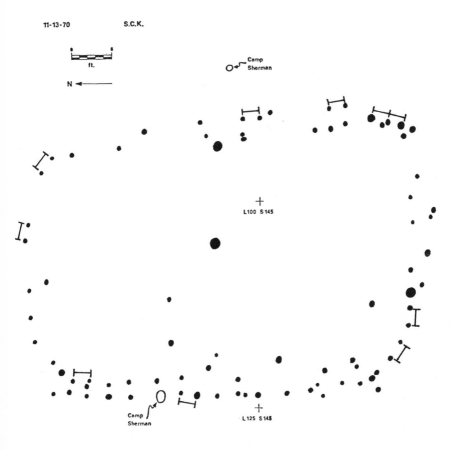

FIG. 3.11. Posthole pattern of the charnel house structure found at the base of Mound 20, Mound City, with superimposed tick marks at intervals equal to the basic Hopewell unit of length of 2.106 feet. *Posthole plan from Baby, Potter, and Koleszar 1971: n.p. Reprinted by permission of the Ohio Historical Society.*

SUBUNITS

In addition to the basic unit of length of 2.106 feet, the Hopewell appear to have used a subunit or lesser multiple of this length. This subunit, which is equal to 1.053 feet, is one-half of the basic unit of length. Interestingly enough, if we multiply the subunit of 1.053 feet by 1,000, the result is 1,053 feet, which is the unit of length that we found earlier in the large-scale enclosures. The large-scale 1,053-foot unit of length, therefore, is directly related to the smaller, basic Hopewell unit of

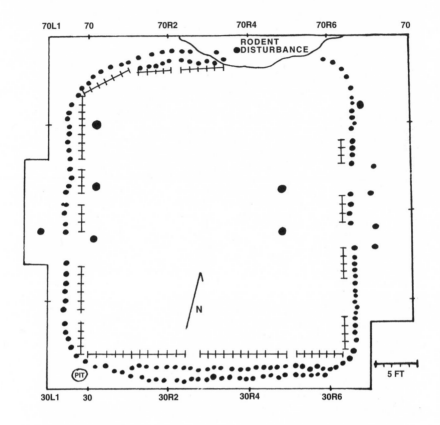

FIG. 3.12. Posthole pattern of the Seip Earthwork, House 3, with superimposed tick marks at intervals equal to 1.053 feet, or one-half of the basic Hopewell unit of length. *Posthole plan from Baby and Langlois 1979:fig 4.3. Reprinted by permission of Kent State University Press.*

length of 2.106 feet and its subunit. Of interest here is that the subunit or lesser multiple of the basic Hopewell unit of length shows up in the posthole separation distances in several charnel house structures.

At the Seip Earthwork, for example, excavations in the area between the central mound and the large circular embankment revealed several house structures (Baby and Langlois 1979). The floor plans for two of these structures—namely, House 3 and House 4—are shown here in figures 3.12 and 3.13. Superimposed on these figures are lines with tick marks at intervals of 1.053 feet, or again, as close to that

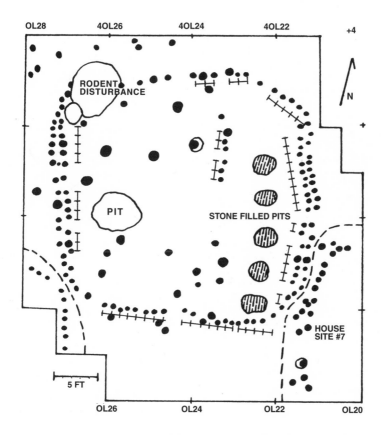

FIG. 3.13. Posthole pattern of the Seip Earthwork, House 4, with superimposed tick marks at intervals equal to 1.053 feet, or one-half of the basic Hopewell unit of length. *Posthole floor plan from Baby and Langlois 1979:fig. 4.4. Reprinted by permission of Kent State University Press.*

interval as the scales in the figures allow. As can be seen, these tick marks closely match the posthole patterns. Hence, the impression is that these two structures were built by setting wooden posts into the ground at intervals equal to one-half the basic Hopewell unit of length.

Much to their credit, after they excavated the house structures at Seip, Ohio Historical Society archaeologists proceeded to set actual wooden posts into the very same postholes that were laid out by the Hopewell. The OHS archaeologists did this for three of the houses they

FIG. 3.14. Posthole separation at the Seip Earthwork, House 2. As can be seen, the distance that separates these two postholes is precisely 12.6 inches, or about 1.053 feet, which is one-half of the basic Hopewell unit of length. Not every set of postholes is separated by this exact distance. *Photo by the author.*

discovered. As a result of these efforts, we can now go back and physically measure the posthole separation at these sites.

Figure 3.14, for example, shows one instance of the post hole separation at Seip House 2. As can be seen, the distance separating these two postholes is precisely 12.6 inches, or about 1.053 feet. This unit of length, of course, is the proposed Hopewell subunit of length. In this structure, then, we have direct photographic evidence for the use of the proposed Hopewell subunit.

Returning to Mound City, we find that the 1.053-foot subunit was also used there. In their report concerning the charnel house located under Mound 22, Ohio Historical Society archaeologists found that "the structure related to Mound City 22 was rectangular, round-cornered in ground plan . . . the walls were formed by single posts . . . and placed on an average of 1.1 feet apart" (Baby, Drennen, and Langlois 1975:2). Of course, if we round off the 1.053-foot unit to the nearest tenth, the result is 1.1 feet. Hence, what Baby, Drennen, and Langlois found was further evidence for use of the proposed subunit of length. What makes this

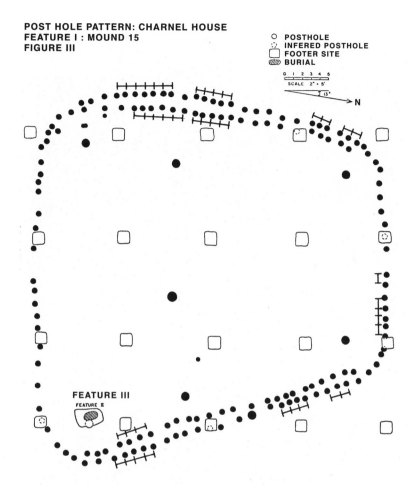

POST HOLE PATTERN: CHARNEL HOUSE
FEATURE I : MOUND 15
FIGURE III

○ POSTHOLE
∴ INFERED POSTHOLE
▢ FOOTER SITE
▨ BURIAL

FEATURE III

FIG. 3.15. Posthole pattern of the charnel house structure found at the base of Mound 15, Mound City, with superimposed tick marks at intervals equal to 1.053 feet, or one-half of the basic Hopewell unit of length. *Posthole plan from Drennan 1974: fig. 3. Reprinted by permission of the Ohio Historical Society.*

finding especially significant is that it is one of the very few published references that provides posthole separation data for a Hopewell charnel house. Unfortunately, most records of Hopewell mound excavations do not include this information, at least in narrative form.

Also at Mound City, it appears that the charnel house under Mound 15 was likewise built using the subunit length of 1.053 feet. Mound 15 was excavated in 1974 by Bert Drennan of the Ohio Historical

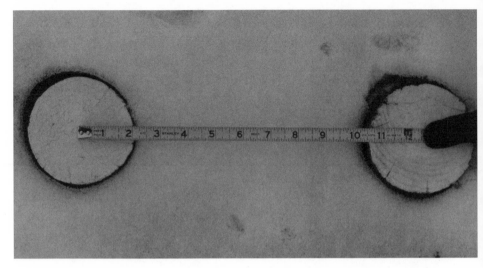

FIG. 3.16. Posthole separation at the Mound City Mound 15 charnel house. As can be seen, the distance that separates these two postholes is precisely 12.6 inches, or about 1.053 feet, which is one-half of the basic Hopewell unit of length. *Photo by the author, in company with Bob Petersen, Mound City Group National Monument Park Ranger.*

Society. Drennan's floor plan of the submound charnel house is shown in figure 3.15. As in previous figures, I have superimposed on this figure lines with tick marks at intervals equal to the subunit of length. As can be seen, these tick marks closely coincide with the postholes.

Even more impressive is the photographic evidence for the 1.053-foot subunit of length shown in figure 3.16. As was done at Seip, OHS archaeologists placed wooden posts into the actual postholes revealed under Mound 15. Like the exhibit at Seip, they did this in order to illustrate the size and shape of an actual charnel house. What we see in figure 3.16 is that the Mound 15 posthole separation for the illustrated posts is again equal to 1.053 feet or 12.6 inches, which is equal to the proposed Hopewell subunit of length.

Of course, not every posthole at the Seip and Mound City structures just mentioned is separated by 1.053 feet or 12.6 inches. The point, however, is that many are.

MULTIPLES OF THE SUBUNIT

It is difficult to say why the Hopewell used different multiples or subunits of the basic Hopewell unit of length. Perhaps the situation is analogous to our use of the inch, foot, and yard. When we build something, we can make the linear distances of our structure equal to either the inch, foot, or yard. The decision to use any one of these particular units—or alternatively, the basic Hopewell unit of length, or its multiples, or subunit—is simply a matter of convenience. Certainly, there are all kinds of possible explanations. What I can explain, though, is how these smaller multiples might have been measured.

The Hopewell subunit of length, for example, could have been measured by doubling back on itself a string that was equal in length to the basic Hopewell unit of length of 2.106 feet. By doubling the string back on itself, the resulting length of string would be equal to 1.053 feet. Greater multiples of either the basic unit or the subunit could have been measured by similar procedures.

Next I will look at what the Hopewell may have used as a standard for their measurements.

THE MEASURE OF MAN

Safely stored away in the recesses of a government building near Paris, France, is a strange-looking cylindrical object. Made from an alloy of platinum and iridium, this unique object is the official standard for the unit of mass known as a kilogram. It is of some historic interest that this object is the last physical standard in use today. In fact, by the time this book is in print, even this physical standard will probably have been replaced by a more sophisticated standard such as the standard for the length of a meter.

By international agreement, the length of a meter is the distance that light travels in $1/299,792,458$ of a second. Before that, a meter was defined as the length of 1,650,763.63 wavelengths in a vacuum of the orange-red line in the spectrum of krypton-36.

So what, then, is a standard of measurement? According to the definition we will use here, a "standard of measurement is an object which, under specified conditions, serves to define, represent, or record the magnitude of a unit" (*American Heritage Dictionary* New College Edition 1976:812).

In earlier times, standards of length were directly related to the human body. This was because body parts provide the most convenient way of measuring things. For example, the Egyptian cubit, devised in about 3000 B.C., was based on the length of the arm as measured from the elbow to the extended fingertips. This unit of measure was memorialized in a block of granite known as the royal master cubit. This singular block of granite, or standard, was then used to set the length of all cubit sticks throughout Egypt. The royal cubit, which was equal to 20.62 inches, was subdivided in a complex way. However, the basic subunit was the digit, which was equal to the width of one finger.

From what we can tell, the Greeks derived their system of measurement in part from the Egyptians. In the Greek system, the basic unit of length was the width of one finger. Sixteen fingers equaled one foot. The Romans, in turn, adopted much of the Greek system, but divided the foot into twelve inches. For the most part, Western civilization adopted the Roman system of feet and inches. And so, every time we use the foot or inch, we, too, are using standards that have their origins in the dimensions of the human body.

In fact, it was the Roman architect Vitruvius who proposed that architectural elements be based on the proportions of the human body. Vitruvius went on to illustrate, for example, how the human body with outstretched arms fits into a square and circle centered on the navel. Vitruvius's work greatly influenced the architecture of the Renaissance and, in turn, many of our own architectural designs.

The point here is that many people throughout history have based their systems of measurement on the human body. In North America, the Maya, Aztecs, and many of the Indians north of Mexico likewise used different parts of the body as physical standards. Given this, it seems logical that the Hopewell too might have used the body to establish their standards of measurement. In the case of the Hopewell, however, the question is: What part of the human body is equal to the proposed basic unit of length of 2.106 feet?

As it turns out, it may be that the answer to this question is found in the length of the human arm. Now I cannot absolutely prove that the Hopewell used the length of the arm as a standard of measure. But consider the following. To begin with, there are some very provocative data suggesting that adult males of at least some Hopewell populations may (and I emphasize "may") have averaged about 66.5 inches, or five feet, six inches in height. This figure is derived from the stature estimates provided for two Hopewell populations. Notably, these two Hopewell populations are the largest for which modern archaeologists currently have published stature information.

The first population is comprised of fifty individuals recovered from the Fairchance Mound (Baby and Langlois 1984). The Fairchance Mound is located about eighty miles east of Newark, Ohio, near Moundsville, West Virginia. Radiocarbon dates from the Fairchance Mound indicate the site dates to about A.D. 150 (Hemmings 1984:10). Characteristics that tell us that these people were Hopewell include their physical type (Lenid); their participation in the Hopewell exchange network as evidenced by findings of exotic flint, copper, mica, and marine shell; and a "true Hopewellian blade industry," featuring characteristic prismatic, parallel-sided blades struck from pyramidal cores (Hemmings 1984:36,48).

Of the fifty recorded Fairchance Mound burials, Ohio Historical Society archaeologist Raymond Baby was able to determine the stature for a total of fourteen adult males, based on measured tibia lengths and using standard formulae (Genoves 1967). Statures ranged from 169.80 cm to 172.54 cm, with a mean of 168.86 cm. The height of 168.86 cm, in turn, is equal to five feet, six inches.

The second Hopewell population for which we have sufficient population size for meaningful interpretation was recovered from the Gibson site in the Lower Illinois Valley (Buikstra 1976). In this case, stature estimates were made by physical anthropologist Jane Buikstra for twenty-four adult Hopewell males, again using standard formulae (Genoves 1967).

Buikstra's stature estimates (1976:appendix H) for each of the recovered Gibson site males ranged from 157.67 cm to 181.56 cm, with a

FIG. 3.17. Photo showing how the basic Hopewell unit of length may be related to the length of the human arm. Because the plumbed line forms a true perpendicular, the distance on the ground between the edge of the author's wife's right foot and the plumb bob will be equal to the shoulder joint to distal metacarpal bone length. For a person who is 66.5 inches in height, or the average height of an adult Hopewell male, this distance on the ground will be about 25.27 inches (or 38 percent of their height), which is equal to the basic Hopewell unit of length of 25.3 inches, or 2.106 feet. *Photo by the author.*

mean of 168.74 cm. The height of 168.74 cm, in turn, is equal to about 66.5 inches, or about five feet, six inches.

Using the tentative working hypothesis that West Virginia, Ohio, and Illinois Hopewell populations were about the same size, we can further hypothesize that the height of the average adult Hopewell male was about five feet, six inches.

Admittedly, this conclusion derives from only two, relatively small and widely separated populations. And even one six-footer in either group could have seriously skewed the results. Nevertheless, whether it is by coincidence or not, and in spite of the arguments that we can easily bring to bear against the idea, the current data suggests that five feet, six inches is a reasonable stature estimate for the typical adult Hopewell male.

Next, consider that the human arm, as measured from the proximal end of the humerus (that is, the shoulder joint or armpit) to the distal end of the metacarpal bones (where the fingers meet the palm of the hand) is equal to about 38 percent of the height of the human body. This percentage was determined from illustrations provided by Bass (1971:fig. 6) and Ubelaker (1978:fig. 124). (For a further discussion of this percentage, see Romain 1991a:n. 4).

If the average height of an adult Hopewell male was 66.5 inches (subject to the caveats I mentioned earlier), then 38 percent of that figure is 25.27 inches. In other words, the length of an average adult male

Hopewell arm from shoulder joint to distal metacarpals was 25.27 inches. As it happens, this length is identical to the basic Hopewell unit of 25.3 inches, or 2.106 feet. Each span of the average Hopewell arm, therefore, was equal to the basic Hopewell unit of length.

All of this becomes really interesting in the observation that the standard of length I have proposed for the Hopewell was, in fact, used by certain North American Indians. Ethnologist J. Peter Denny (1986:175), for example, reports the use of a canoe-building length by the Canadian Cree Indians that was measured from the "armpit to first joint of the fingers [when] gripped around an object." Denny's description is less technical than mine, but whether we say from armpit or shoulder joint, to either the "first joint of the fingers when gripped around an object" or "distal ends of the metacarpal bones," the meaning is the same. In fact, Denny's description of the Cree unit of length is identical to the arm-length standard I proposed for the Hopewell. Moreover, this is an important piece of information because it tells us that the standard of measure that I proposed for the Hopewell is not some imaginary concept but a very real standard of measure used by other Native Americans.

Finally, it is useful to observe that the standard of measure suggested here—that is, from shoulder joint to the distal end of the metacarpals—provides a very practical and consistently accurate means of measure. Figure 3.17 illustrates my point.

In figure 3.17, my wife, Evie, has her right arm extended horizontally. Suspended from her closed fist is a weighted line, or plumb line. This vertical line is in line with the distal end of her metacarpals or the "first joint of the fingers when gripped around the weighted line." Because the plumbed line forms a true perpendicular between her arm and the ground, then the distance on the ground between the edge of Evie's right foot and the plumb bob will be equal to the shoulder joint to distal metacarpal bone length. For a person who is 66.5 inches in height—or the average height of an adult Hopewell male—this distance on the ground will be 25.27 inches (38 percent of 66.5 inches = 25.27 inches) which, again, is equal to the basic Hopewell unit of length of 25.3 inches, or 2.106 feet.

Using this method of measure, it is a very simple matter to lay out long lines that are accurate multiples of the basic Hopewell unit of length. To lay out, for example, a line that is 1,053 feet in length, a Hopewell geometer would simply step off five hundred of the arm-length units demonstrated in figure 3.17. In this hypothetical scenario, I am reminded of the method used by the Cherokee to lay out their sacred areas: "a fitting location having been selected, the chiefs and magicians congregate together . . . and the medicine men then proceed to walk in single file, and *with measured steps*, completely around the spot which they would render sacred, and which is generally half a mile in diameter" (quoted in Swanton 1946:769, emphasis added).

Below we will look at how the Hopewell may have kept track of their units of measurement by counting. But first, it might be of interest to look at a possible continuity in the systems of measurement used by the Hopewell and later Mississippian peoples.

THE TOLTEC MODULE

Mississippian cultures flourished throughout the Southeast and Midwest regions of North America from about A.D. 1000 to A.D. 1600. Thus the Mississippian period began about 500 years after the demise of the Hopewell. Some of the better-known Mississippian sites include Cahokia, Etowah, Spiro, and the Toltec Mounds site.

During the 1980s, archaeologists P. Clay Sherrod and Martha Ann Rolingson, of the Arkansas Archaeological Survey, surveyed both the Toltec Mounds and Cahokia sites and then analyzed the maps and published reports of more than two dozen other sites. What they found in every location they looked at was evidence that Mississippian peoples located their burial mounds and other site features at distances that are multiples of 47.5 meters. In other words, Sherrod and Rolingson found that Mississippian peoples used a unit of length equal to 47.5 meters to lay out their sites. Sherrod and Rolingson named this unit of length the "Toltec Module."

Of special interest here is the possible correspondence between the Toltec Module and the Hopewell system of measurement. This correspondence is suggested by the following calculation (again derived from the formula provided by O'Brien and Christiansen 1986:140): Toltec Module = 47.5 meters = 155.8 feet; 155.8 feet/150 = 1.0386 feet; 1.0386 feet = 98.6 percent of the Hopewell subunit of 1.053 feet. Hence, the correspondence between the two systems is to within 1.5 percent (100% – 98.6% = 1.4%). According to Sherrod and Rolingson (1987:134), the "actual distance of the Toltec Module varies by up to 10% or ±4.75 m from a precise 47.5 m." As can be seen, the Hopewell system of measurement fits well within this 10 percent variation.

Given this, it seems possible that the Toltec Module and the basic Hopewell unit of length are actually manifestations of the same system of measurement that was used for thousands of years by the people of Eastern North America, from Mississippian times back into the Middle Woodland Period.

NUMERATION

It was about forty thousand years ago. In one hand, the man held a piece of animal bone. In his other hand, he held a broken fragment of rock. Slowly and deliberately, the man drew the sharp stone across the softer bone fragment. He then repeated the action several more times. The result was a series of tally marks, each engraved mark a symbol for something the man was keeping track of. Maybe he was counting the number of animals killed in a hunt. Or maybe he was counting the number of days away from home. What he was counting is no longer important. What is important, however, is that, for the first time, human beings were storing numerical information in a form that could be transmitted across time. From this simple beginning, we would discover, or invent, algebra, geometry, trigonometry, calculus, and a dozen other branches of mathematics. We would then use these new languages to unlock the secrets of the universe.

Direct physical evidence that the Hopewell knew how to count is meager. And, too, there may be other explanations for the marks I am about to describe. Nevertheless, it is possible that direct physical evidence that the Hopewell knew how to count exists in the form of tally marks found on various Hopewell stone gorgets.

On the other hand, indirect evidence that the Hopewell knew

how to count is ubiquitous and includes the observation that, if the Hopewell intended to lay out an earthwork with a perimeter, for example, of five times the 1,053-foot unit of length—such as found in the Liberty Circle—then they must have had some way of counting so that the desired perimeter length would incorporate five units of 1,053 feet. Likewise, we can infer from the occurrence of both greater and lesser multiples of the basic Hopewell unit of length in the distances between charnel house postholes that, again, the Hopewell had some method of counting.

Pursuing this idea a bit further, I would like to offer a possible explanation of how the earthwork builders may have counted out thousands of feet of linear distances without recourse to multiplication or use of any numbers larger than twenty. In fact, the earthwork builders could have easily laid out these distances simply by counting on their fingers and toes.

To establish, for example, a straight line that was 1,053 feet in length, the following procedure might have been used. First, the basic Hopewell unit of length is established by the outstretched arm and plumb bob method illustrated in figure 3.17. Next, a series of twenty basic Hopewell units of length are laid out either by use of a cord equal in length to 2.106 feet or by repeating the outstretched arm and plumb bob method. The twenty basic Hopewell units are kept track of by counting on all ten fingers and all ten toes. When the twenty units are reached, then one finger on the right hand is extended from a closed fist. Thus one outstretched finger is equal to twenty arm lengths, or twenty basic Hopewell units of length. This procedure is repeated, but this time, when we have counted twenty units or arm lengths on our fingers and toes, a second finger on our right hand is extended. Again and again the procedure is repeated until all of the fingers on our right hand have been extended, thus accounting for 100 units of 2.106 feet. When all of the fingers on the right hand have been extended, then we also extend one finger from the closed fist of our left hand. Thus, each extended digit on the left hand is equal to 100 units. When all five fingers of the left hand have been extended, we will have counted a total of five hundred units. Since each unit is equal to 2.106 feet, then the distance that we will have kept track of on our digits will be a total of 500 times 2.106 feet, or 1,053 feet. Thus, by counting only on our fingers and toes, and only up to twenty, we can generate huge multiples of the basic Hopewell unit of length. Equally significant, this method of counting yields the large, 1,053-foot unit of measure so often found in the Hopewell earthworks.

The system of counting just described is not imaginary. It is known as the 5–20, or base 20 system. As we have seen, large numbers are built up by multiples of twenty. What makes this system especially relevant to the Hopewell is that the base 20 system of counting was used by a large number of diverse Native American groups throughout North America, including the Aztecs, Maya, and even the Eskimo. It is not unreasonable to think that perhaps the Hopewell used a similar system.

CONCLUSION

In summary, it was proposed that the basic Hopewell unit of length was 2.106 feet. A subunit which is equal to one-half of the basic unit of length appears to have been used. And either the subunit or the basic unit were used to lay out at least nine small house-like structures which may have been charnel houses. In actuality though, not all charnel houses always incorporate these smaller units and, as I have pointed out, not all postholes even in the illustrated charnel houses are always separated by the smaller units of measure. Quite simply, without more data in the way of very accurate site maps, it is difficult to know how widespread or common the use of these smaller units of measure actually was.

It was suggested that the basic Hopewell unit of length may have its origins in the length of the human arm. However, again more data is needed before we can establish that conclusion with any real certainty.

At the other end of the scale, large multiples of the basic unit of length were clearly used to lay out the large geometric enclosures. At least twenty-four of the large earthworks were found to incorporate the great length of 1,053 feet. The length of 1,053 feet, in turn, is equal to five hundred times the basic unit of 2.106 feet. And, as I have shown, five hundred could have easily been counted in groups of twenty by use of the fingers and toes.

In a later chapter, we will explore the idea that the circular and square earthworks were meant as symbols of the earth and sky. Suffice it to say at this point that, by incorporating these special units of length into their earthworks, the Hopewell, in effect, synthesized the dimensions of their physical being with their universe.

Chapter 4

HOPEWELL ASTRONOMY

Consider the true picture. Think of myriads of tiny bubbles, very sparsely
scattered, rising through a vast black sea. We rule some of the bubbles. Of the
waters we know nothing.

—Niven and Pournelle, *The Mote in God's Eye*

In the dream world existence between conception and birth, each
of us floated in a formless darkness surrounded by warm amniotic fluid.
Suspended between consciousness and eternity, we had little or no
awareness of up and down, front and back, left and right, future or past.
We did not relate to the universe in those terms.

All that changed, however, when we entered the world of air-
breathing creatures. Confronted with the openness of space and an
ever-changing present, we needed to orient ourselves. Of course, it was
easy to orient ourselves in space—after all, our bodies have a front and
back, left and right, top and bottom. Imposed on the world around us,
these directions provide the spatial references we need to function effec-
tively. As it happens, these directions are at right angles to each other.
And so from these directions we can further establish the cardinal directions of north, south, east, and west, as well as the zenith and nadir.

Orienting ourselves in time was a bit more involved. Looking to
nature, we found oscillating, cyclic phenomena that gave us a way to

relate to the future and the past. Night and day, the monthly changes of the moon, and the advance of the seasons—these phenomena gave us a sense of time.

Moreover, because the sun and moon, and some of the stars and planets, have predictable rising and setting positions on the horizon, these celestial bodies allow us to orient not only ourselves but also our sacred structures in time and space. In some instances, we aligned our structures to the rising or setting of the sun at the solstices or equinoxes. In other instances, we aligned our structures to the lunar maximums or minimums. Other times, we aligned our structures to a star like Sirius or a planet like Venus. Regardless of what celestial body we used, though, the effect of orienting our structures to oscillating celestial phenomena was to bring our sacred structures into harmony with the great cycles of time and into harmony with the visible universe.

In earlier chapters, I proposed a possible sequence of events involved in building a sacred structure. First, a location is identified that is in some way sacred or special. Second, a shape is given to that place; that is, we define the geometric form of the area. Next, we establish the size of the space. This is the step that allows us to bring our abstract geometric shape into the physical world. Finally, we give a direction to our shape. In other words, the final step is to decide in what direction our geometric figure will face.

In the case of the Hopewell, it is clear that they aligned many of their earthworks to the sun and moon. In this chapter, we will look at these celestial alignments in some detail. But first, it might be useful to consider some of the mechanics that are involved.

SOLAR AND LUNAR MECHANICS

The annual movement of the sun from north to south and back again and the way this apparent movement defines the solstices and equinoxes is generally understood by most people. Figures 4.1 and 4.2 show how the solstice positions in particular are defined by various rising and setting azimuths.

The important point is that, by watching the sun over a period of just a couple of years, we can easily identify these solstice and equinox

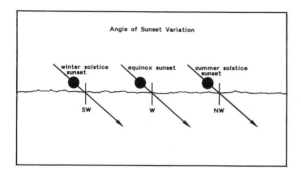

FIG. 4.1. Illustration showing how the sun sets at an angle to the horizon, and the relative positions of the sun at the winter solstice, equinox, and summer solstice. *Drawing by the author, after Reed 1974:fig. 24.*

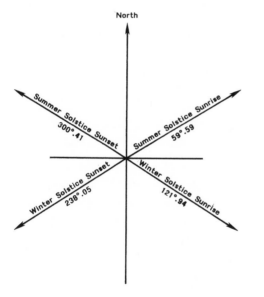

FIG. 4.2. Solstice azimuths for 39° north latitude, 1° horizon elevation, A.D. 1, and lower limb tangency. *Drawing by the author, based on data from Aveni 1972.*

positions on the horizon. Once these positions are identified, it is then a simple matter to align a building, or a wall, or an enclosure to any of these points on the horizon.

The motions of the moon are more complicated. The most obvious lunar cycle is its monthly metamorphosis from new moon to waxing, to full, to waning, and back again to new. On another scale, though, there is a lunar cycle that is counted in years. This cycle is 18.61 years in length, and it is this one that we are especially concerned with here. Hively and Horn give a good description of this cycle:

The rising point of the Moon as marked along the horizon oscillates between a northerly and southerly extreme during each sidereal month (27⅓ days). Due to a slow precession of the Moon's orbit, these extreme northerly and southerly rising points oscillate between two fixed azimuths with a period of 18.61 years. A similar variation occurs in the setting point of the Moon.(Hively and Horn 1982:S11)

In figure 4.3, I have illustrated the angular variation in the lunar cycle that Hively and Horn describe. As can be seen, the lunar standstills are comparable in a way to the sun's solstice extremes.

METHODS

While contemporaneous observation of the sun or moon is straightforward enough, it is quite another matter to predict exactly where the sun or moon will rise or set in relation to the Hopewell earthworks. Yet this is exactly what we need to do if we want to find out how closely some particular earthwork is aligned to the sun or moon on any future or past date, such as the date of the sun's equinox or solstice. To make these kinds of predictions, we need to take into account such variables as horizon elevation, date, and latitude of the site. Spherical trigonometry gives us a way to take these variables into account by use of the following formula, where A stands for the azimuth, h is the angular elevation of the horizon, ϕ represents the latitude of the site, and δ is the declination of the sun or moon (see Wood 1978:61):

$$\cos A = \frac{\sin \delta - \sin \phi \sin h}{\cos \phi \cos h}$$

In short, this formula will give us the exact azimuth for the sun's solstice and moon's standstill positions from any given location.

For further clarification, azimuth means "the angular distance between north and any other horizontal direction . . . [it] is measured clockwise around the horizon from 0 degrees at north through 360 degrees" (Bowditch 1966:385).

We could use the above formula for our analysis of each Hopewell earthwork, but the task would be mind-numbing. Better to

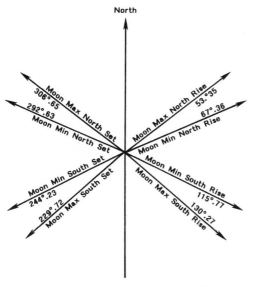

FIG. 4.3. Maximum and minimum lunar standstill azimuths for 39° north latitude, 1° horizon elevation, A.D. 1, and lower limb tangency. *Drawing by the author, based on data from Aveni 1972.*

leave this kind of number crunching to computers. Indeed, most of the time-consuming calculations have already been done for us and are available in convenient table form. The tables I am referring to were computer-generated, based on a program that was written by Colgate University physics and astronomy professor Dr. Anthony F. Aveni.

First published in 1972, Aveni's tables provide the exact azimuth for the rising and setting of the sun and moon at the solstices and standstills for the years 1500 B.C. to A.D. 1500, for latitudes 0° through 60° north and south, and for horizon elevations from 0° to 3°. To use these tables we simply enter and interpolate according to the latitude, horizon elevation, and date of our site. Additional corrections can also be made by reference to the tables for refraction and variations from standard values of temperature and barometric pressure as a function of altitude.

For the analyses presented here, the location of each site was established to the nearest 10' of latitude by reference to United States Geological Survey topographic maps. Horizon elevations were measured in the field using a Suunto Model PM-5 optical reading clinometer. Measurements were typically made to the top of the distant tree line.

All horizon elevation measurements were made from the actual locations identified on the aerial photos or topographic maps to follow as
point A, point B, and so on. I would estimate that, in those instances
where the earthworks are not visible on the ground due to agricultural
plowing but are still visible in aerial photos, I was able to establish the
point A or point B locations on the ground to within plus or minus ten
feet of the actual earthworks by measuring distance and angle from
identifiable landmarks visible on both the aerial photos and on the
ground. Since, in almost every instance, the distant horizons as viewed
from points A or B are all flat, even if elevated (with the exception of
the Hopewell site and, to a lesser extent, Marietta), establishing these
locations to within plus or minus ten feet provides more than sufficient
accuracy for measuring horizon elevations which are typically several
miles distant. For future reference, in all instances a photographic
record was made of each horizon elevation as viewed from points A
or B.

The date of construction for each site was presumed to be A.D.
250, which was about the height of the Hopewell florescence. Rising
and setting events were considered to occur at the instant of the sun or
moon's lower limb tangency with the horizon, where lower limb tangency refers to the instant when the bottom part of the sun or moon
touches the horizon.

As tables 5 and 6 show, the rising and setting positions for the sun
and moon change at relatively small increments in response to changes
in latitude and date. A change of one full degree of latitude, for example, results in a change in rising or setting azimuth of less than one-half
of one degree. For comparative purposes, consider that the north-south
separation between Cincinnati and Columbus, Ohio, is slightly less than
one degree of latitude. The point here is that rounding the latitude of
our sites to the nearest 10' increment provides calculated azimuths that
are accurate to about one-twentieth of one degree.

Similarly, over the course of 1,000 years, the sun's rising and setting positions on the horizon change by less than two tenths of one
degree in azimuth as the result of a phenomenon known as precession.
Aveni's tables (1972) take this change into account, and the tables are

Table 5. Changes in the sun's azimuth as a function of latitude (summer solstice sun, A.D. 250, 1° horizon elevation, lower limb tangent)

	39°00′N latitude	39°30′N latitude	40°00′N latitude
Rise	059°.639	059°.406	059°.172
Set	300°.361	300°.594	300°.827

Source: Aveni (1972)

Table 6. Changes in the sun's azimuth as a function of date (summer solstice sun, 39°N latitude, 0° horizon elevation, lower limb tangent)

	500 B.C.	A.D. 1	A.D. 500
Rise	058°.483	058°.566	058°.666
Set	301°.516	301°.433	301°.333

Source: Aveni (1972)

entered by date, which in this case is A.D. 250. Accordingly, we would not expect any significant change in the calculated azimuth of the sun, even if the Hopewell earthworks were built two or three hundred years earlier or later than the assumed date of A.D. 250.

By far the greatest change in azimuth results from variations in horizon elevation. Because the sun and moon rise and set at an angle to the horizon, the horizon elevation affects the apparent rising and setting azimuth of those bodies. As table 7 shows, at 39° north latitude, a change of one degree in horizon elevation results in a corresponding change of about one degree in the sun's or moon's rising or setting position on the horizon.

Spherical trigonometry and observational astronomy can be understood, given sufficient study. With respect to Hopewell archaeoastronomy, however, the more difficult task is to find sites that are still sufficiently intact as to allow accurate angular measurements to be made of their walls, passageways, and other features. Because of agricultural plowing, it usually happens that the walls of the Hopewell enclosures are very difficult to see at ground level. Indeed, many times

Table 7. Changes in the sun's azimuth as a function of
horizon elevation (summer solstice sun, 39°N latitude,
A.D. 500, lower limb tangent)

	0° horizon elevation	1° horizon elevation	2° horizon elevation	3° horizon elevation
Rise	058°.667	059°.689	060°.711	061°.733
Set	301°.333	300°.311	299°.289	298°.267

Source: Aveni (1972)

they are not visible at all. In such instances, though, these same walls
can sometimes be seen from the air and may be visible in aerial photographs. Typically, in aerial photos, the ancient wall remnants appear as
ghostly white lines.

Except for the Marietta Earthworks, which are considered sepa-
rately, what I have done here is to measure the proposed alignments as
well as the orientation of the individual earthworks themselves on
eight-by-ten-inch aerial photos, using a ten-inch diameter circular pro-
tractor. (For publication purposes these photos have been greatly reduced from their original 8" x 10" sizes.) This ten-inch diameter protrac-
tor is divided into marked increments of one-half degree; hence, it was
possible to discern angles on the aerial photos to an accuracy of one-
quarter of a degree, plus or minus about one-eighth of a degree.
Because the sun's diameter is equal to about one-half of one degree, the
maximum potential rounding error associated with this method is less
than one-half of one sun diameter.

As to the aerial photos themselves, in all cases I selected those
photos that best showed the individual sites from among several series
of photos taken by the United States Department of Agriculture during
the years from 1938 to 1988 (also see Taylor and Spurr 1973). The photos
were taken by the Agriculture Department for making soil survey
maps, land-use planning, and other such purposes. All of the photos I
selected have been rectified.

Rectification means that a procedure known as aerotriangulation
was used to correct for any deviation from the true vertical that may
have occurred in the picture-taking as the aircraft camera passed over
the site. This correction is made in the print-making process by the

Photogrammetric Branch of the Aerial Photography Field Office. The result is a photograph that is accurate to better than 99 percent (USDA 1983).

It will be noted in several instances that the corners of what I refer to as "square" earthwork enclosures are actually rounded. In these cases, I bisected the rounded corners by extending a line along the angle of each embankment wall. The intersections of these lines helped define the diagonal of each earthwork, and in turn, the diagonals bisected the rounded corners, thereby yielding points A and B on the rounded corners. The same procedure is used in chapter 5 with reference to Hopewell charnel house alignments, and in those figures the extended guidelines are actually drawn on to the figures.

SEAL

Visiting the Seal Earthwork brings to mind an interesting irony in space, time, and worldviews. The Seal Earthwork is located on the east bank of the Scioto River in Pike County, Ohio, just a few miles south of Chillicothe. Less than half a mile away, however, is an Atomic Energy Commission nuclear facility.

What I find so ironic is that here, at Seal, technicians from two very different worldviews were both using the same space to explore their respective universes, but in radically different ways. Two thousand years ago, the Hopewell were dealing with unseen forces and entities associated with the otherworld; whereas today, in almost the exact same space, we are exploring the equally mysterious world of subatomic particles and quantum mechanics. Moreover, through our respective territorial imperatives, we have both left our mark on the land.

The mark left by the Hopewell is beginning to fade. In fact, most of the Seal Earthwork has been destroyed by gravel mining and agricultural plowing. From what is left of the site, however, it is clear that the square enclosure is very precisely oriented to the cardinal directions and to the vernal and autumnal equinoxes. This is one of the very few Hopewell earthworks so oriented.

Figure 4.4a shows Squier and Davis's map of the earthwork; figure 4.4b shows a section of the USGS map for the area with the Seal

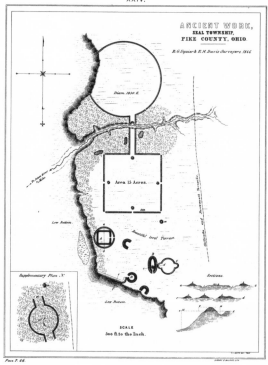

FIG. 4.4A. *Squier and Davis's map (1848:plate 24) of the Seal Earthwork.*

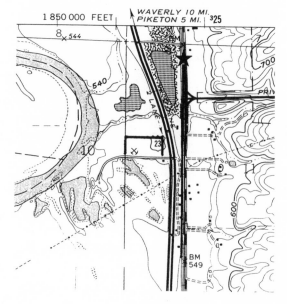

FIG. 4.4B. *Section of USGS Wakefield Quadrangle map with what remains of the Seal Earthwork sketched in by the author.*

FIG. 4.5. Aerial view of what remains of the Seal Square. The walls of the square appear as ghostly white lines. Extending from points A to B and from B to C, the walls of the square are in alignment with the cardinal directions. Wall A-B is aligned east-west, while wall B-C is aligned north-south. *Enlarged detail of U.S. Department of Agriculture aerial photograph, 1976.*

Earthwork sketched in; and figure 4.5 presents a 1976 aerial view of what is left of the square enclosure. Using the USGS topographic map in conjunction with the aerial photo gives us a fairly straightforward way of determining the exact orientation of the earthwork. Specifically, we find by reference to the USGS map that the one mile section of the Norfolk and Western railroad just to the east of the Seal enclosure extends along an azimuth of 359° as measured from true north. Using the known azimuth of the railroad as a reference, we next draw a true north-south line onto the photo in figure 4.5. With a north-south line established on the aerial photo, we are now able to directly measure the azimuth of the square enclosure's north wall from point A to point B. This azimuth is 270°. In other words, the wall that extends from point A to point B extends along a precise east-west azimuth in exact alignment with the rising and setting position of the sun on the days of the vernal and autumnal equinoxes. Correspondingly, it also happens that the wall extending from point B to point C is aligned along a true north-south axis. Hence, the Seal Square is aligned to cardinal directions and to both equinoxes.

As already mentioned, the Seal Earthwork is the only Hopewell earthwork for which there is clear evidence of alignment to the cardinal directions. Squier and Davis (1848) show a few other earthworks that might be similarly aligned. However, without aerial photos or reliable ground surveys, we cannot state with certainty that these other sites are, in fact, aligned to the cardinal directions.

This brings us back to the problem of how much weight we should give to one example of any phenomenon, as contrasted to the obvious significance implicit in a series or pattern of occurrences. Clearly, we would always prefer to find more than one occurrence of any phenomenon.

In the case of the Seal Earthwork, I don't know why the Hopewell chose to align this particular earthwork to the equinoxes. Maybe further research will reveal other sites similarly oriented. And maybe, through further study, we will one day be able to answer the question why this earthwork was oriented to the cardinal directions, while others were oriented to the solstices. For now, all we can do is note the data for what it is, and point out those features of the equinoxes that might have been recognized and considered important by the Hopewell.

Most noticeably, at the time of the equinoxes, night and day are of equal length: twelve hours of night and twelve hours of day. As the equinoxes mark the beginning of spring and the beginning of fall, they also mark the two halves of the year. Moreover, as already mentioned, on the days of the equinoxes, the sun rises at an azimuth of 90°, or due east, and sets at the reciprocal azimuth of 270°, or due west, thereby establishing the cardinal directions. On the days of the equinoxes, therefore, night and day are in balance, the seasons are in balance, and the cardinal directions are established. In other words, through the alignment of the earthwork to the equinoxes, a synchronicity is established wherein the earth, sky, and earthwork are all in harmony. Perhaps this synchronicity is related to the orientation of the Seal Earthwork.

DUNLAP

According to local legend, sometime in the late 1800s, a local Ross County family barely escaped the raging floodwaters of the Scioto River when they climbed to the top of an ancient Indian mound near the Dunlap Earthwork. Given that Dunlap is located on the banks of the Scioto River, and that the river is subject to rapid and severe flooding, I do not doubt that the story could be true.

Today, the scene is much more tranquil and, in fact, due to years of agricultural plowing, very little of the Dunlap Earthwork can be seen. Traces of the earthwork, however, are still visible in older aerial photos. Specifically, figure 4.6a shows my plan of the earthwork made by tracing an aerial photograph. Figure 4.6b shows a section of the USGS map for the area with the Dunlap Earthwork sketched in, and figure 4.7 shows an aerial photo of the earthwork as it appeared in 1938.

By using the same method as outlined earlier for the Seal Earthwork, we are able to establish the orientation of the Dunlap Earthwork by reference to the USGS topographic map and aerial photo. As shown by the USGS map, Infirmary Road—which is just to the south of the square embankment—extends along an azimuth of 263° as measured from true north. Using this known value, we next draw a true north-south line on to the aerial photo. Using this north-south line as a reference, we measure the azimuth of the diagonal sightline that extends from point A to point B in figure 4.7. The corners of the Dunlap Earthwork are difficult to make out. However, from what I can tell, the azimuth of the diagonal sightline is 60°.5. As measured in the field from point A, the horizon elevation along this sightline is 1°.5.

From Aveni's tables, and given a date of A.D. 250, 39°20' north latitude, lower limb tangency, and 1°.5 horizon elevation, it is found that the summer solstice sun would have risen at a point on the horizon at an

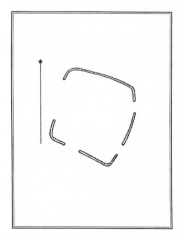

FIG. 4.6A. Map of the Dunlap
Earthwork made by tracing an aerial
photograph. *Drawing by the author.*

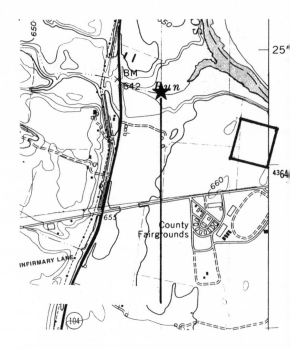

FIG. 4.6B. *Section of USGS Anderson Quadrangle map with the
Dunlap Earthwork sketched in by the author.*

azimuth of 60.00138 degrees as viewed from point A. If I have correctly
identified the corners of this earthwork, then the accuracy of this sightline is to within one-half of one degree ($60°.5 - 60°.00138 = 0°.49862$). In
other words, the diagonal of the Dunlap enclosure is aligned to the summer solstice sunrise to within one-half of one degree.

HOPETON

The Hopeton Earthwork is located in Ross County, Ohio, on the
east bank of the Scioto River, diagonally across from Mound City. Again,
years of agricultural plowing have greatly reduced the height of the
earthwork. But fortunately, recent efforts by the Archaeological Conser-

FIG. 4.7. Aerial view of the Dunlap Earthwork. The diagonal of the Dunlap enclosure, shown here as line A-B, is aligned to the summer solstice sunrise to within one-half of one degree. *Enlarged detail of U.S. Department of Agriculture aerial photograph, 1938.*

vancy and the National Park Service have resulted in the acquisition of the site and its incorporation into the Hopewell Culture National Historic Park. Figure 4.8a shows Squier and Davis's map of the earthwork; figure 4.8b shows a section of the USGS map for the area with the Hopeton Earthwork sketched in; and figure 4.9 shows an aerial photo of the earthwork as it appeared in 1938.

Using the same methods as discussed earlier, we find from the

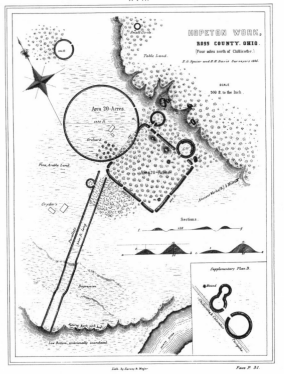

FIG. 4.8A. *Squier and Davis's map (1848: plate 17) of the Hopeton Earthwork.*

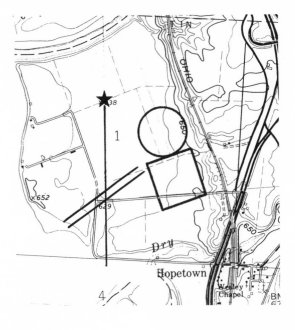

FIG. 4.8B. *Section of USGS Chillicothe West Quadrangle map with the Hopeton Earthwork sketched in by the author.*

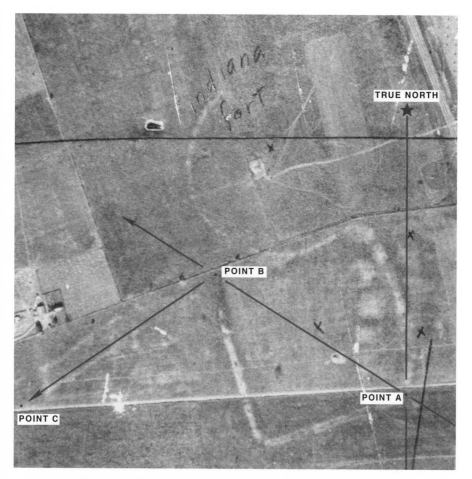

FIG. 4.9. Aerial view of the Hopeton Earthwork. The diagonal of the Hopeton enclosure, shown here as line A-B, is aligned to the summer solstice sunset to within three-quarters of one degree. The parallel walls, shown here as extending parallel to line B-C, are aligned to the winter solstice sunset to within one-third of one degree. *Enlarged detail of U.S. Department of Agriculture aerial photograph, 1938.*

USGS map that the road that cuts through the south part of the square enclosure extends along an azimuth of 86°.5 as measured from true north. With this known value, we draw a true north-south line onto the aerial photo. With this north-south line as a reference, we measure the azimuth of the diagonal sightline that extends from point A to point B in figure 4.9. The northwest corner of the square in the area of point B is somewhat difficult to discern and the Hopeton Square is not exactly symmetrical. But from what I can tell, the azimuth of line A-B is 301°.0.

Unfortunately, the distant horizon at Hopeton is partially blocked by a newly created hill of debris from a nearby gravel mining operation. Still, this mound of dirt is no higher than 1°.25 as viewed from point A. Further, by measuring the horizon elevation along either side of this obstructing hill, and by plotting the horizon profile from USGS maps, it can be established that the horizon elevation along sightline A-B is 1°.25.

Using a date of A.D. 250, 39°20' north latitude, lower limb tangency, and 1°.25 horizon elevation, we find from Aveni's tables that the summer solstice sun would have set at a point on the horizon at an azimuth of 300°.2576 as viewed from point A. The accuracy of this sightline is to within 0°.75 (301°.0 − 300°.2576 = 0°.7424). In other words, the diagonal of the Hopeton Square is aligned to the summer solstice sunset to within three-quarters of one degree.

The parallel walls at Hopeton have long been of interest to investigators. Clearly, they head toward the Scioto River. Perhaps equally important, they are also in alignment with the winter solstice sunset. More specifically, if we measure the azimuth of line B-C in figure 4.9, we find that the parallel walls extend along an azimuth of 237°. As measured in the field from point B, the horizon elevation along line B-C is 1.5°. Given a date of A.D. 250, 39°20' north latitude, lower limb tangency, and 1°.5 horizon elevation, it is found from Aveni's tables that the winter solstice sun set at an azimuth of 237°.3778. The parallel walls, therefore, are aligned to the winter solstice sunset to within about one-third of one degree (237°.3778 − 237°.0 = 0°.3778).

In addition to the alignment of the parallel walls to the sun, yet another interesting discovery is that two Hopewell burials were found approximately fifty feet from the southwest end of the parallel walls (Goodman 1973). In the case of the first burial, the only things left were the remains of an arm and some mica debitage. Evidence of recent digging suggests that the rest of the skeleton had been removed by vandals. In the case of the second burial, however, the skeleton was mostly intact. The remains were those of a female in her mid-twenties. She had been buried with a variety of grave goods, including a ball of red ocher, an eight-inch diameter piece of mica, part of a conch shell, a bone awl, and pottery. What is especially intriguing, however, is that not only were these burials located in association with the parallel walls just mentioned, but, by virtue of their location, these burials are also at the terminus, or end, of a winter solstice sightline.

ANDERSON

It looked like a gorgeous day for a flight, and so I thought it was going to be a great trip. I was wrong.

The plan was for Evie and I to fly down to Ross County, take some aerial photos of the earthworks, and return home to Cleveland later that same evening. We departed Cleveland and, after a couple of hours, landed at the Ross County airport. Along the way, we hit a bit of turbulence and, by now, Evie was feeling airsick. Still, she insisted that I go on, while she would wait for me in the pilot's lounge. I was all right with that decision, because I could tell from the greenish tinge to her face that she would need this break before attempting the return flight.

Anxiously, I refueled the plane, checked the charts, and took off. First Dunlap, then Mound City, Cedar Bank, and Hopeton. I circled Chillicothe a couple of times, flew over the confluence of the Scioto River and Paint Creek, and skimmed the mountains to the east of the city. Then on to High Bank, Hopewell, and Frankfort. I was thrilled to fly over and photograph the very same earthworks I had walked over, wondered about, and studied so intently on the ground. I was having a spectacular time.

Then I saw it. While following Paint Creek at an altitude of about two thousand feet, I looked for Anderson. What I found was incredible. In the space of a heartbeat, my soaring spirit was shot through with the finality of what unfolded before me.

I lowered the flaps and circled like a great vulture. There was the Anderson Earthwork—an ancient ceremonial ground—being torn apart by bulldozers. For almost two thousand years, the earthwork had withstood the ravages of time and the elements. Wind and sun and rain had not erased the geometric figure that once connected the Hopewell people to their universe. Now, in a matter of moments, the walls that

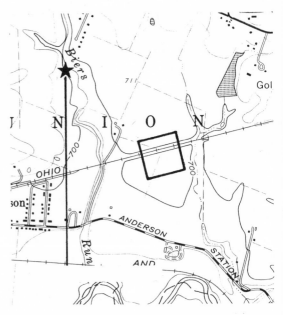

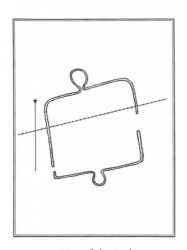

Fig. 4.10a. Map of the Anderson
Earthwork made by tracing an aerial
photograph. *Drawing by the author.*

Fig. 4.10b. *Section of USGS Chillicothe West Quadrangle map
with the Anderson Earthwork sketched in by the author.*

defined this sacred space were being ripped down and crushed under
the steel treads of enormous yellow machines.

Eventually, I turned the plane away from the destruction I witnessed and headed back to the airport. But I couldn't help it—scattered
in with the radio traffic, bits and pieces of the words attributed to Chief
Seattle came to mind:

> Every part of this earth is
> sacred to my people. . . .
> What befalls the earth befalls
> all the sons of the
> earth. . . . Man did not weave
> the web of life—he is merely a
> strand in it. Whatever he
> does to the web—he does to himself.

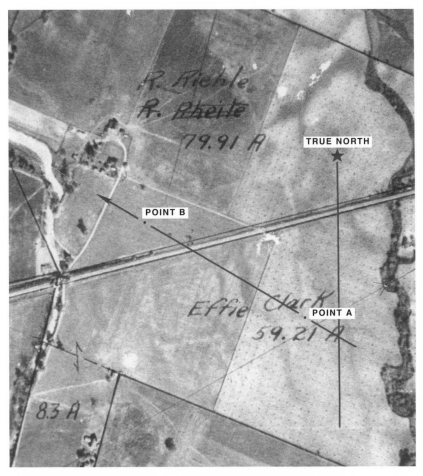

Fig. 4.11. Aerial view of the Anderson Earthwork. The diagonal of the Anderson enclosure, shown here as line A-B, is aligned to the summer solstice sunset to within one-half of one degree. *Enlarged detail of U.S. Department of Agriculture aerial photograph, 1938.*

Today, of course, the earthwork is almost entirely destroyed and has been replaced by a housing development. About the only good thing I can report is that, before the site was totally destroyed, I was able to visit it, photograph it, and take several horizon elevation measurements.

Located in Ross County, Ohio, the Anderson Earthwork was situated on the north fork of Paint Creek. Figure 4.10a shows my plan of the earthwork made by tracing an aerial photograph; figure 4.10b shows a section of the USGS map for the area with the Anderson Earthwork sketched in; and figure 4.11 shows an aerial photo of the earthwork as it appeared in 1938.

From the USGS map, we find that the Baltimore and Ohio railroad tracks that cut through the earthwork extend along an azimuth of 76°.8 as measured from true north. Using this known value, we draw a true north-south line on to the aerial photo. Using this north-south line as a reference, we measure the azimuth of the diagonal sightline that extends from point A to point B in figure 4.11. In figure 4.11, the northwest corner of the enclosure is somewhat difficult to make out. However, careful examination shows that the azimuth of line A-B is 300°.5. As measured in the field from point A, the horizon elevation along this sightline is 1°.5.

Using a date of A.D. 250, 39°20' north latitude, lower limb tangency, and 1°.5 horizon elevation, it is found from Aveni's tables that the summer solstice sun would have set at a point on the horizon at an azimuth of 299°.9986 as viewed from point A. The accuracy of this sightline, therefore, is to within about one-half of one degree (300°.5 − 299°.9986 = 0°.5014). In other words, the Anderson Earthwork is aligned to the summer solstice sunset to within about one-half of one degree.

HOPEWELL

Throughout this book, "Hopewell" has been used to identify both a people and a particular earthwork. In both instances, the term "Hopewell" is derived from the name of the former owner of the property on which the Hopewell Earthwork is located, namely, Captain M. C. Hopewell.

The Hopewell site is located on the north side of the north fork of Paint Creek, in Ross County, Ohio. Squier and Davis's map of the site is shown in figure 4.12a, while figure 4.12b shows a section of the USGS map for the area with the Hopewell Earthwork sketched in. Figure 4.13 shows an aerial photo of the site as it appeared in 1976.

The USGS map shows that the Baltimore and Ohio railroad tracks just to the south of the square embankment extend along an azimuth of 76°.25 as measured from true north. Using this known value, we draw a

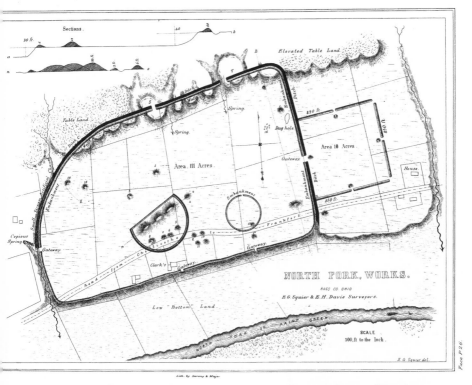

Fig. 4.12a. *Squier and Davis's map (1848:plate 10) of the Hopewell Earthwork.*

Fig. 4.12b. *Section of USGS Chillicothe West Quadrangle map with the Hopewell Square sketched in by the author.*

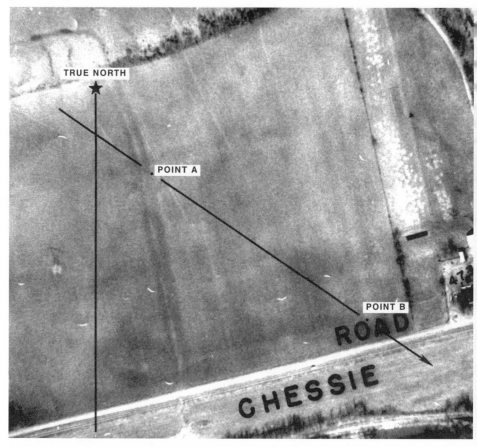

Fig. 4.13. Aerial view of the Hopewell Square. The diagonal of the earthwork, shown here as line A-B, is in almost perfect alignment to the winter solstice sunrise. *Enlarged detail of U.S. Department of Agriculture aerial photograph, 1976.*

true north-south line on to the aerial photo. Using this north-south line as a reference, we find that the azimuth of the diagonal sightline that extends from point A to point B in figure 4.13 is 123°.5. As measured in the field from point A, the horizon elevation along this sightline is 2°.25.

From Aveni's tables, we find that, given a date of A.D. 250, 39°20' north latitude, lower limb tangency, and 2°.25 horizon elevation, the winter solstice sun would have risen at a point on the horizon at an azimuth of 123°.4416 as viewed from point A. The accuracy of this sightline, therefore, is almost perfect (123°.5 – 123°.4416 = 0°.0584). In other words, the Hopewell Square is aligned to the winter solstice sunrise.

MOUND CITY

Mound City is located in Ross County, Ohio, on the west bank of the Scioto River. Figure 4.14a presents Squier and Davis's map of the site; figure 4.14b shows a section of the USGS map for the area with Mound City sketched in; and figure 4.15 shows an aerial photo of the earthwork as it appeared in 1988.

Since its discovery, the Mound City enclosure and its associated burial mounds have been plowed down for agricultural purposes, excavated for their burial goods, and graded by bulldozers to make room for Camp Sherman, a World War I training camp. At one time, too, both a small road and a set of railroad tracks cut through the enclosure.

In the late 1920s, the embankment walls were reconstructed. But, unfortunately, the reconstructed south embankment was placed north of where it should have been, while the reconstructed northwest corner of the enclosure was incorrectly placed too far to the southeast.

Thus the structure remained until the 1960s, when a series of excavations and restorations were made that corrected the earlier errors. It is important to note that these later restorations—made by Brown and Baby (1966), Hanson (1966, 1965), and Drennen (1972)—were constructed by piling earth on top of remnants of the original walls. The original walls were successfully located by excavation. Concerning the east wall of the square enclosure, Brown and Baby (1966:11) note that "the east wall . . . could be traced with some certainty." Regarding the southeast corner of the enclosure, Brown and Baby explain that "The base of the original embankment was finally located in the unit east of the tracks where it was indicated by a midden at its base. This unit was extended to continue the tracing of the embankment base. . . . It was successfully followed west of the tracks and to the point where it straightens out into the south wall" (Brown and Baby 1966:6). Regarding the south wall, they offer these observations: "The network of profiles . . . managed to reveal the outer slope of the embankment over a distance of 220 feet on the east end and a distance of 165 feet on the west" (Brown and Baby 1966:11). Having clearly identified the base of the original wall on the east, southeast, and south sides of the enclosure, Brown and Baby leveled the incorrectly placed 1920's wall and

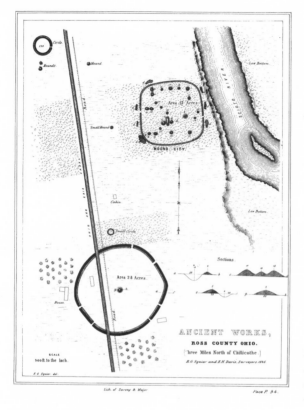

Fig. 4.14a. Squier and Davis's map (1848:plate 19) of the Mound City Earthwork.

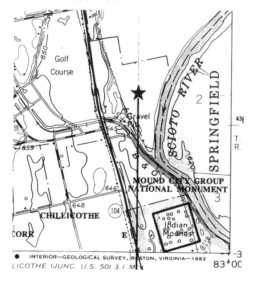

Fig. 4.14b. Section of USGS Andersonville Quadrangle map with the Mound City enclosure sketched in by the author.

Fig. 4.15. Aerial view of the Mound City Earthwork. The diagonal of the enclosure, shown here as line A-B, is aligned to the summer solstice sunset to within about three-quarters of one degree. *Enlarged detail of U.S. Department of Agriculture aerial photograph, 1988.*

restored the wall to its original location by piling earth on top of the traceable remnants of the original wall.

Regarding the northwest corner of the enclosure, Hanson's report is quite clear: "Testing revealed traces of the original wall on the northern side of the enclosure with evidence that it had been cut down in height with a drag scraper" (Hanson 1965:14). Hanson then explains how he restored the northwest corner to its original curve.

The crucial point here is that, even though the Mound City walls have been partially reconstructed and restored, the available evidence tells us that what we see in the 1988 aerial photograph is indeed an accurate reflection of the original configuration of the enclosure.

The USGS map shows that the section of State Route 104 just to the west of Mound City extends along an azimuth of 345°.25 as measured from true north. Using this known value, I drew a true north-south line on to the 1988 aerial photo. Using this north-south line as a reference, I found that the azimuth of the diagonal sightline that extends from point A to point B in figure 4.15 is 300°.25. (As mentioned earlier, points A and B are established by extending the lines of the embankment walls to the point where those lines intersect, thereby establishing the diagonal, which then locates points A and B on the curved sections of wall.) As measured in the field from point A, the horizon elevation along sightline A-B is 2°.0.

By reference to Aveni's tables, and using a date of A.D. 250, 39°20' north latitude, lower limb tangency, and horizon elevation of 2°.0, I found that the summer solstice sun would have set at an azimuth of 299°.4806 as viewed from point A. The accuracy of this sightline, therefore, is to within about three-quarters of one degree (300°.25 − 299°.4806 = 0°.7694). In other words, Mound City is aligned to the summer solstice sunset to within about three-quarters of one degree.

The finding that Mound City is aligned to the summer solstice sunset is intriguing enough. But what makes the situation even more fascinating is the discovery of several skeletons that were buried at each end of the summer solstice sightline.

These burials were found underneath and just to the outside of the original embankment walls in both the southeast and northwest corners of the Mound City enclosure, in the areas of points A and B (see Drennen 1972; Brown and Baby 1966; Hanson 1965). Four burials were found in the southeast corner, while one burial was found in the northwest corner. The assessment that the burials were Hopewell was made by principal investigator James A. Brown (1982), based on the location of the burials underneath sections of the enclosure's walls, as well as the finding of Hopewellian cache bifaces with one of the burials.

One of the interesting things about these burials is that all five burials were articulated skeletons, whereas all of the burials located within the Mound City enclosure were cremated. As Brown (1982:10) points out, a distinction was being made between the burials within the enclosure from those at the southeast and northwest corners.

Given the corner placement of the burials as well as their articulated condition, the intriguing possibility exists that maybe the Hopewell placed these burials to further emphasize the significance of the summer solstice sightline, in much the same way as appears to have been done at Hopeton.

MARIETTA

The Marietta Earthworks are located in Washington County, Ohio, at the confluence of the Muskingum and Ohio Rivers.

The best representation of the earthworks is a map that was published in Squier and Davis's (1848) book, although, for some unknown reason, Squier and Davis mistakenly attributed the map, shown here as figure 4.16, to Charles Whittlesey. Research by archaeologist James L. Murphy (1977) has shown that the map was actually made in 1838, by General Samuel R. Curtis. Curtis was a West Point graduate who was, for a time, employed as a civil engineer for the State of Ohio.

Most of the embankments that make up the square enclosures shown on the Curtis map have long since disappeared under the urban expansion of Marietta. However, a few features—including the Quadranaou Mound, the Capitoleum Mound, and the Sacra Via—can still be seen. We begin with the Quadranaou Mound.

QUADRANAOU MOUND

The Quadranaou Mound is a rectangular-shaped mound with a flat top. Although some minor damage to the mound occurred during the early 1800s as the result of plowing, the Quad Mound was very soon thereafter preserved in a city park. As a result, the mound has mostly remained intact. Figure 4.17 shows two views of the Quad Mound as it appears today. Squier and Davis (1848:74) give the measurements of the mound as 188 feet long, 132 feet wide, and 10 feet in height. At the center

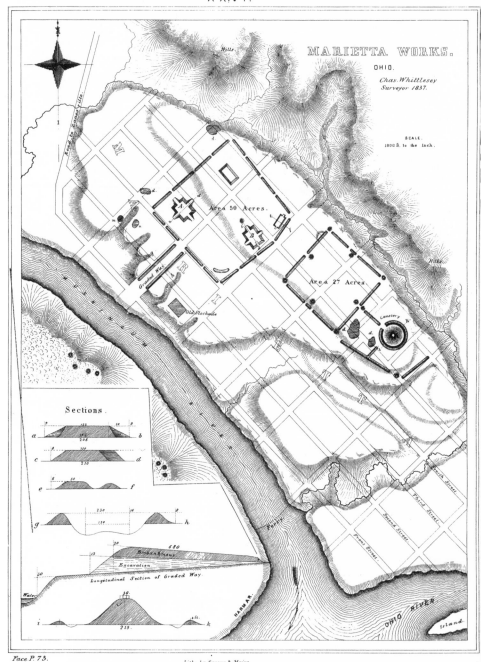

Lith. by Sarony & Major

Fig. 4.16. Samuel R. Curtis's map of the Marietta Earthworks. *From Squier and Davis 1848:plate 26.*

of each of its four sides, earthen ramps project outward, providing access to the top.

On the Curtis map in figure 4.16, the Quadranaou Mound is identified as feature A. Figure 4.18 provides an enlarged detail.

Operationally, what is important here is that, as shown by the photographs in figure 4.17, the major or longitudinal axis of the Quad Mound extends parallel to Fourth Street. Correspondingly, the minor axis of the mound extends parallel to Warren Street. From the USGS map detail provided in figure 4.19, we find that Warren Street extends along an azimuth of 231°.5 as measured from true north.

As measured from the base of the Quad Mound facing Third Street, the horizon elevation looking along the 231°.5 azimuth is 7°.0. This relatively high horizon is the result of a tremendous mountain ridge located just across the Muskingum River. This mountain ridge forms the visible horizon to the west, not only for this mound, but also for the Capitoleum Mound and for the Sacra Via (see figure 4.20). (This ridge, by the way, is not exactly level, and so that factor, too, affects the horizon elevation. In the case of the Quad Mound, for example, the horizon elevation along the 231°.5 azimuth is higher than might otherwise be expected because of a small knoll located on top of the distant ridge. This results in the circumstance whereby the horizon elevation is 7°.0 both from the base of the Quad Mound and from the intersection of Sacra Via and Second Street, which is closer to the ridge.)

In any event, from Aveni's tables we find that given a date of A.D. 250, 39°20' north latitude, lower limb tangency, and a 7.0 degree horizon elevation, the winter solstice sun would have set at an azimuth of 231°.3463. Recall that the azimuth of the Quad Mound's minor axis is 231°.5. Accordingly, the Quad Mound is aligned to the winter solstice sunset to within two-tenths of one degree (231°.5 – 231°.3463 = 0°.153).

CAPITOLEUM MOUND

Like the Quadranaou Mound, the Capitoleum Mound is also a rectangular-shaped mound with a flat top (see figure 4.21). In about 1916, a small building that houses the Washington County public library was built on top of the mound. Some additional fill may have been

Fig. 4.17. *Top*, view of the Quadranaou Mound from Warren Street. *Bottom*, view of the Quadranaou Mound from Third Street. *Photos by the author.*

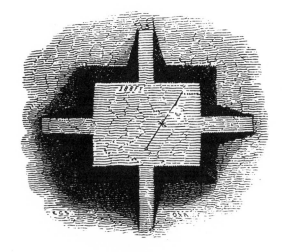

Fig. 4.18. Drawing of the
Quadranaou Mound.
*From Squier and Davis
1848: fig. 17.*

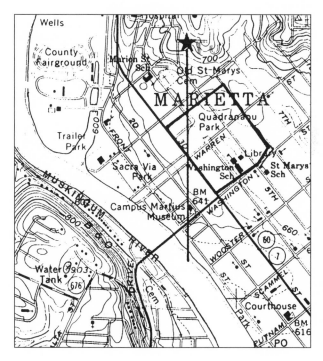

Fig. 4.19. *Section
of USGS Mariet-
ta Quadrangle
map with the
Marietta Large
Square sketched
in by the author.*

Fig. 4.20. View of the southwest horizon from the intersection of Third Street and the Middle of the Sacra Via. *Photo by the author.*

added to the mound at that time. From what I can tell, however, the original orientation of the mound was maintained.

In figure 4.16, the Capitoleum Mound is identified as feature B. As can be see, Curtis shows the mound skewed to the northeast relative to Fifth Street. By field survey, my measurements show that this skew is on the order of about 1°.5.

From the USGS map, we find that Fifth Street extends along an azimuth of 141°.5 as measured from true north. Since the Capitoleum Mound is skewed about 1°.5 from the azimuth of Fifth Street, the longitudinal axis of the mound is therefore 143°.0. Necessarily, then, the minor axis of the mound extends along an azimuth of 233°.0, since the minor axis is at a 90° angle to the longitudinal axis.

Today, the distant horizon as viewed from the center of the base of the Capitoleum Mound is blocked by a school building. As measured, however, from the closest unobstructed location, which in this

Fig. 4.21. View of the Capitoleum Mound looking along Fifth Street. *Photo by the author.*

case is at the intersection of the two alleyways at the immediate north-west corner of the mound, we find that the horizon elevation is $4°.5$. From Aveni's tables, we find that, given a date of A.D. 250, $39°20'$ north latitude, lower limb tangency, and $4°.5$ horizon elevation, the winter solstice sun would have set at an azimuth of $234°.09$. Recall that the azimuth of the Capitoleum Mound's minor axis is $233°.0$. As a result, the Capitoleum Mound is aligned to the winter solstice sunset to within about one degree ($234°.09 - 233°.0 = 1°.09$).

SACRA VIA

In addition to the two mounds just discussed, there is yet another major feature of the Marietta Earthworks that is aligned to the winter solstice sunset, and that is the Sacra Via, or Sacred Way (see figure 4.22).

The Sacra Via was a passageway that extended from the Marietta Large Square down to the Muskingum River. Curtis's map shows both

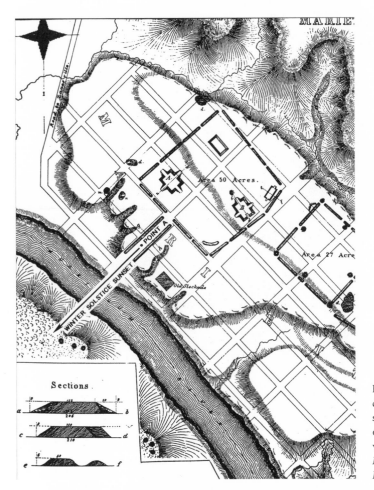

Fig. 4.22. Enlarged
detail of Curtis map
showing the alignment
of the Sacra Via to the
winter solstice sunset.
*Modified after Squier and
Davis 1848:plate 26.*

profile and longitudinal views of the Sacred Way (see figure 4.16); while
Squier and Davis provide the following description:

> Leading from [the Large Square] . . . towards the river, and at right angles
> to the embankment, is the "Sacra Via," *a graded way* . . . of singular con-
> struction. It is six hundred and eighty feet long by one hundred and fifty
> wide between the banks, and consists of an *excavated passage* descending
> regularly from the plain, upon which the works just described are situat-
> ed, to the alluviuns [sic] of the river. The earth, in part at least, is thrown
> outward upon either side, forming embankments from eight to ten feet
> in height. The center of the excavated way is slightly raised and round-
> ed. . . . (Squier and Davis 1848:74, emphasis added)

It was originally intended that the Sacra Via was "never to be disturbed or defaced, as common ground" (resolution quoted in part in MacLean 1903:37). Unfortunately, this resolution was not strictly adhered to, and, sometime in the 1800s, the parallel embankments of the Sacred Way were leveled and a set of two parallel cobblestone roadways were laid inside the excavated portion of the Sacred Way. Still, several lines of evidence suggest that the orientation of the Sacred Way as it appears today is, in fact, the same as it was originally.

First, the Curtis map (figure 4.16) clearly shows the city street now known as Sacra Via to extend parallel to the original raised embankments of the graded way. If Curtis's map is correct, then we can presume that the current orientation of the Sacra Via is the same as the orientation of the original parallel walls that flanked the excavated passageway.

Second, it may be that remnants of the original parallel walls are still extant. Of course, ground testing is needed to be certain, but during my reconnaissance of the area I noticed a slight ridge that looks like it may have been part of the original south embankment wall. It is about two feet in height, ten feet in width, and perhaps thirty feet in length (see Figure 4.23). The remnant is located just west of Allan Street in an area that was never paved. It extends along the same azimuth as the Sacra Via.

Third, it is important to keep in mind that, as explained by Squier and Davis, MacLean, and others, the Sacra Via was not just a set of parallel embankment walls. It was also a "graded way." This means it was a "broad avenue, excavated so as to descend by a perfect grade to the lower or latest formed terrace" (History of Washington County 1881:440). In other words, the surface of the earth had actually been cut into and excavated in order to provide a sloping passageway to the river, much like a ramp. According to MacLean (1903:64), who visited the site in 1882, "the depth of the excavation near the square was eight feet, but gradually deepened towards the farther extremity where it reached eighteen feet on the interior—the average depth of the avenue being about ten feet."

Although the embankment walls that were on top of the flanking

Fig. 4.23. Photo of what may be a remnant of the Sacra Via's parallel walls. In this view, we are looking along the top of the wall remnant as it extends toward the Muskingum River. Mrs. McNutt, the property owner, is standing at the far end of the wall segment. *Photo by the author.*

sections of the Sacra Via are now mostly gone, the original grade, or excavation, still remains and can be seen to form a very distinct series of cuts into the earth. Thus, the orientation of the Sacra Via is yet preserved in the shape and form of the original excavation.

Based on the above lines of evidence, it seems certain that the present appearance of the Sacra Via does indeed reflect the original orientation of the parallel walls and the graded way.

Given this, we find from the USGS map that the Sacra Via extends along an azimuth of 231°.5 as measured from true north. By field survey, it is found that the horizon elevation as measured along this azimuth varies from about 6°.0 to 7°.0. Quite simply, the horizon elevation depends on where one stands to take the measurement. As mentioned earlier, a tremendous mountain ridge looms across the Muskingum River. This ridge forms the visible horizon (see figure 4.20). Naturally, when looking down the Sacra Via along the 231°.5 azimuth, the closer one stands to the ridge, the higher the horizon elevation will be. For example, from the intersection of Sacra Via and Third Street, the horizon elevation is 6°.0. From the intersection of Sacra Via and Second Street, the horizon elevation is 7°.0. For my purposes here, I used the intersection of Sacra Via and Second Street as the vantage point. My reasoning was that this location is midway between the Large Square and the river. This location is identified in figure 4.22 as point A.

In the case of the Sacra Via, then, given a date of A.D. 250, 39°20' north latitude, lower limb tangency, and 7.0 degree horizon elevation, it is found from Aveni's tables that the winter solstice sun would have set at an azimuth of 231°.3463, as viewed from point A. Recall that the azimuth of the Sacra Via is 231°.5. The accuracy of the Sacra Via sightline, therefore, is to within two-tenths of one degree (231°.5 – 231°.3463 = 0°.153). In other words, the Sacra Via is aligned to the winter solstice sunset to within two-tenths of one degree.

The above calculations told me that, in ancient times, the winter solstice sun would have set in alignment with the Sacra Via. The best evidence for any suggested alignment, however, will always be an eyewitness observation of the event as it occurs. And so it was on Saturday, December 21, 1996, that I set out for Marietta with the hope of verifying by actual observation what my calculations predicted.

I arrived in Marietta late in the afternoon. As I set up my equipment in the middle of the Sacra Via, I watched with a worried eye as dark and ominous clouds moved in from the west. It was going to be close. Ever so slowly the sun began to sink in the western sky, inching its way toward the horizon. However, at the same time, I could also see the storm clouds as they twisted and churned and drew closer.

Luck was with me, though. As the sun finally set on the cliff that forms the horizon, I could see through the viewfinder of my camera that its spearlike rays were beaming down in alignment with the Sacra Via. Indeed, just as predicted by Aveni's tables, the winter solstice sun was setting in exact alignment with the ancient passageway. There was no mistake. The Hopewell would have seen the same thing. (To be precise about it, due to the effects of precession, in Hopewell times the sun

Fig. 4.24. Winter solstice sunset in alignment with the Marietta Sacra Via. *Photo by the author, December 21, 1996.*

would have set three-tenths of one degree farther north than it does today. Since the sun's diameter is equal to about one-half of one degree, then the difference between the sunset alignment as seen today along the Sacra Via and what the Hopewell would have seen fifteen hundred years ago is equal to about one-half of one sun diameter.)

Figure 4.24 shows the alignment as it occurred on that cold day in December. But a photograph alone cannot sufficiently convey the sense of awe or wonder that overtakes a solitary witness to the moment when the sun, ever so gently, touches the horizon in alignment with an ancient earthwork. At that moment, time almost seems to stop as the warm solar energy pulses and races across the landscape and into the heart of the ancient figure. As the sun's rays enter through the sacred passageway, it seems as though everything within the boundary of the geometric figure is suddenly charged and revitalized with the life force of the sun. Is it too much to think that maybe the Hopewell recognized the same thing?

As I drove home that night, the implications of what I witnessed began to dawn on me. A quick look at the Curtis map showed that the southwest facing wall of the Large Square was built perpendicular to the Sacra Via. As a result, the Large Square itself was oriented to the winter solstice sun. That is, the minor axis of the Large Square was oriented along the same azimuth as the Sacra Via, which is aligned to the winter solstice sunset.

Actually, I was hardly aware of the long drive home as yet another pattern in the data began to emerge. Yes, I had just verified that the Sacra Via or parallel walls at Marietta were aligned to the winter solstice sunset. But then I remembered that the same winter solstice alignment is also found in the long parallel walls at Hopeton. Later, I could barely contain my excitement when I realized that, like Marietta and Hopeton, the long parallel walls at Fort Ancient are also aligned to the winter solstice sunset.

My findings relevant to Fort Ancient are based on my analysis of Robert Connolly's map of the Fort Ancient site (Connolly 1997: fig. 10.2) which shows the parallel walls to extend along an azimuth of 237°.0. Because of agricultural plowing, the Fort Ancient parallel walls are not very visible at ground level. However, Connolly successfully located the walls through extensive excavations and soil core sampling. By reference to features shown both on the USGS topographic map for the area and Connolly's map, I was able to determine that Connolly's map used true north as its reference. By actual field survey, I was further able to establish that the horizon elevation along the 237°.0 sightline, as measured from within where the parallel walls were located, is 1°.5.

Using a date of A.D. 250, 39°20' north latitude, lower limb tangency, and 1°.5 horizon elevation, it is found from Aveni's tables that the winter solstice sun set at an azimuth of 237°.3778. The Fort Ancient parallel walls therefore, are aligned to the winter solstice sunset to within about one-third of one degree (237°.3778 − 237°.0 = 0°.3778).

In other words, the parallel walls at Marietta, the parallel walls at Hopeton, and the parallel walls at Fort Ancient are all aligned to the winter solstice sunset.

For me, this was pretty exciting stuff. But I became even more fascinated with the possibilities when I remembered that human burials were found at the ends of at least some of the parallel walls and/or solstice sightlines. Recall, for example, that two burials were found at the end of the parallel walls at Hopeton; and burials were also found at both ends of the solstice alignment at Mound City. Next, notice how, on the map of Marietta, a group of mounds is shown located in approximate alignment with the Sacra Via, just across the Muskingum River. In all likelihood, these are burial mounds, although admittedly we do not know that for certain. Nor do we know that they are Hopewell. Still, it strains the imagination to think that the discovery of burials at the ends of two, or possibly even three solstice sightlines is mere coincidence.

As I made my way through the darkness, it occurred to me that maybe the orientation of the dead along the solstice sightlines at Mound City, Hopeton, and perhaps Marietta was somehow meant to help integrate the deceased into the otherworld. Maybe the solstice sightlines were, in effect, azimuths to the otherworld.

Chapter 5

AZIMUTHS TO THE OTHERWORLD

I heard the dogs howl in the moonlight night,

And I went to the window to see the sight;

All the dead that I ever knew

Going one by one and two by two.

On they pass'd, and on they pass'd;

Townsfellows all from first to last;

Born in the moonlight of the lane

And quench'd in the heavy shadow again.

On, on, a moving bridge they made

Across the moon-stream, from shade to shade.

—Allingham, "A Dream"

Among all the powers of the heavens that are visible to the naked eye, surely the sun is the most awesome. Still, there comes a time, at the end of the day, when the sun disappears and yields its dominion of the sky to the mysterious, silver moon.

Given that the moon rules the night, it should come as no surprise that the Hopewell might align some of their earthworks to this celestial body. Indeed, impressive evidence for lunar consciousness is found at the Newark Earthworks and the High Bank Earthwork.

NEWARK

The Newark Earthworks were originally comprised of several geometrically shaped enclosures of varying size and complexity. These enclosures, in turn, appear to have been connected to each other by a series of parallel walls. Today, the most visible of these earthworks and the ones we are concerned with here are the Observatory Circle and its connected Octagon; and a second, nearby earthwork known as the Fairground Circle.

The definitive work on the archaeoastronomy of the Newark Earthworks was published in 1982 by Ray Hively and Robert Horn. In their paper, Hively and Horn report a total of seventeen lunar alignments evident in the designs of the Observatory Circle and Octagon and the Fairground Circle.

Of these proposed lunar alignments, perhaps the most impressive finding is that the longitudinal axis of the Observatory Circle and Octagon is in alignment with the moon's maximum north rise position. According to Hively and Horn (1982:table 2), the measured azimuth of this longitudinal axis or sightline is 52°.0, while, from Aveni's tables, they find that the moon's maximum north rising azimuth was 51°.8— given a computed horizon elevation of 0°.51, upper limb tangency, and a date of A.D. 250. In other words, the longitudinal axis of the Observatory Circle and Octagon is aligned to the moon's maximum north rise position to within two-tenths of one degree (52°.0 – 51°.8 = 0°.2). Figure 5.1 shows this alignment.

Yet another impressive alignment is found in the sightline that extends along the Fairground Circle's gateway or entrance. As pointed out by Hively and Horn (1982:table 2), the axis of the entranceway to the Fairground Circle extends along a measured azimuth of 66°.6. From Aveni's tables, Hively and Horn found that the moon's minimum north rising azimuth was 65°.7 given a computed horizon elevation of 0°.11, upper limb tangency, and a date of A.D. 250. According to Hively and Horn, therefore, the alignment of the Fairground Circle entranceway to this lunar rise event is to within nine-tenths of one degree (66°.6 – 65°.7 = 0°.9). Figure 5.2 shows this alignment.

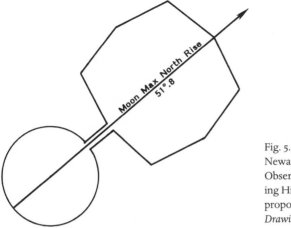

Fig. 5.1. Plan of the
Newark Octagon and
Observatory Circle show-
ing Hively and Horn's
proposed lunar alignment.
Drawing by the author.

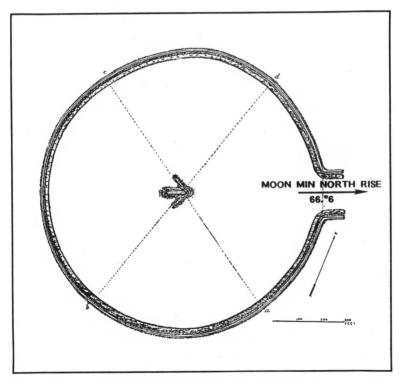

Fig. 5.2. Plan of the Newark Fairground Circle showing Hively and Horn's proposed
lunar alignment of the gateway. *Modified after Thomas 1894:plate 31.*

Hively and Horn used a computed horizon elevation for their analysis. Perhaps, though, we can improve on Hively and Horn's work by using actual measured horizon elevation data.

Today, the view of the horizon along the 66°.6 azimuth as measured from the Fairground Circle entranceway is obstructed by the Newark Earthworks Museum. By measuring the horizon elevation on both sides of this small building, however, I found the horizon elevation on either side of the building to be about one-half of one degree. Since the horizon elevation in the direction of the building is flat, we can use the two adjacent readings to establish that the horizon elevation along the 66°.6 azimuth is also about one-half of one degree. Using this horizon elevation value, we find from Aveni's tables that the moon's minimum north rising azimuth is 66°.6 given a date of A.D. 250, lower limb tangency, and 40°00' north latitude. So, it turns out that Hively and Horn's proposed alignment is really more accurate than they thought. Indeed, their alignment is exact (66°.6 − 66°.6 = 0°.0).

In a way, it makes sense that the entrance to the Fairground Circle would be aligned to a celestial event. As discussed earlier, the geometrically shaped walls of the Hopewell earthworks serve to separate the sacred space within from the mundane or profane space outside. A boundary wall without any point of access, however, is self-defeating. Accordingly, sacred structures are usually provided with gateways that allow entrance into the sacred area. Necessarily, the sacred nature of such gateways is enhanced by their alignment along celestial azimuths. Perhaps, then, the lunar orientation of the Fairground Circle gateway was meant to sanctify further the sacred nature of that entranceway and the inner earthwork.

Related to this thought is my finding that the charnel house structure once located underneath the Eagle Mound in the center of the Fairground Circle also appears to have been aligned along its longitudinal axis to the moon's minimum north rise position. Figures 5.3, 5.4, and 5.5 show this possible alignment. For this analysis, I used Greenman's field sketch of the Eagle Mound charnel house, which he excavated in 1928, and Thomas's (1894) map of the overall earthwork. I wish I could

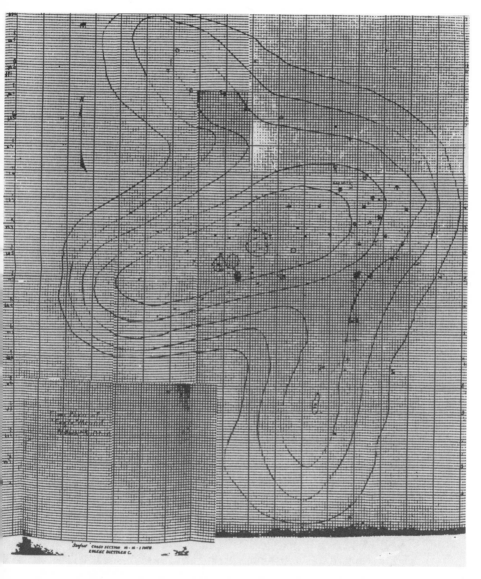

Fig. 5.3. Emerson F. Greenman's floor plan and outline of the Eagle Mound located in the center of the Newark Fairground Circle. *From Greenman's unpublished field notes, courtesy of Bradley T. Lepper.*

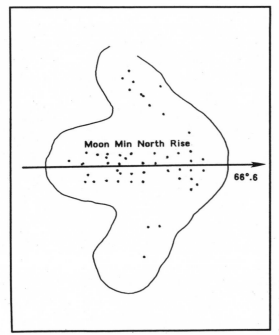

Fig. 5.4. *Tracing of Green-man's floor plan and outline of the Eagle Mound by the author.*

be more definitive about the Eagle Mound charnel house alignment. Unfortunately, Greenman's (1928) floor plan fails to show true north accurately, while Thomas' map of the earthwork does not show the postholes underneath the Eagle Mound. By combining the two figures, however, it is possible to reconstruct the likely orientation of the char-nel house structure. Simply stated, I traced Greenman's outline of the Eagle Mound and post mold pattern onto a sheet of vellum. Next, by using a copy machine and translucent carrier sheets, I equalized in scale my tracing of Greenman's figure with the Thomas figure of the Eagle Mound, while at the same time superimposing my now-reduced tracing of Greenman's mound outline and post mold floor plan onto the enlarged Thomas figure. Figure 5.5 shows the resulting compound image, demonstrating that the Eagle Mound charnel house and the entranceway to the Fairground Circle are both aligned to the moon's minimum north rise position. (Interestingly enough, as pointed out by

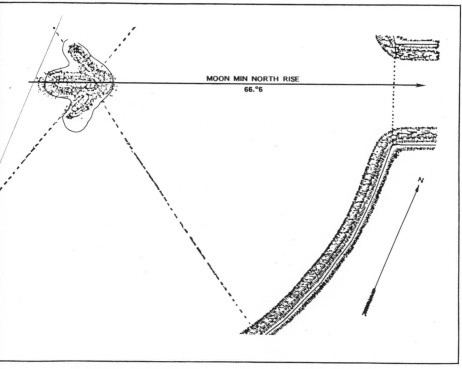

MOON MIN NORTH RISE
66.°6

Fig. 5.5. *Compound image made by superimposing Figure 5.4 on an enlarged section of Thomas's map of the Newark Fairground Circle (see figure 5.2).*

Hively and Horn [1982:S15], "the avenue axis does not pass through the centre of the Fairground Circle." Hence, the azimuths of the Eagle Mound charnel house and the Fairground Circle entranceway both extend along an azimuth of 66°.6, but the two sightlines are parallel to each other rather than being one and the same.) In any event, later in this chapter we will find additional lunar alignments at other Hopewell charnel houses.

HIGH BANK

The High Bank Earthwork is located about fifty-eight miles south-west of the Newark Octagon Earthwork, in Ross County, Ohio, about five miles south of Chillicothe. Although separated from each other by a respectable distance, High Bank and Newark can in many ways be considered sister sites. Their similarities are remarkable. To begin with, the High Bank Circle and Newark Observatory Circle are virtually the same size. Whereas the High Bank Circle is 1,052 feet in diameter, the Newark Observatory Circle is 1,054 feet in diameter. Second, the High Bank Circle is connected to an octagon-shaped enclosure and so is the Newark Observatory Circle. Further, as demonstrated in chapter 2, the size of the High Bank Octagon and the size of the Newark Octagon can both be related geometrically to their respective circular components.

Even more intriguing, however, is that the longitudinal axis of the Newark Observatory Circle and Octagon extends along an azimuth of about 52°, while the longitudinal axis of the High Bank Circle and Octagon extends along an azimuth of 140°. This places the axis of the High Bank Circle and Octagon at a near right angle to the axis of the Newark Circle and Octagon (140° − 52° = 88°). The similarities and relationships between the two sites, however, do not end here.

Two years after their article on Newark, Hively and Horn published a second article (1984) wherein they reported a total of nine lunar alignments and four solar alignments evident in the layout of the High Bank Earthwork. Among the alignments claimed by Hively and Horn for High Bank is an alignment to the moon's maximum north rise position.

According to Hively and Horn (1984:table 3), the azimuth of the High Bank Octagon's minor axis is 53°.4. From Aveni's tables, Hively and Horn find that the moon's maximum north rise azimuth is also 53°.4 given a computed horizon elevation of 1°.13, lower limb tangency, and a date of A.D. 250. The alignment, therefore, is perfect. Notably, this lunar alignment is the same one that was found in the longitudinal axis of the Newark Observatory Circle and Octagon. In other words, both the Newark Octagon and Circle and the High Bank Octagon are aligned to the same lunar north rise phenomenon.

It is interesting to find that the Newark Octagon and the High Bank Octagon are both associated with the moon by virtue of their alignments; but there is yet another association with the moon in terms of geometry. That is, because they are octagons, both the Newark Octagon and the High Bank Octagon have eight sides. This number coincides with the number of lunar phases visible to the naked eye during the course of a month. These phases are new moon, waxing crescent, first quarter, waxing gibbous, full moon, waning gibbous, last quarter, and waning crescent. It is intriguing to speculate that perhaps the Hopewell recognized and counted these same lunar phases; and that, in addition to actually aligning both of these octagons to the moon, by giving the Newark and High Bank figures eight sides they purposefully intended a further symbolic association between these earthworks and the moon.

THE GREAT HOPEWELL ROAD

As we have seen, the correspondences between Newark and High Bank are impressive. Size, geometry, and astronomical alignments all correspond. Could it be that these two sites were once physically connected? Surely such a thing is possible. In fact, Ohio Historical Society archaeologist Dr. Bradley T. Lepper is currently investigating just such a possibility. According to Lepper (1995), a long, straight road may have linked Newark to the Chillicothe area and maybe even to High Bank itself. Appropriately, Lepper has named this structure the Great Hopewell Road.

Several lines of evidence suggest the possible existence of the Great Hopewell Road, including early aerial photos that clearly show a set of ancient parallel walls beginning near the Newark Octagon and extending southwest toward Chillicothe. In 1862, James and Charles Salisbury (1862:15) followed these walls on foot for six miles "over fertile fields, through tangled swamps and across streams," and they, too, noted that the walls head toward Chillicothe. Other evidence for the road includes infrared aerial photos commissioned by Lepper that show possible segments of the road at several locations between Newark and Chillicothe.

Additional work needs to be done to further locate connecting segments of the road. However, the pieces may soon come together. Aerial photography, ground reconnaissance, and excavation of features that look like they might be part of the road all offer exciting possibilities.

CHARNEL HOUSE ALIGNMENTS

To return to the matter of lunar alignments, it may be that other large-scale geometric earthworks also incorporate lunar alignments in their designs. But without aerial photographs, or very accurate maps of these sites, it is impossible to know for sure.

We do have, however, some very reliable floor plans of Hopewell charnel houses made by recent investigators, including Raymond Baby, former head of the archaeology department of the Ohio Historical Society; Martha Potter Otto, current head of the archaeology department of the Ohio Historical Society; N'omi B. Greber, archaeology curator for the Cleveland Museum of Natural History; and James A. Brown, professor of archaeology at Northwestern University. From the floor plans of the charnel houses excavated and mapped by these archaeologists, it appears that quite a few were oriented to the moon. Figures 5.6–5.13 show several of these charnel houses and their alignments.

For the analyses presented here, where the original floor plans use magnetic north as their reference, I corrected for true north using declination correction tables published by the United States Geological Survey (1991). These tables take into account the yearly change in declination. As in previous analyses, azimuthal data was derived from Aveni's tables using a date of A.D. 250 and lower limb tangency. However, for these analyses, I used an estimated horizon of 1°.

On another matter, all of the charnel houses have rounded corners, perhaps related to the building methods employed. For the purposes of this analysis, in order to better define the corners of these structures, in each case I drew a line extending along the same angle of each wall as revealed by the postholes. The intersections of these lines then became the reference points for the proposed lunar sightlines. For further clarification, I included these extended guidelines on each of the charnel house floor plans.

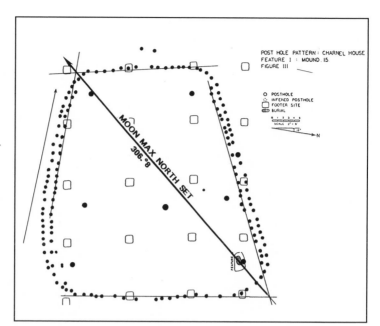

Fig. 5.6. Lunar alignment of the charnel house located under Mound 15 at Mound City. *Modified after Drennan 1974: fig.3. Reprinted by permission of the Ohio Historical Society.*

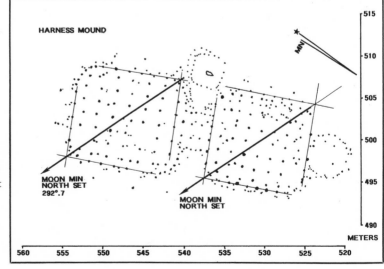

Fig. 5.7. Lunar alignment of the charnel house located under the Harness Mound, at the Liberty Earthwork. *Redrawn after Greber 1983: fig. 2.6.*

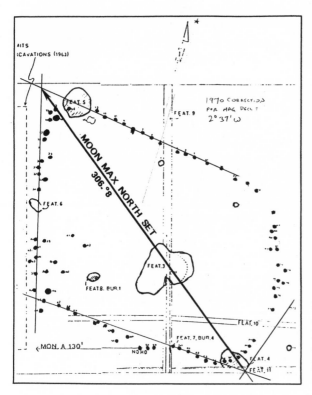

Fig. 5.8. Lunar alignment of the charnel house located under Mound 12 at Mound City. *Modified after Otto 1980: fig. 4. Reprinted by permission of the Ohio Historical Society.*

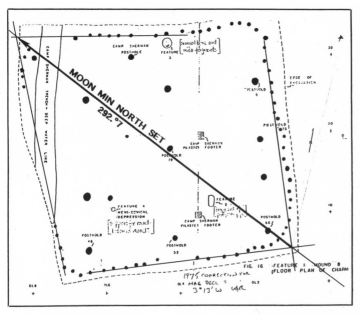

Fig. 5.9. Lunar alignment of the charnel house located under Mound 8 at Mound City. *Modified after Baby and Langlois 1977: fig. 16. Reprinted by permission of the Ohio Historical Society.*

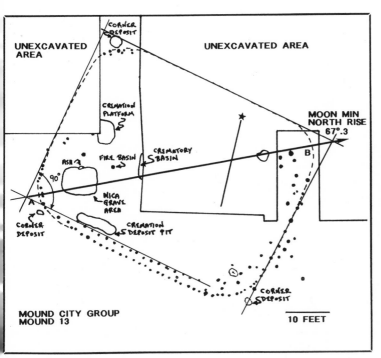

Fig. 5.10. Lunar alignment of the charnel house located under Mound 13 at Mound City. Presumed configuration of north and west walls is indicated by the dashed line. *Drawing by the author, modified after Brown 1979:fig. 27.2.*

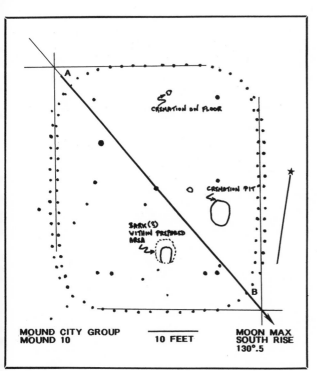

Fig. 5.11. Lunar alignment of the charnel house located under Mound 10 at Mound City. *Drawing by the author, modified after Brown 1979:fig. 27.1.*

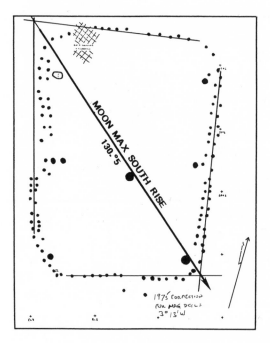

Fig. 5.12. Lunar alignment of the charnel house located under Mound 14 at Mound City. *Modified after Baby, Drennan, and Langlois 1975: fig. 6. Reprinted by permission of the Ohio Historical Society.*

Fig. 5.13. Lunar alignment of the charnel house located under Mound 9 at Mound City. *Modified after Baby and Langlois 1977: fig. 6. Reprinted by permission of the Ohio Historical Society.*

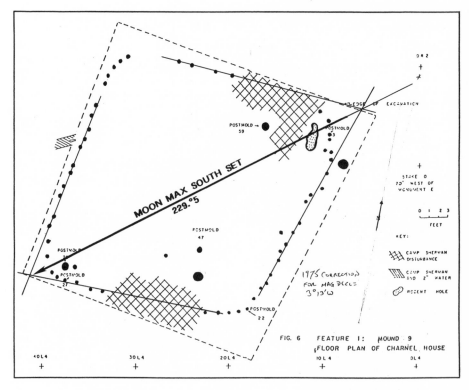

Assuming that the floor plans made by our experts are correct in terms of orientation, and knowing from field surveys that no horizon elevations at these sites are greater than 3.5 degrees, I am confident that the alignments I have proposed are accurate to within one or two degrees. As shown by figures 5.6–5.13, at least eight more charnel houses, in addition to the Newark Eagle Mound charnel house, appear to be aligned to the moon.

One of the peculiar things that stands out about these alignments is that, even though the structures are all aligned to the moon, there does not seem to be any discernible pattern in terms of which lunar standstill event any particular house is aligned to. In other words, out of nine alignments, two charnel houses are aligned to the moon's minimum north rise; two are aligned to the maximum north set; two are aligned to the maximum south rise; two are aligned to the minimum north set; and one is aligned to the maximum south set. The best explanation I can offer for these alignments is that each charnel house might have been aligned to whatever lunar event was closest to the date when each structure was built. Notably, the temporal cycle between minimum and maximum lunar positions is about 9.3 years.

In the next section, I will present a possible explanation as to why the charnel houses might be aligned to the moon in a more general sense.

AZIMUTHS TO THE OTHERWORLD

Chapter 3 touched upon the use of charnel houses by the Hopewell, and, in this regard, Kent State University archaeologist Mark Seeman (1979:43) has made some observations that are especially relevant. As Seeman explains, "charnel houses were widespread throughout the Southeast during the historic period." They extended from the Atlantic coast of Virginia to Florida, around the Gulf, and to the lower Mississippi Valley. Further, according to Seeman, charnel houses were an important part of the late prehistoric Mississippian period, extending north to the lower Ohio Valley and west as far as Oklahoma. As the reader will recall, the Mississippian period began a few hundred years after the demise of the Hopewell.

The point here is that charnel house interment is a practice that was geographically widespread—across most of eastern North America —and it apparently had its origins deep in the prehistory of eastern North America. From the data at hand, it appears that charnel house interment represents a continuity of ritual that extends back from historic times, through the Mississippian period, and into Hopewell times.

The continuity being emphasized here is important because in the Southeast there was a clear and definite association between charnel house rituals and the moon. This association is documented by references such as the following, which refer to food offerings presented at the "temple" houses of the Natchez and Taensa Indians. We know from further descriptions of these structures that the "temples" referred to are actually charnel houses that contain the bones of the dead and other sacred objects:

> At the *last quarter of the moon* all the cabins make an offering . . . which is placed at the door of the temple. (Swanton 1911:260–261; emphasis added)

> [At] every *new moon* presents . . . are made at the Temple. (Swanton 1911:159; emphasis added)

> They give the dishes to the guardian who carries them to the side of the basket in which are the bones of the dead; this ceremony lasts only *one moon*. (Swanton 1911:269; emphasis added)

> The seeds are in like manner offered before the temple with great ceremony, but the offerings which are made there of bread and flour *every new moon* are for the use of the keepers of the temple. (Swanton 1911:166; emphasis added)

In each of the above descriptions of these historic period charnel houses, we find references to the moon. Again, the point is that the Southeastern Indians clearly associated their charnel houses, which were used for the processing of the dead, with the moon and lunar cycles. Likewise, the same association is seen in the lunar-aligned charnel houses of the Hopewell, who, at the very least, were the indirect ancestors of later Mississippian peoples.

As to why the moon would be associated with the dead, either by the historic Indians of the Southeast or the Hopewell, there are a couple of observations that can be made.

To begin with, it is clear that charnel houses, both historically and prehistorically, were associated with death. So, too, death is often associated with the color black and the night. The moon, of course, is a phenomenon of the night. Hence, the association of charnel houses with the moon. A link diagram of these associations takes the following form: charnel houses = death = black = night = moon.

That the Indians of the Southeast recognized these same associations is documented by anthropologist Charles Hudson, in connection with Cherokee cosmology: "east was the direction of the Sun, the color red, sacred fire, blood, and life and success; its opposite, the west, was associated with *the Moon*, the *souls of the dead*, the color *black*, and *death"* (Hudson 1976:132, emphasis added).

We also find that, among many Native Americans, the otherworld was thought of as a mirror image of this world. As Hultkrantz explains, "The peculiar character of the Otherworld is also expressed by describing everything there in reverse. . . . During the day the dead are skeletons, but at night they look like humans, alive and energetic, they walk upside down, they do not hear speech but listen to yawnings and so forth" (Hultzkrantz 1979:135).

If the sun is the primary life-giving body in this world, as suggested by the quote from Hudson, then it follows that, in the reversed otherworld, the moon would be the primary celestial body there. Accordingly, it would make sense to orient the dead to the primary celestial body of their new, otherworld home. Hence, the alignment of the charnel houses to the moon.

There is yet another piece of the puzzle to consider here. At Seip, Mound City, Hopewell, Tremper, Newark, Liberty, and elsewhere, clay basins are found dug into the floors of the charnel houses. Many of the Hopewell dead were cremated in these clay basins. We know this from the dozens of instances where cremated bones are found within the basins, and from the basins themselves, which show extensive evidence of long-burning fires.

Imagine, then, the ritual of an honored shaman or medicine man, who, in passing to the otherworld, was cremated within the most sacred inner chamber of a Hopewell charnel house. As the crematory fire burned, it melted flesh from bone and thereby transformed it. In this way, perhaps, the soul was released in the form of billowing clouds of smoke, sacred smoke that rose upward on the wind, higher and higher until it forever vanished into the otherworld. If we view it in this way, we can perhaps understand the thoughts of the Oglala medicine man who explained that the life soul "is like smoke and it goes upward until it arrives at the stars" (quoted in Hultkrantz 1953:184).

In the same way—who knows?—maybe the Hopewell thought that the charnel house alignments would provide the deceased with a sense of the direction they needed to travel to reach the otherworld, which was there, in alignment with the shadow of the moon.

Part Two

THE HOPEWELL WORLDVIEW

Chapter 6

SYMBOLS OF EARTH AND SKY

The great function of symbols is to point beyond themselves, in the power of
that to which they point, to open up levels of reality which otherwise are
closed, and to open up levels of the human mind of which we otherwise are
not aware.

    —Paul Tillich

I love cosmology: there's something uplifting about viewing the entire universe as a single object with a certain shape. What entity, short of God, could
be nobler or worthier of man's attention than the cosmos itself? Forget about
interest rates, forget about war and murder, let's talk about space.

    —Rudy Rucker, *The Fourth Dimension*

It has been called the God principle. And, while that may be over-
stating things a bit, the idea may still go a long way toward explaining
why the Hopewell earthworks are geometric in shape.

Essentially, the idea is that our brains are hardwired in such a way
that we find geometric patterns in visual fields, even when such patterns do not objectively exist. Consider, for example, the design shown
in figure 6.1. Most people see a square. But, in reality, what we see as a
square has no existence by itself. Take away the funny little circle shapes

Fig. 6.1. Kanizsa-square illusion used to illustrate the
God-principle. *Redrawn after Kosko 1993:fig. 15.3.*

and the square is gone. Hence, the square is an illusion—a creation of
our minds.

Expanding on this idea, mathematician Bart Kosko (1993:278–79)
has suggested that perhaps our discovery of geometric order in the universe is the functional equivalent of the square we see in figure 6.1—
that is, the God principle.

Today it is very difficult for us to imagine a universe that has a finite boundary or a comprehensible geometric shape. But let us keep in
mind that before relativity and the big bang, most ancient peoples believed the universe to be geometrical in shape with a finite border, just
as we might expect as per the God principle. Further, many of these ancient peoples built their temples, shrines, and even cities to reflect, on a
smaller scale, the geometric order they believed to exist in the universe
at large.

Anthony Aveni (1992:18) refers to such structures as cosmograms—that is, buildings or architectural works that incorporate into
their design a map or plan of the cosmos. Examples of cosmograms
(Clancey 1994) include the Indonesian stupa of Borobudur. There, the
magnificent hemispherical dome is meant as a symbol of the sky, while
the supernal balcony represents the hub of the earth. The Cambodian
temple at Angkor Wat is also a cosmogram symbolizing the nested levels of the universe, which are represented as squares. Yet another cosmogram is found in the architecture of the Forbidden City at Beijing,

where streets, buildings, and even gateways are cosmic symbols, and where the Imperial Palace was said to be modeled after heaven itself.

In North America, the tradition of designing architectural structures so they incorporate beliefs about the shape of the universe is widespread. Indeed, several well-known Mesoamerican ceremonial centers were laid out as cosmograms. The Mayan Pyramid of Inscriptions, for example, symbolizes in its interior stairway and exterior terraces the number of upperworld and underworld levels (Clancey 1994:48). Similarly, at Teotihuacán, the Pyramid of the Sun metaphorically incorporates ideas about the three primary levels of the universe—namely, the celestial, terrestrial, and underworld (Clancey 1994:46).

North of Mexico, many Native American peoples likewise designed their ceremonial areas, ritual lodges, and individual dwellings to reflect their beliefs about the structure of the universe. As explained by anthropologist Peter Nabokov and architect Robert Easton: "The buildings of the Native Americans encoded not only their social order but often their tribal view of the cosmos. . . . Thereafter Indian peoples held the ritual power to renew their cosmos through rebuilding, remodeling, or reconsecrating their architecture" (Nabokov and Easton 1989:38).

In the case of the Indians north of Mexico, we are not talking about a few isolated instances of symbolic architecture randomly scattered across the landscape. Quite the contrary: the majority of Native American peoples are found to have modeled various architectural structures as symbols of the cosmos. As Nabokov and Easton again point out, "The idea that houses served as models of the universe is suggested by the folklore and architectural terms of native groups as distant from one another as the Eskimo, the Mohave, the Navajo, the Hopi, the Delaware, and the Blackfeet" (Nabokov and Easton 1989: 38). To this list we can add many other peoples, including the Haida, Kwakiutl, Crow, Cheyenne, Sioux, Arikara, Pawnee, Hidatsa, and Mandan (Nabokov and Easton 1989), the Tewa (Ortiz 1969), the Ojibway (Grim 1983), and the Creek, Seminole, Natchez, Yuchi, and Chickasaw (Howard 1968). All of these peoples, and more, re-created their vision of the universe in the design of their ceremonial areas, ritual lodges, and individual dwellings. What I am proposing here is that, in a similar fash-

ion, the Hopewell also designed their ceremonial enclosures, or geometric earthworks, to reflect their vision of the universe.

We will return to the matter of the Hopewell earthworks. First
though, consider how some other Native American peoples have symbolized the universe in their ceremonial structures. For the Delaware,
the floor of their "big house" ceremonial lodge represented the earth,
the roof the sky, and the four walls the "four sides of the horizon"
(Nabokov and Easton 1989:89).

Similarly, the dome-shaped roofs of Navajo hogans symbolize the
sky, the flat dirt floor represents the earth, and each of the four wooden
posts that support the roof are aligned to one of the four cardinal directions (Suzuki and Knudtson 1992:155).

Among the Pawnee, their earth lodges connected the heavens to
the earth through the smoke hole in the top of their lodges. The circular walls of their lodges represented the horizon, while the western-
most roof-supporting pole became the evening star, and the eastern-
most pole was the morning star (Nabokov and Easton 1989:139).
Archaeoastronomer Ray Williamson (1984:221) has likened the Pawnee
earth lodges to "miniature models of the cosmos."

The Apache ceremonial lodge was supported by four main poles
intended to represent "the four directions of the universe, the four seasons, and the four stages of life" (Farrer and Second 1981:140).

The Midewiwin lodge of the Ojibway also was meant as a symbol
of the universe. Its four walls represented the four directions, the open
roof was expressive of the sky, and the floor symbolized the earth below our own earth (Grim 1983:130).

Characterizing the architectural designs of North American Indians in general, Ake Hultkrantz explains that

> The ritual lodge may symbolize the universe and this is to some extent
> true as well of the open ceremonial area where the annual rites are cele-
> brated. Sometimes the cosmic symbolism is extended to include the
> whole village or camp site. The camp circle of the Plains Indians at the
> time of the Sun Dance and the arrangement of houses around an open
> plaza by the southeastern Indians are thus perceived by the inhabitants as
> miniature reproductions of the great cosmic room. (Hultkrantz 1979:111)

More examples could be cited, but I think the point is clear—many Native American peoples designed their architectural structures to reflect their view of the cosmos. Given this, it makes sense that perhaps the Hopewell, too, would design their ceremonial or ritual areas to reflect what they believed to be the shape of their universe or their vision of the earth and sky.

As to the exact nature or shape of the cosmos that the Hopewell envisioned, I think it will be useful to keep in mind the larger view that most Native Americans had of their universe. As explained by David W. Penny:

> Throughout the Americas, traditional Native thought has conceived of the universe as a layered structure with the terrestrial domain suspended below the celestial vault of the sky-world and above the watery realm of the underworld. The horizontal axes of the earth have been defined by the four cardinal directions, whose conjunction has been thought of as creating the center—the world navel or world tree—connecting the earth with those above and below it. (Penny 1985:180)

A FORMAL HYPOTHESIS

Specifically, what I am proposing is that the large square Hopewell enclosures were meant as symbols of the sky or heavens; correspondingly, the large circular enclosures represent the earth. (Tripartite earthworks such as Frankfort, Works East, Seip, and Liberty may, in their symbolic geometry, represent a division of the cosmos into three levels—namely, the upperworld, the earth, and the underworld.)

I am not proposing that each and every Hopewell earthwork of every size and configuration was meant as a cosmic symbol. Surely, there are structures that were built for reasons that we have yet to fathom. Rather, it is only the large, classic circle, square, and octagon enclosures that I am suggesting are symbols of the heavens and earth. Three observations in particular lead me to believe that the geometric earthworks might be cosmic symbols.

First, as discussed in chapter 2, many of the earthworks are not perfect geometric figures. Hopeton, for example, is not a perfect circle and square. Nor are Shriver and Milford perfect circles. Likewise, Anderson and Dunlap are not perfect squares. However, it is apparent from earthworks such as the Newark Octagon and Fairground Circle, which are very close to being perfect figures, that the Hopewell were entirely capable of constructing very precise large-scale geometric figures if they so desired. What seems to have been of central importance, then, was the idea of a circle, or a square, or an octagon, rather than absolute perfect execution on the ground in each and every instance.

Second, in connection with the astronomical alignments found at many of the earthworks, after spending a sufficient amount of time among these behemoths, I realized that it simply is not necessary to have such tremendous earthworks for celestial observations. For example, it seems peculiar, and in some ways counterproductive, to have an earthwork the size of three football fields just to observe a lunar alignment that occurs once every nineteen years.

Moreover, given the frequent haze, fog, and cloud cover that occurs along the Ohio and Scioto River Valleys, reliance on such observations might not have been very practical. In fact, my own experience, over roughly fifteen years, is that poor visibility has resulted in cancellation of about half of my planned trips to make either solstice or equinox observations. To my way of thinking, something other than celestial alignments alone motivated the building of the earthworks.

Third, as discussed in chapter 1, there seems to be a fairly clear association between the location of the geometric earthworks and nearby geophysical features, including river confluences, outcroppings of unusual rocks, and special soils. Located in juxtaposition to these features, the geometric earthworks call attention to the special or unusual nature of the earth at these locations.

Considered together, these observations suggest the likelihood that the earthworks were symbols. But symbols of what? Therein is the mystery.

Anyone can come up with a reasonably good theory or hypothesis as to what the earthworks might represent. Indeed, I am not the only person ever to have proposed such a thing. Stephen D. Peet, Charles C. Willoughby, and Warren K. Moorehead come to mind as early theorists who attributed symbolic meanings to the earthworks. Peet (1891), for example, proposed that certain crescent-shaped earthworks were meant to symbolize the moon. Willoughby (1919) proposed that the Adams County Serpent Mound is a representation of the Great Horned Serpent of North American Indian legend. And Moorehead (1922) suggested that the circle and square enclosures of the Hopewell might represent the sun and four corners of the earth, respectively.

More recently, a number of anthropologists and archaeologists have addressed various aspects of Hopewell symbolism. Hall (1979), for example, proposed several important symbolic continuities between Hopewell and historic Indian groups; Penny (1985) provided a very interesting overview of Hopewell artifact symbolism; Cowan (1996) has looked at how certain Hopewell artifacts conveyed meanings within social groups; Byers (1996) has looked at the symbolism of the earthworks as manifestations of an "iconic warrant" between the living and ancestral generations; Greber (1996) found some interesting symbolic contrasts in the spatial patterning of offerings, including mica and obsidian, grave goods, and prepared mound floors; and Seeman (1995) has discussed some of the symbolism associated with certain classes of artifacts recovered from the GE Mound.

It is encouraging to see these recent endeavors. However, with the possible exception of Byers, the above-noted papers do not address in any real depth the symbolism of the earthworks as a whole. Instead, they are focused on smaller pieces of the puzzle.

In contrast, the early theorists do present more general theories regarding the symbolism of the earthworks, but their shortcoming is that they fail to provide any sort of tests for their theories. This is important, because what separates science from speculation is testability. In other words, for a hypothesis to be supportable, we have to be able to establish testable predictions. If the testable predictions generated from the hypothesis are found to be true, then we can consider the hypothesis to be supported.

With regard to the hypothesis I have suggested, four test implications or predictions can be made relevant to the hypothesis that square enclosures were meant as symbols of the sky or heavens, whereas circular enclosures were meant as symbols of the earth.

Relevant first to the square enclosures, the test implications are: (1) if the square enclosures were meant to represent the sky, then we should find that they are associated with observable sky phenomena; and (2) if the square enclosures were meant to represent the sky, and if it is assumed that there is some continuity in the belief systems of historic Native Americans and their prehistoric ancestors such as the Hopewell, then we should find ethnographic evidence that historic Native Americans likewise associated the geometric shape of the square with the sky.

Relevant to the circular enclosures, the test implications are as follows: (1) if the circular enclosures were meant to represent the earth, then we should find that they are associated with earth phenomena; and 2) if the circular enclosures were meant to represent the earth, and again, if it is assumed that there is some continuity in the belief systems of historic Native Americans and their prehistoric ancestors, including the Hopewell, then we should find ethnographic evidence that historic Native Americans likewise associated the geometric shape of the circle with the earth.

Before proceeding too much further, allow me to qualify something. That is, the hypothesis testing that follows may seem rather simple. Indeed, some may argue that the hypotheses are not falsifiable in a scientific sense, that the test implications are too vague, that concepts like "sky phenomena" are not explicitly defined, or that the evidence simply needs to be stronger. In general, I agree with such sentiments. However, I would also point out that what follows is meant as a beginning, rather than a definitive picture of the Hopewell worldview. A great deal of additional work needs to be done before we can truly, if ever, know the thoughts of the Hopewell. With that caveat in mind, let us see what the data reveal.

SQUARE ENCLOSURES

Looking first to the square enclosures, we find that they are indeed physically associated with observable sky phenomena. Recall that, in chapters 4 and 5, we found solar and lunar alignments to occur predominantly among the square earthworks.

More to the point, it was shown that the square, or truncated square, enclosures at Newark, High Bank, Hopeton, Mound City, Hopewell, Anderson, and Dunlap are all oriented to either solar or lunar events. The rectangular-shaped Capitoleum and Quadranaou Mounds at Marietta were shown to be aligned to the winter solstice. And recall that the square-shaped Seal Earthwork was found to be oriented to the sun's equinox positions and the four cardinal directions. All are sky phenomena.

This is not to say that circles are never associated with the sky. Clearly some are. The Newark Observatory Circle and Newark Fairground Circle, for example, are both oriented to sky phenomena. However, in the case of the Newark Observatory Circle, we note that that circular earthwork is connected to the octagon, and that the octagon's major axis is aligned to the moon. The location of the Observatory Circle along this axis can, therefore, be interpreted as further emphasizing the significance of the lunar axis established by the orientation of the octagon.

With regard to the Newark Fairground Circle, it was noted earlier that the opening into the circle is oriented along a lunar azimuth. What may have been important to the Hopewell, however, was not so much where this opening was in relationship to the circle, but rather that the opening allowed an unrestricted view of the horizon from the charnel house located at the center of the circle. Hence, the opening in the circle is a function of, or incidental to, the intended alignment, which is the longitudinal axis of the charnel house aligned to the moon's minimum north rise position.

The point here is that the majority of the circular enclosures—such as those at Seip, Frankfort, Hopeton, High Bank, Baum, Liberty, and Shriver—do not demonstrate alignments to celestial events. On the other hand, at least eight Hopewell squares, or truncated squares in the case of the Newark and High Bank octagons, are clearly oriented to sky phenomena such as solstice positions, equinox positions, and lunar standstills. In short, the finding that the square enclosures are associated with sky phenomena supports the hypothesis of square = sky.

The second test implication relevant to the square enclosures is that, if the hypothesis is correct, and if it is assumed that there is some continuity in the belief systems of historic Native Americans and their prehistoric ancestors, including the Hopewell, then, in addition to finding an association of the squares with sky phenomena, we should also find ethnographic evidence that historic Native Americans likewise associated the geometric shape of the square with the sky.

Looking to the ethnographic literature, we find that the square was indeed associated with sky phenomena, especially by the historic Indians of the Southeast, including the Creek, Seminole, Natchez, Yuchi, and Chickasaw. According to firsthand accounts—documented, for example, by ethnologist John R. Swanton (1946, 1931) and anthropologist James H. Howard (1968)—all of the above-mentioned people laid out the most important of their ceremonial areas in the shape of large, open squares. Moreover, these squares were oriented to the cardinal directions. The cardinal directions, in turn, can only be established by reference to sky phenomena.

THE SQUARE GROUNDS

The best-known examples of the square ceremonial areas mentioned above are those of the historic Creek Indians. Known as "square grounds," these sacred areas were defined by a series of wooden shelters, or clan lodges, which were open in the front and laid out to form a square. Typically, the square grounds averaged several hundred feet across, comparable in size, for example, to the Seal enclosure. Like the Seal enclosure, too, the Creek square grounds were oriented to the cardinal directions. As Swanton (1931:11) explained, "the cabins are placed normally toward the four points of the compass."

An illustration of a wooden clan shelter or lodge is shown in figure 6.2, while the manner in which these lodges were arranged in a square is shown in figure 6.3. Figure 6.2 shows an Alabama square ground lodge from the 1700s, while figure 6.3 shows the plan of a typical Creek square ground.

Figure 6.4 provides an illustration of several of the square grounds shown by Swanton in his 1931 paper on the Creek square

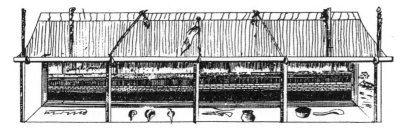

Fig. 6.2. "Square ground" cabin of the Alabama Indians used in the eighteenth century. *From a sketch in the French archives, reproduced in Swanton 1946:plate 59.*

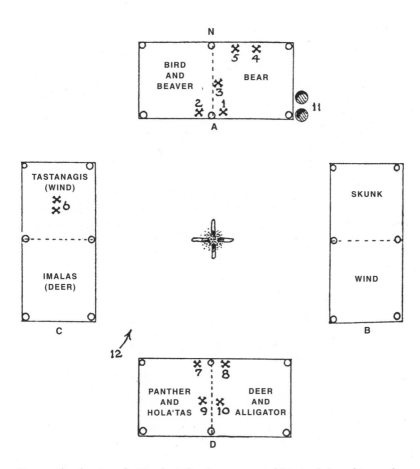

Fig. 6.3. Plan drawing of a Nuyaka Indian "square ground." Animal clan cabins, such as the one shown in figure 6.2, are arranged in a square around a central fire. *From Swanton 1931: fig. 4.*

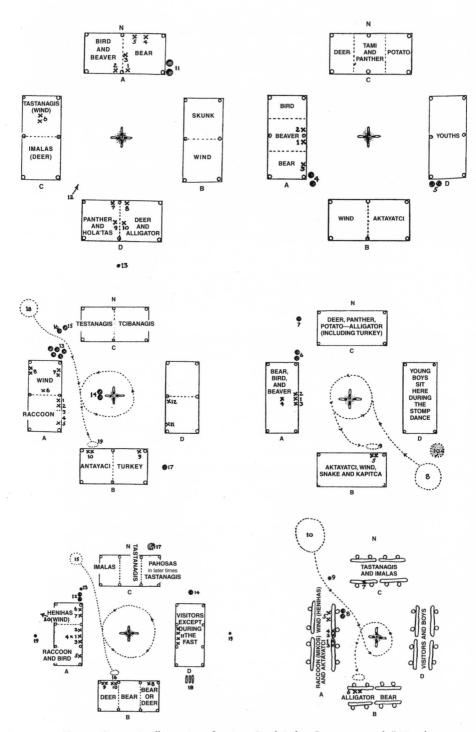

Fig. 6.4. Composite illustration of various Creek Indian "square grounds." Note how the square grounds are all oriented to the cardinal directions. *From Swanton 1931.*

grounds. In most instances, the wooden clan lodges are named after some special animal. As can be seen, though, each square is clearly oriented to the cardinal directions. As explained by Nabokov and Easton: "The Creek of the Southeast constructed their ceremonial 'square grounds' to reflect the directional order in the universe" (Nabokov and Easton 1989:40).

Also important to the symbolism of the square grounds was the sacred fire. Appropriately enough, this fire was located in the middle of the square ground. Throughout the Southeast, fire was considered to be an earthly representative of the sun. As we will see in the next chapter, the sacred fire was an important feature of the Green Corn Ceremony that was performed within the square grounds. Of interest to us here, however, is that the logs of the traditional sun-fire within the square ground were arranged in a crisscross fashion so that they also pointed to, and thereby reiterated, the four cardinal directions. Indeed, as Howard (1968:19) explains, "the concept of a sacred fire, identified with the sun, and fed with four logs oriented to the four cardinal points, thus forming a cross is the most widespread and basic ceremonial concept in the Southeast."

In summary, we find that the square grounds of the historic Southeastern Indians were associated with sky phenomena in several ways. First, they were associated with the sky through their connection to the sacred fire, which was a manifestation of the sun. Second, they were associated with the sky through the sacred fire logs which were oriented to the cardinal directions. Third, the square grounds were associated with the sky by virtue of their orientation to the cardinal directions, which can only be established by reference to sky phenomena.

A CONTINUITY OF BELIEF

In this chapter, I have taken the position that there is a continuity of thought in the meanings of certain symbols extending from historic times back to the prehistoric Hopewell. This assumption underlies the second test implication. I do not have the space here to present all the data that support this position. However, the opinion that there is a continuity in Native American thought that goes back thousands of years is shared by a number of authorities, including David W. Penny (1985), Robert Hall (1979), James A. Ford (1969), James H. Howard (1968), William S. Webb and Raymond Baby (1957), and A. J. Waring and Preston Holder (1945). Further, the link between the Hopewell and later historic Indians appears to be found in Mississippian culture. Looking to the Mississippian culture, we come to Cahokia.

Cahokia is one of the largest prehistoric Mississippian sites known. Located on the east side of the Mississippi River, across from St. Louis, Missouri, Cahokia flourished from about A.D. 800 to A.D. 1500. At its height, its population reached well over ten thousand people. Of special interest here is that Cahokia's primary mounds are laid out along the cardinal axes (see Sherrod and Rolingson 1987:91; also see figure 6.5). Moreover, where the north-south and east-west axes intersect, there is a tremendous square-based mound. Known as Monks Mound, this 100-foot-high earthen pyramid is itself closely oriented to the cardinal directions, as are several other square-based mounds nearby.

In both the layout and design of its square-shaped mounds, we find in Cahokia the geometric figures of the cross and square which are oriented to the cardinal directions, just like the layout of the earlier Hopewellian Seal square, and like the later ceremonial grounds of the Creek, Chickasaw, and other Indians of the historic Southeast.

Links across time in the symbolic meanings of the square are also found on a smaller scale. For example, shell gorgets recovered from Mississippian sites are found to have cross as well as bent-arm cross designs carved into their surfaces. According to historic Indian accounts (see Willoughby 1897:10), these designs were meant to symbolize the four cardinal directions, the four world quarters, and the four winds. Several of these cross designs are shown here in figure 6.6, while figure 6.7 shows one of the more complicated of these designs. The gorget shown in figure 6.7 was recovered from the Spiro Mound in Oklahoma. According to the late Joseph Campbell, "the Spiro Mound gorget . . . is an unmistakable representation of the mythologi-

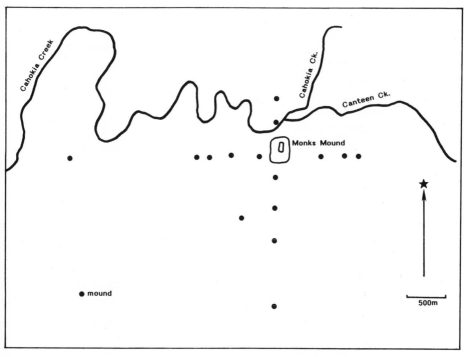

Fig. 6.5. Plan view of the Cahokia site showing how the main axes of the site form a cross that is closely oriented to the cardinal directions. *Redrawn after Sherrod and Rolingson 1987:fig. 21.*

cal archetype of the quartered cosmos: an 'elementary idea' of which the swastika and equal-armed cross are abstractions" (Campbell 1988: 218).

Mississippian designs like the Spiro gorget look very similar to some of the designs found in earlier Hopewell contexts, especially those which incorporate cross and bent-arm cross features (see figure 6.8). Moreover, a clear geometric relationship can be demonstrated between the cross, the square, and the bent-arm cross (see figure 6.9). Given this relationship, as well as the close proximity in both time and space between the Hopewell and Mississippian cultures—including the southern Ohio-based, Mississippian-influenced Fort Ancient peoples—my

Fig. 6.6. Examples of cross and bent-arm designs found on Mississippian shell gorgets. *From Holmes 1883.*

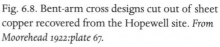

Fig. 6.7. Spiro gorget showing cross and bent-arm cross motifs, symbols of the quartered cosmos. *Drawing by the author from a photograph.*

Fig. 6.8. Bent-arm cross designs cut out of sheet copper recovered from the Hopewell site. *From Moorehead 1922:plate 67.*

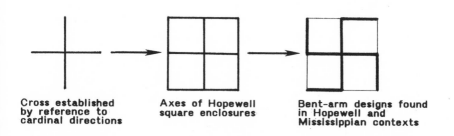

Cross established by reference to cardinal directions

Axes of Hopewell square enclosures

Bent-arm designs found in Hopewell and Mississippian contexts

Fig. 6.9. Illustration showing how the cross, square, and bent-arm cross are geometrically related. *Drawing by the author.*

thought is that the symbolic meanings of the cross, the square, and the bent-arm cross were the same for historic Indians of the Southeast, the prehistoric Mississippians, and the Hopewell: namely, symbols of the sky, the four world quarters, the four cardinal directions, and the four winds.

To summarize this section in another way, we know from ethnographic accounts that many historic southeastern Indian peoples laid out their ceremonial grounds in the shape of a square and that these square grounds were thought of as symbolic microcosms of the universe. Moreover, these square ceremonial grounds were oriented to sky phenomena, including the cardinal directions.

Likewise, prehistoric Mississippian peoples also laid out certain of their architectural structures, like Cahokia, to sky phenomena, including the cardinal directions and the solstices (Sherrod and Rolingson 1987).

A time period of only a few hundred years separates the end of Hopewell from the beginning of Mississippian culture. And, as we have seen, the Hopewell also laid out their square enclosures, as well as certain square-shaped mounds, to sky phenomena, including the solstices and cardinal directions.

Given the above, it seems reasonable to conclude that there very well could be a continuity of belief in the meaning of the square which extends from the historic Indians of the Southeast back to Mississippian times, and back even further to the Hopewell. This belief includes association of the square with the sky, the sun, the cardinal directions, the four world quarters, and the four winds. In this view, the Hopewell squares are sky symbols.

GATEKEEPERS

My final observation in this section relates to the "gateway" mounds that are found inside many of the square enclosures. Figure 6.10 shows the location of these mounds as per Squier and Davis (1848). Below, I will show how burial mounds—especially ones that are located within circular enclosures—are related to themes involving the earth

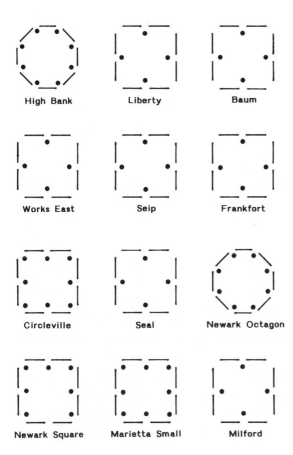

Fig. 6.10. Gateway mounds at the entranceways to Hopewell enclosures. *Drawing by the author, based on Squier and Davis 1848.*

and the Earth Diver myth. But the question must be asked as to how we are to account for the mounds within the square enclosures.

Probably the most revealing thing about these gateway mounds is that nothing of substance is found in them. In figure 6.10, there are a total of sixty-seven gateway mounds. But, as far as I can tell, there is not a single reference in the literature to any artifact or burial ever being found in even one of these mounds. The closest thing to a report of anything found in these mounds is from Squier and Davis (1848:142), who note that a thin layer of "fine-grained, carbonaceous material . . . resembling burned leaves or straw" is sometimes found at the base of some mounds. However, it is not clear in this passage whether Squier and Davis are referring to gateway mounds or not. Still, even if some of the gateway mounds do have this thin burned layer at their base, the fact remains that no burials, no caches, no artifacts, no charnel houses, no debris pits, no postholes—indeed, nothing of real substance—is found in the gateway mounds.

At first this might seem strange, until we consider a point briefly touched on in an earlier chapter. Walls without openings are self-defeating even when they define sacred space. Without an entranceway, no one would be able to enter the sacred space. Hence, sacred areas are usually provided with some means of entrance—that is, a gateway.

Entranceways, however, need to be protected. The sacred space, after all, must not be desecrated or trespassed upon by the profane, or by ghosts, demons, or other malevolent spirits. Accordingly, entranceways to sacred areas are often protected by gateway guardians of one sort or another. To understand the principle, we need only consider the torii gates of Japan that guard the passageways to temple shrines, or the colossal stone creatures that guard the gates to ancient Sumerian cities.

Given this, my thought is that maybe the empty mounds that stand opposite to the entranceways of the Hopewell squares were meant as protective devices or gatekeepers, symbolic guardians that limited casual access into the geometric enclosures, which were passageways to the otherworld.

It is also interesting to note an ancient belief among many peoples that spirits can only travel in straight lines and not in zigzags. To obtain entrance or exit, however, into or out of a Hopewell enclosure that has a gateway guardian mound, a zigzag path is required. Could it be, then, that the gateway mounds at the entranceways to the enclosures also served to keep spirit entities from crossing from the otherworld back into this world?

CIRCULAR ENCLOSURES

In the preceding pages, it was shown how the square Hopewell enclosures are associated with sky phenomena. But what about the second part of the hypothesis, that the circular enclosures represent the earth?

Following the same protocol used for the squares, the test implications for the circular enclosures are: (1) if the circular enclosures were
meant to represent the earth, then we should find that they are associated with earth phenomena; and (2) if the circular enclosures were
meant to represent the earth, and if it is assumed that there is some
continuity in the belief systems of historic Native Americans and their
prehistoric ancestors, including the Hopewell, then we should find
ethnographic evidence that historic Native Americans likewise associated the geometric shape of the circle with the earth.

Looking to the first of these test implications, we are immediately
faced with the problem of what constitutes an "earth phenomenon."
The earth is all around us. And, too, the earthworks themselves are
made of earth. So how can we, or, in the case of the Hopewell, how
could they make the point that the circular earthworks represent the
very earth that they are made out of and built on? Clearly, alignments
will not do because, by its very nature, a circle points in all directions
and it has an infinite number of axes. Circles point to everything and
everywhere.

The answer, I think, might be found in the centrally located burial
mounds sometimes found within the circular enclosures. At Newark,
for example, there is a mound in the center of the Fairground Circle
(Thomas 1894:plate 31). When this mound was opened, calcined bones
and ashes, as well as what appears to have been a crematory basin, were
found within it (Smucker 1881:266; Greenman 1928). Early maps and reports describe a large burial mound at the center of the Circleville Circle (Atwater 1820:178, plate 5). At Seip, a tremendous burial mound was
located in the center of the Seip Large Circle (Squier and Davis
1848:plate 21). And, at Marietta, a large burial mound still remains at the
center of the Circle Earthwork (Squier and Davis 1848:plate 26). Additionally, early maps show an earthen mound in the center of the Shriver
Circle (Squier and Davis 1848:plate 19), and there was a large conical
mound at the center of the Portsmouth Large Circle (Squier and Davis
1848:plate 28). Last, a burial mound is located in the center of the Great
Mound Circle Earthwork near Anderson, Indiana (Cochran 1992; Lilly
1937). Figure 6.11 shows these circular earthworks with their centrally

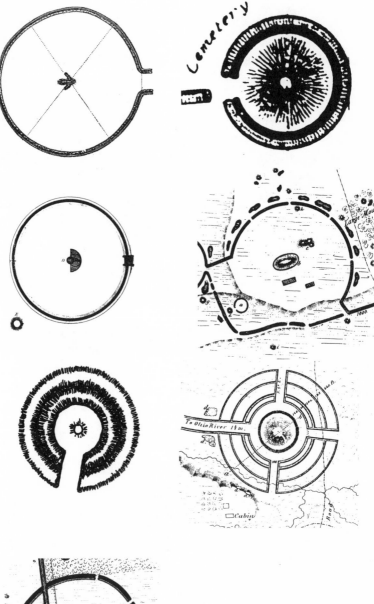

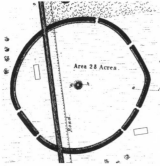

Fig. 6.11. Circular enclosures with centrally located burial mounds. *Drawings by Thomas (1894:plate 31); Atwater (1820:plate 26); Squier and Davis (1848:plates 21, 26, 19, and 28); and the author after Levette in Lilly (1937).*

located mounds. (The Shriver Earthwork and the Great Mound Circle at Anderson, by the way, appear to have been used by both the Adena and Hopewell.)

What I am getting at is that if these centrally located mounds are thought of as symbols, or effigies, of real mountains found in the Hopewell territory, then what we have is an association between the Hopewell circular enclosures and earth phenomena. Two concepts are involved here: (1) mountains as the center of the earth, or axis mundi; and (2) burial mounds as symbols of mountains. Both concepts are widely distributed around the world and across time.

Millions of Hindus and Buddhists, for example, believe that a mountain forms the divine axis, or cosmological center, of the universe. The Hindus call this mountain Mount Meru, while Buddhists know it as Mount Sumeru. Likewise, tens of millions of Chinese believe that the center of the universe is located in the Kunlun Mountains. Among the ancient Greeks, Mount Parnassus was identified as the center of the world, while in Palestine, Mount Gerizim was known as the "navel of the earth." Closer to home, the Sioux medicine man Black Elk identified Harney Peak in the Rocky Mountains as the center of the earth for his people.

The second concept—that is, burial mounds as symbols of mountains—also has a long history among peoples around the world. In Japan, for example, the burial mounds of the ancient emperors were intentionally shaped like mountains. Indeed the mausoleums of later Japanese rulers were called *yama*, which means "mountains" (Bernbaum 1990:58).

Closer to the Hopewell, it has often been suggested that the large conical mound at the Olmec center of La Venta was built as an effigy of a volcanic mountain. Similarly, it is often pointed out that the Pyramid of the Sun at Teotihuacán closely resembles in its shape nearby Mount Patlachique.

Mountains, then, have a long tradition of being considered the axis mundi, or center of the earth. And there are clear instances where man-made pyramids or earthen mounds were made to reproduce, on a smaller scale, real mountains that were important to various mound builders.

What makes the idea of Hopewell burial mounds as effigies or symbols of real mountains especially attractive is the observation that some of the centrally located Hopewell mounds are conical in shape, while others are loaf-shaped. Figures 6.12 and 6.13 show these two mound types. I submit that these distinctions are not accidental but, rather, reflect the actual shapes of two distinct mountain types found in the Hopewell heartland. As shown by figure 6.14, some mountains in southern Ohio are conical in shape and look like the centrally located mound at Marietta, while other mountains, like the one shown in figure 6.15, are loaf-shaped and resemble the centrally located mound at Seip. (Additional examples of these two mound types can be seen at Mound City. Unfortunately, however, all of the loaf-shaped mounds have been excavated, and so what we see today at both Seip and Mound City are reconstructions, made either by their original excavators or by later archaeologists based on early photos.)

In any event, we must always be careful about reading too much into visual resemblances. Certainly, the final shape of a Hopewell mound was, at least to some extent, related to the shape of its underlying charnel house, or burial feature. Nevertheless, it would be foolish to ignore what our eyes tell us—that the centrally located Hopewell burial mounds do, in fact, look like miniature mountains. Again, some of the central burial mounds look like nearby conical-shaped mountains, while others resemble nearby loaf-shaped mountains. Indeed, that may have been exactly what the Hopewell intended.

In summary, it was noted that at least seven major circular enclosures have associated burial mounds. And, just as would happen if these burial mounds were intended to represent the axis mundi of the circular earth represented by the circular enclosures, these mounds are located in the centers of the enclosures. Further, these centrally located mounds closely resemble, in their conical and loaf shapes, the shape or outline of real mountains in the Hopewell heartland. Based on the above, it seems reasonable to suggest that maybe the Hopewell

Fig. 6.12. Conical-shaped burial mound at Marietta. *Photo by the author.*

Fig. 6.13. Loaf-shaped burial mound at Seip. *Photo by the author.*

Fig. 6.14. Conical-shaped mountain at Chillicothe, typical to southern Ohio. *Photo by the author.*

Fig. 6.15. Loaf-shaped mountain near the Seip Earthwork, typical to southern Ohio. *Photo by the author.*

intended the centrally located burial mounds to be symbols, or effigies, of either idealized or specific real mountains. If this is the case, then an association is established between the circular enclosures which contain the mountain-effigy burial mounds and the earth.

The second test implication related to the hypothesis that circles represent the earth is that, if we again assume a continuity in the belief systems of historic Native Americans and their prehistoric ancestors, including the Hopewell, then we should find ethnographic evidence that historic Native Americans likewise associated the geometric shape of the circle with the earth.

Looking to the ethnographic literature, we find that the circle was indeed associated with the earth by both Northeastern and Southeastern Indians. The Iroquois (Beauchamp 1922:9), for example, believed the earth was created when mud was spread on the back of a turtle. The turtle expanded and became the island we know as earth.

Similarly, the Tuscarora (Count 1952:60) said the earth was made on the back of a turtle. And the Seneca (Hewitt 1918:411) believed that the circular earth-turtle floats on an endless sea. In a Wyandot version of the story (Connelley 1899:122), earth was rubbed on the edges of Big Turtle's back, and from this island, earth was formed. To my way of thinking, the back of a turtle is a pretty good approximation of a circle.

Even more to the point are the comments of anthropologist Charles Hudson with reference to the Indians of the Southeast: "The southeastern Indians conceived of This World as a great, flat island. . . . Most of them evidently thought that the island (earth) was *circular* in shape" (Hudson 1976:122; emphasis added).

Based on his studies of the Muskogean Indians—which includes the Creek, Choctaw, Chickasaw, and Seminole—Charles C. Willoughby provides an equally explicit picture of the Southeastern Indians' view of the world:

> the world was a body of land like a great island entirely surrounded by water. . . . The four cardinal points were determined by the course of the sun, and the direction of the winds, which came from the north,

south, east, and west. *The Indians therefore graphically represented the world by one or more circles enclosing a cross.* (Willoughby 1932:59; emphasis added)

Again, the point is that, as predicted by the second test implication, historic references to the earth as a circle are found in the ethnohistoric literature. Indeed, we find that the idea of the earth as a circle is widespread.

Before someone objects and points out that it seems naive to think of the earth as a Great Turtle floating in an endless sea, or a flat circular island surrounded by water, let us keep in mind that, up until a few hundred years ago, most of the civilized Western world likewise believed the world to be flat and surrounded by water. In fact, the fear was that, if a ship sailed far enough, it might fall off the edge of the earth.

Most likely, the idea of the earth as a flat circle arises from the fact that, as we look around us to the horizon, and as we turn, the figure that we trace between the edge of the earth and the sky is a circle. In other words, from each individual's perspective, the earth really does look like a flat circle. Hence, the association of the earth with the figure of a circle is natural.

In this brief analysis, we have seen how the circular enclosures may represent the earth. Certainly, both test implications relevant to the circular enclosures support the hypothesis.

A really good hypothesis, though, not only explains the known facts but should also result in the happy circumstance whereby unknown and even unsuspected data fall into place within the newly proposed hypothesis. Let me give you an example.

If we accept the idea that the circular enclosures were meant as symbols of the earth, then we are able further to explain several features that have long been a mystery. These features include the so-called moats that surround some of the circular earthworks and the waterborne nature of some of the soils that cover burials found in many of the Hopewell mounds. First, though, we need to know something about the Earth Diver myth.

THE EARTH DIVER

According to some of the most brilliant minds of this century, the universe came into existence around fifteen billion years ago, when a quantum flux resulted in the big bang. Matter, energy, and time were thus created, as were the galaxies, stars, and star systems. After several billion years, when things cooled down a bit, the earth and planets were formed out of leftover star dust.

Maybe it happened that way. But the Indians of North America tell a different story.

According to many Native Americans, the earth was created from a tiny bit of mud or sand that was brought up from the bottom of the primal waters. One very typical version of the story goes like this:

> In the beginning . . . water covered everything. Though living creatures existed, their home was up there, above the rainbow, and it was crowded. "We are all jammed together," the animals said. "We need more room." Wondering what was under the water, they sent Water Beetle to look around.
>
> Water Beetle skimmed over the surface but couldn't find any solid footing, so he dived down to the bottom and brought up a little dab of soft mud. Magically the mud spread out in the four directions and became this island we are living on—this earth. (Cherokee legend quoted in Erdoes and Ortiz 1984:105–106)

There are many versions of this story. Among the Iroquois, for example, a toad dives into the primal water, brings up a piece of mud, and makes the earth on the back of a turtle (Erdoes and Ortiz 1984:75). Among the Crow, Old Man Coyote sends a duck to the bottom of the waters. On the duck's third try, he manages to bring up a tiny bit of earth. Old Man Coyote blows on the fragment of earth, which grows and spreads all over (Erdoes and Ortiz 1984:88–89). Depending in large measure on the geographical location of the people who are telling the story, the Earth Diver is variously described as a duck, toad, water beetle, otter, beaver, turtle, or other creature.

One of the most impressive things about the Earth Diver myth is its wide distribution. Earl W. Count (1952), for example, collected close to 230 examples of the tale from northern Eurasia and North America. In fact, according to Count: "the cosmogonic notion of a primal sea out of which a diver fetches material for making dry land, is easily among the most widespread concepts held by man. It stretches from Finland across Eurasia—roughly, over the USSR, the Balkans, Mongolia and Turkistan; it even appears in India and southeastern Asia" (Count 1952:55).

Ethnographers Count (1952:55) and Eli K. Kongas (1960:151) both go on to say that the Earth Diver myth also appears to be the most widely distributed of all North American Indian myths. No doubt they are correct, given that a review of just one anthology of stories (for example, Coffer 1978) reveals the Earth Diver myth, or significant elements of it, in the creation stories of the Cherokee, Delaware, Hopi, Navajo, Omaha, Yakima, Seneca, Kansa, Shawnee, and Acoma.

Such a wide geographical distribution implies a deep time depth. And Count and Kongas both make the point that the Earth Diver appears to be one of humankind's oldest myths, with elements of the story found in many ancient texts, including the Gilgamesh legend and the biblical story of the Great Flood. Given the wide geographical distribution of the tale and its deep temporal origins, could it be that the Hopewell knew the Earth Diver story?

Drawing upon the Earth Diver myth, my thought is that the circular enclosures themselves, as well as any associated central burial mounds, represent the ever-expanding earth that was brought up from the primeval waters by the Earth Diver. Circular perimeter walls define the boundary between the primordial waters and the earth. Everything outside the boundary of the circular enclosures is equivalent to the primal waters.

In this scenario, it really does not matter if burial mounds are found within the circular enclosures or not. As we have seen, some circular enclosures—like the Newark Fairground Circle—do have a centrally located mound, while other enclosures—such as the Newark Observatory Circle—do not. In either case, though, the symbolism of the circle remains the same: the circular enclosure itself represents the earth. Where they occur, centrally located mounds are simply a further embellishment or reiteration of the basic idea of the circular earth being created out of the bit of primal mud.

We now come to the matter of the deep ditches, or moats, that surround some of the circular earthworks. Circular Hopewell earthworks that have such moats include Shriver (Squier and Davis 1848), Circleville (Shetrone 1930:252), Turner (Willoughby and Hooten 1922:5), the Great Mound at Anderson (Lilly 1937), and the Newark Fairground Circle (Thomas 1894:461).

Sometimes these moats extend along the interior side of the circular perimeter walls, as at Newark, while other times they are found along the outside of the perimeter walls, such as at Shriver. In either case, though, these moats are not small features. The moat that extends along the inside perimeter wall of the Newark Fairground Circle, for example, was measured by Thomas (1894:461) to average ten feet deep and thirty-five feet across, and that is after almost two thousand years of accumulated debris having partially filled it.

In any event, my thought is that, where they exist, moats around the circular earth-island enclosures were meant to further emphasize the distinction between the earth within and the primal waters outside.

FLOODWATERS AND THE EARTHWORKS

In addition to what we have already discussed, yet another factor leads me to believe that the Hopewell circular earthworks and burial mounds incorporate elements of the Earth Diver myth, and that is the personal experience the Hopewell may have had with real flooding.

Review of flood data for the Scioto and other southern Ohio rivers shows that these rivers are subject to frequent and severe flooding (see, for example, Cross and Mayo 1969; Cross and Webber 1959). This flooding is no small matter. Photos of the 1913 flood, for example, show much of the city of Chillicothe under water. In fact, according to data for the Bridge Street gauge station (located on the Scioto River at Chillicothe) during the period from 1908, when records were first kept, through 1956, the Scioto River reached flood stage on ninety different occasions (Cross and Webber 1959:240–41). Flood stage is reached when the waters are sixteen feet or more above datum. As one can imagine, some of the worst flooding occurred when the Scioto River reached heights above datum of 39.8 feet in 1913; 31.3 feet in 1898; 27.6 feet in 1937; 25.8 feet in 1945; 26.6 feet in 1952; 32.5 feet in 1959; and 25.2 feet in 1963. Over the years, this flooding has resulted in thousands of people being evacuated from Chillicothe and millions of dollars worth of property damage (ODNR 1959). Recently, three major reservoirs and a series of flood control levees have been built at Chillicothe and Frankfort to protect those cities. However, the problem is still significant.

Looking back to Hopewell times, we do not know if flooding was quite so severe. Maybe increased forest cover mitigated some of the worst flooding. Still, given the climate and topography of the area, it is likely that periodic flooding did occur.

Because most of the geometric enclosures are built on the second river terrace level, when severe flooding occurs, many of these earthworks are also subject to flooding. As noted in chapter 1, floodwaters do not reach the second terrace level very often, but when they do, the effect is dramatic. More specifically, review of the data shows that out of twelve geometrically shaped Hopewell earthworks in Ross County, as many as nine would have been inundated by flood levels equal to historically known floods. These sites include Baum, Dunlap, Frankfort, Hopeton, Mound City, Seip, Shriver, and probably Anderson and Hopewell.

Imagine, then, the stunning effect during a flood of the Scioto River of seeing the Hopeton or Shriver circles, or the Seip or Harness burial mounds, as they slowly emerged from the surface of a retreating expanse of floodwater. As the Hopewell looked on, they would have been witness to an ever-expanding bit of earth, slowly growing in size as the lowering floodwaters revealed more and more of a circular earthwork or burial mound. What better visual metaphor could there be for the creation of the earth, just as is told in the Earth Diver myth?

Indeed, I am reminded of our own Western cosmology, in the

story of how the Great Flood receded from the slopes of Mount Ararat, thereby resulting in a rebirth of the world.

WATERBORNE SOILS

In the scenario above, I mentioned the appearance of burial mounds as they emerged from the floodwaters, and that brings us to the second feature of the earthworks that may be explained by the circle = earth hypothesis and the Earth Diver myth. This feature is the occurrence of waterborne soils that are sometimes found either in association with, or actually covering, burials located within the Hopewell mounds.

At the base of the Eagle Mound located in the center of the Newark Fairground Circle, for example, Emerson F. Greenman (1928:6) found a prepared floor layer comprised of a "well packed muck."

At the Hopewell site of Mount Vernon, in Posey County, Indiana, it was discovered that part of the central burial mound was comprised of a dark "gummy clay" which had "apparently been brought to the site from some low lying wet area" (Tomak 1990:9). Notably, the Mount Vernon Mound is one of the largest Hopewell burial mounds ever discovered.

At the Liberty Earthwork, a layer of puddled clay—meaning clay that is mixed with water when it is laid down—was found within the Harness Mound (Greber 1983:24). At the Hopewell site, layers of puddled clay were found to overlie other, nonpuddled soil layers within the Great Burial Mound (Greber and Ruhl 1989:44). Puddled clay was also used in the construction of Mound 7 at Mound City (Mills 1922:481). And puddled clay was used to cover burials in the Seip Mound (Mills 1909:288).

Anthropologist Robert L. Hall (1979:260) has pointed out several other instances of waterborne soils—including puddled clay, muck, and mud—being used to cover Hopewell burials, notably in Illinois. Even more importantly, though, Hall (1979:260) has proposed that the use of such waterborne soils suggests analogies to the Earth Diver myth. Hall's suggestion is that the waterborne soils used to cover the

Hopewell dead represent the bit of primal mud that was originally brought up by the Earth Diver. For reasons that I will explain later in this chapter, I think the idea makes sense.

A QUESTION OF IDENTITY

So far, we have followed the trail of the Earth Diver across two thousand years of time. But we are still left with a mystery as to the identity of the Hopewell Earth Diver. Was it a bird? Or an animal? Or a frog or a toad? Definite answers are hard to come by, but maybe a clue is found in the designs on Hopewell pottery.

Decorated Hopewell pottery is usually cord-marked, rocker-stamped, or incised with very simple patterns. Representations of living creatures are rare. Occasionally, though, a pottery vessel is found that shows a living creature, and in those rare instances, the only creatures that are ever represented are two kinds of birds. One bird is clearly raptorial, given its curved beak. The other bird, however, is a broad-billed creature that might be either a shoveler duck or a roseate spoonbill.

The shoveler duck is common to northern climates. However, in a very interesting case in Illinois, the actual physical remains of a roseate spoonbill were found buried with two Hopewell individuals in one of the Gibson mounds (Parmalee and Perino 1971). Moreover, there are several instances where the roseate spoonbill is clearly represented on Hopewell effigy pipes recovered, for instance, from the Hopewell site in Ohio. In any event, my proposal is that the Hopewell Earth Diver was either the shoveler duck or the roseate spoonbill. My argument follows.

Many sorts of vessels can hold things. Baskets, for example, can hold solid items like food or wood. Bags made from animal skins can also be used to hold things. Pottery vessels, however, are the best vessels for holding liquids such as soup, paint, or water. Accordingly, it seems appropriate that Hopewell pottery, which was probably used to hold water or water-based substances, might be decorated with representations of the creature who was responsible for bringing substance, or earth, out of the primal world of water. As mentioned, representations of the roseate spoonbill and/or shoveler duck are found on Hopewell pottery. Hence, one of these birds seems a likely candidate for the Hopewell Earth Diver.

EQUAL EXPANSION OUTWARD

Before leaving the subject of the circular earthworks, the Earth Diver myth, and the shape of the world, I would like to make a couple of additional observations. The first has to do with the principle of equal expansion outward.

In nature, the principle of equal expansion outward is found in a variety of phenomena, including splashes, bubbles, craters, exploding volcanoes, and even stars. Consider, for example, what happens when we toss a pebble into a pool of water. Subsequent to impact, ripples rush outward in a series of ever-expanding circles. Expanding from a single point at its center to the infinite points of its circumference, the circle is thus the geometric figure that best represents an ever-expanding earth, just as told in the Earth Diver myth. Thus, we find yet another reason why the Hopewell might choose a circle to represent the earth.

INTERNESTED CIRCLES AND SQUARES

My second observation relates to our earlier finding that many Indian peoples believed the earth to be circular in shape. In fact, the Cherokee (see Mooney 1900:239), as well as a number of other Southeastern Indian groups, further believed that the circular earth is supported by four cords attached to the four cardinal directions. As explained by Charles Hudson:

> The southeastern Indians conceived of This World as a great, flat island resting rather precariously on the surface of the waters, suspended from the vault of the sky by four cords attached at each of the cardinal directions. Most of them evidently thought that the island was circular in shape, but that it was crosscut by the four cardinal directions. (Hudson 1976:122)

A more detailed and somewhat later version told by the Cherokee includes a warning:

Earth is floating on the waters like a big island, hanging from four rawhide ropes fastened at the top of the sacred four directions. The ropes are tied to the ceiling of the sky, which is made of hard rock crystal. When the ropes break, this world will come tumbling down, and all living things will fall with it and die. Then everything will be as if the earth had never existed, for water will cover it. Maybe the white man will bring this about. (quoted in Erdoes and Ortiz 1984:105)

Of interest here is the image of the earth as a circle attached to the sky and crosscut by the four cardinal directions. Although it may be pushing the analogy pretty hard, maybe this image can help explain the geometric interrelatedness of the Hopewell earthworks, wherein the circular enclosures neatly nest within the squares, just as though the corners of the square sky were holding up the circular earth by means of ropes or cords extending from each of the corners, or cardinal directions. Figure 6.16 illustrates this idea, wherein an idealized Hopewell geometric construct is presented with its typical nesting circle and square. In this fig-

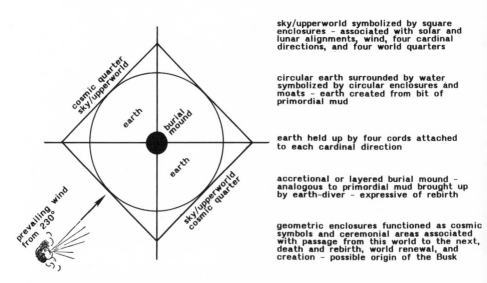

Fig. 6.16. Idealized geometric construct showing how the square sky/upperworld symbol is interrelated to the circular earth symbol. *Drawing by the author.*

ure, we see how the cardinal axes that extend from each of the cardinal directions intersect and thereby hold up the circular earth. Perhaps the Hopewell were trying to express a similar idea through their geometrically interrelated circle and square earthworks.

SUMMARY

According to the hypothesis I have offered, square Hopewell earthworks were meant as symbols of the sky. As such, the squares incorporate alignments to the sun and moon and the cardinal directions. Today, a continuing belief in the square as a sky symbol is found in the layout of Southeastern Indian square ceremonial grounds that are likewise oriented to the sun and the cardinal directions.

The complementary opposite of the square is the circle. Accordingly, circular Hopewellian enclosures were likely meant as symbols of the earth. As such, circular earthworks sometimes incorporate conical or loaf-shaped mounds within their perimeters. It was suggested that these mounds are effigies, or symbols, of real mountains. Hence, the association of the circular enclosures with the earth. Today, continuing use of the circle as an earth symbol is found in the ethnographic accounts of various Southeast Indian groups, who describe the earth as a flat, circular island surrounded by water.

It was also suggested that belief in the earth as a circular island surrounded by water may explain the occurrence of moats around some of the Hopewell earthworks and the use of waterborne soils to cover many Hopewell burials.

In the widely distributed Earth Diver myth, the earth is said to have magically expanded from a bit of earth brought up from the bottom of the primordial waters. By analogy, the circular moats around the perimeters of the circular Hopewell enclosures can be interpreted as symbols of the primordial waters that surround the earth. So, too, the use of waterborne soils in Hopewell burial mounds may be analogous to the expanding bit of mud from which the earth was created.

According to this interpretation, then, each burial mound within a circular enclosure—or even within a square enclosure, if it is a burial mound—represents a reenactment of the mythical creation of the earth. That is to say, when an individual Hopewell burial is incorporated into the symbolic structure of a mound which, in turn, is located within a circle or square earthwork figure, the deceased is, in effect, returned to the mythological beginning—the creation of the world. The individual's soul, or spirit, may continue to the otherworld, but the physical remains of the body are symbolically returned to the beginning.

Chapter 7

SACRED CEREMONIES

Religious ritual aims at existentially uniting opposites in an effort to gain control over an essentially unpredictable universe. The ultimate union of opposites is that of contingent and vulnerable humanity with a powerful, possibly omnipotent force.

—Eugene G. d'Aquili, "The Myth Complex:
A Biogenetic Structural Analysis"

A creature who has once passed from visible nature into the ghostly insubstantial world evolved and projected from his own mind will never cease to pursue thereafter the worlds beyond this world.

—Loren Eiseley, *The Invisible Pyramid*

The secret of magic—that is, its real essence—is in the manipulation of symbols. Let me give you an example.

Years ago, I was traveling in a remote region of Nepal, in a place where Buddhism is only a thin veneer over a more ancient and sometimes darker religion known as Bön.

Night was beginning to fall and a storm threatened, so I sought shelter in a small, rundown village. I found the local version of a bed and breakfast, and after a simple meal of boiled potatoes, I was getting ready to settle in for the night. That was when he showed up—the local shaman. It was hard to tell how old he was, maybe late sixties or early seventies. What I remember most now is his crooked smile and broken teeth.

He seemed friendly enough. And after a brief introduction, he made himself comfortable by the fire. Soon thereafter, he began to make a little doll figure out of flour and water.

Along with five or six villagers who were in the hut with me, I watched, quite fascinated really, as "Old Broken Tooth" carefully shaped the body and head, and then the arms and legs, of the little dough figure. For final effect, he added a couple of feathers and a few pebbles. The doll was about five or six inches in height. At first I thought, "How quaint." But then a couple of my newfound acquaintances told me that the doll was an effigy of me.

Outside, it was raining. But even so, Old Broken Tooth gathered up the flour image and headed out the door with it. Curious as to what he was going to do next, I followed at a discreet distance. What I witnessed a few minutes later sent a chill down my spine.

We had walked maybe a quarter of a mile outside the village when the shaman placed the flour image in the middle of the footpath. Then, with much animation and jibber-jabber, he smashed the little figure again and again under the heel of his foot. Given that the figure was meant to represent me, I wondered if I had made a wise decision to stay the night.

Later that same evening, after making a few inquiries, helped along with liberal quantities of the local beer, I learned that a local family of five recently died from some unknown fever. The shaman, however, believed, and was able to convince many of the villagers, that the unfortunate family really died from evil spirits brought into the village by strangers.

My new friends went on to explain that, by smashing the little flour image, Old Broken Tooth really meant to exorcize and drive away any evil spirits I may have brought with me into the village. After a while, I was convinced that the old man's intentions were good. Still, I suffered a restless night, broken by strange dreams.

Morning came bright and clear. After a quick cup of tea, I was happy to be on my way. I had made it through the night without incident. But it was there—in a faraway corner of the world, and in the depths of a storm-tossed night—that I learned that the power of magic is in the manipulation of symbols, for ultimately, it was the shaman's antics and his manipulation of the little flour image that, for whatever reason, caused me to leave just as soon as I could.

Magic symbols can take many forms. Sometimes they can be little voodoo dolls. Other times, they might be more breathtaking images, like the animal paintings found deep in the caves of France. In yet other instances, magic symbols can take the form of geometric figures like the pentagrams, hexagrams, and other designs used in medieval alchemy and hermetic magic.

In fact, although the magical symbols used by medieval alchemists and magicians may differ in size from the Hopewell geometric earthworks, the principle is the same. By manipulation of such symbols, the shaman or magician expects to influence or control the forces of nature or the universe. In this sense, the Hopewell geometric earthworks can be thought of as magic symbols. They just happen to be far bigger than the magic symbols we are more used to seeing.

In chapter 6, it was proposed that, for the Hopewell, the magic symbol of the circle represented the earth, while squares symbolized the sky. But the big question remains, and that is, for what purpose were these magic symbols used?

Here things get a bit sketchy. But it seems likely that the circle and square earthworks were used for a variety of purposes, including social and community gatherings of various sorts. Mostly, though, I think the geometric earthworks were used for ceremonies relating to passage from this world to the next, death and rebirth, world renewal, and creation.

PASSAGE FROM THIS WORLD TO THE NEXT

Evidence that the enclosures were used for ceremonies relating to passage from this world to the next includes burials and cremations, mica graves, offerings of precious materials, and transformational symbols and paraphernalia, including animal headdresses, effigies of a very special mushroom, and stone pipes used for smoking.

BURIALS

Walking among the geometric enclosures, one often gets the feeling that these were places for the dead. At Seip and Tremper, for example, burial mounds visually dominate the surrounding landscape, while at Mound City, no matter which way we turn, we are surrounded by tremendous burial mounds—silent reminders that peoples' lives, hopes, and dreams are forever buried here.

Burials and burial mounds are located within many of the geometric enclosures, including Newark, Circleville, Mound City, Hopewell, Liberty, Seip, Tremper, Turner, Frankfort, and Shriver.

Sometimes only one or two individuals are represented by the remains buried within the enclosures. But more often than not, the remains of dozens and sometimes even hundreds of individuals are found within the enclosures. The remains of more than 170 people, for example, were recovered from the mounds within the Seip enclosure (Greber 1979:table 6.3). At the Liberty Earthwork, the remains of at least 178 people were found in the Harness Mound (Greber 1979:table 6.3). At Tremper, the cremated remains of an estimated 375 people were discovered in the central burial mound (Mills 1916:280). And at Turner, the remains of ninety individuals were recovered from mounds within that enclosure (Willoughby and Hooten 1922:99).

Of course, Hopewell burials are also found in mounds located outside of the enclosures. But, by far the vast majority of known Hopewell remains are interred in mounds located within the geometric enclosures. Necessarily, then, the physical relationship between the remains of the dead and the enclosures tells us that the Hopewell did, indeed, associate the geometric enclosures with passage of the individual from life into death.

In fact, as I implied in an earlier chapter, it may even be that the Hopewell considered the geometric enclosures to be actual gateways, or doorways, to the otherworld. Certainly, the idea of architectural structures being used to create entrances to the otherworld was known throughout North America. The circular hole in the top of the Ojibway shaking tent, for example, was specifically meant to allow for "soul-flight travel . . . to the Hole in the Sky and [a]cross the barrier to the spirit realm" (Conway 1992:253). Likewise, the circular hole in the top of the Pawnees' earth lodge was meant as a symbolic link between the heavens and earth (Nabokov and Easton 1989:139). And, too, the wooden pole located in the center of the Plains Indian Sun Dance lodge was meant to connect the earth and sky (Nabokov and Easton 1989:168).

Let us also recall, from chapter 5, that Hopewell charnel houses were often oriented to the moon, perhaps in order to provide a sense of direction to the soul as it ascended through the cremation smoke to the otherworld.

The point here is that the idea of architectural elements, like the Hopewell enclosures, being used as gateways to the otherworld is an idea that was well known throughout Native America. Indeed, one gets the impression that the geometric enclosures were in many ways analogous to the oversized community houses known as *karigi* that are used for ceremonies by the Inuit, Yupik, and other native peoples of Alaska and Canada:

> On ceremonial occasions ... the community gathers at the karigi. It is a nexus between the secular, and sacred worlds; passage by celebrants through the house entrance tunnels, doorways, and smoke holes symbolizes the passage between worlds and between different states of being. The karigi smoke hole serves as a passage permitting movement and communication between the world of the hunter and the hunted, between the world of the living and the dead. (Hirschfelder and Molin 1992:144)

In the same way, to step inside the boundary of a Hopewell geometric earthwork was perhaps to step into a threshold or doorway—a doorway somewhere between this world and the next, a doorway between life and death.

CREMATIONS

Like most people, the Hopewell disposed of their dead in several different ways. Sometimes the dead were interred as extended burials, either singularly or in company with others. In other instances, the dead were dismembered and cremated and then either interred alone or in company with other cremated or noncremated remains. Mostly, though, the Hopewell appear to have preferred cremation. That is to say, most of the Hopewell burials we have found are cremations.

What is interesting about this is that fire is one of the most powerful mechanisms we know of for the transformation of matter. Through fire, matter in one form, such as wood, is changed into other kinds of matter, including smoke and ash.

Within the flames of the cremation fire, the dead body is transformed from a potentially dangerous object that could pose a threat to the living, if it were to become reanimated, into a ghostly manifestation of smoke, flame, and harmless ash. Carried ever upward on the blackened smoke of the cremation fire, the souls of the Hopewell dead were thus transported to the otherworld.

Since the vast majority of Hopewell cremations appear to have taken place within the geometric enclosures—as evidenced by the dozens of crematory basins that are found located within the enclosures—we can again conclude that the enclosures were indeed associated with passage from this world to the next.

MICA GRAVES

Cremation was one way that souls of the dead could reach the otherworld. But perhaps there was also another way.

In many instances, Hopewell remains are found buried with pieces of mica. Extended Hopewell burials, for example, are often found with one or two pieces of mica included in the grave, while cremated remains are sometimes found resting on sheets or beds of mica. In yet other instances, mica sheets are found placed on top of the remains. A splendid example of this burial trait is provided by the Great Mica Grave at Mound City. In this instance, the cremated bones and ashes of four individuals were found carefully placed on a bed of mica that measured almost seven feet in diameter (Mills 1922:448).

Mica is a peculiar mineral that easily breaks apart into flat sheets.

What makes mica really unique, however, is that, in its sheet form, it provides a naturally occurring reflective surface, much like a mirror. Because of this reflective characteristic, it has often been suggested, especially by early investigators, that the mica fragments and sheets found with the Hopewell dead served as mirrors for the person in life.

No doubt that was true in some cases, for many of the mica sheets found with the Hopewell dead would have made fine mirrors. Still, the idea of mica being used for personal mirrors of adornment does not explain why cremated remains, like those within the Great Mica Grave, are found to have been gingerly placed on mound floor surfaces that were first prepared by laying down dozens of mica sheets, much like floor tiles. These mica sheets are typically described as varying from "6 by 6 inches to 16 by 14 inches," as in the case of the Great Mica Grave (Mills 1922:448).

Nor does the idea of mica as personal mirrors explain why, in many instances, mica sheets or fragments are the only objects accompanying the dead. Surely, people had other things that were valued in life besides a simple mirror. But, again, it often happens that all we find with the Hopewell dead is a piece or two of mica and nothing more. Furthermore, much of the mica found with the Hopewell dead occurs in the form of one or two very small fragments that would not have been very useful for looking at one's self.

So why, then, was mica included with the dead? What conceivable purpose could have been served by providing the dead with fragments of this peculiar mineral?

One possibility is that the mica fragments were meant to open a doorway for the deceased into the otherworld. My suggestion is based on a couple of observations.

To begin with, mirrors have long been associated with magic and occult practices. Lao-tzu's mirror, for example, reflected the mind and its thoughts. Merlin's mirror told him of treachery within Arthur's kingdom. And the Aztec god Tezcatlipoca spoke to his worshipers as Lord of the Smoking Mirror.

In fact, the idea of mirrors being used to access the otherworld is familiar even to our Western consciousness. In George MacDonald's 1895 novel *Lilith*, for example, the hero opens an interdimensional window to other worlds by manipulating a series of mirror reflections.

One of the things that makes mirrors so suitable for such purposes is that, whether they are made out of mica, metal, or some other material, mirrors provide a glimpse into a world that has no substance. When we look into a mirror, we see an image peering back at us from somewhere within. But, like a soul, or a ghost, or a spirit, the image we see is without material substance. We can never quite touch it.

Even more strange, though, the world within the mirror seems to be a reversed image of this world. In particular, left and right seem reversed. For example, when we look into a mirror and wink our right eye, the face that looks back at us seems to be winking his or her left eye.

As it happens, many Native American peoples describe the otherworld as being the reverse, or opposite, of this world. According to the Cherokee, for example, when it is daytime in this world, it is nighttime in the otherworld. When it is winter in this world, it is summer in the otherworld. As empirical proof of this otherworld reversal, the Cherokee (Mooney 1900:239–40) point out that water from underground springs feels cool in the summer but warm in the winter.

Thus, the world within the mica mirror and the otherworld of the deceased are equivalent. Both are the dwelling places of beings without substance. And both are the reverse of this world.

Perhaps, then, in the case of the Hopewell, it was thought that, by placing the remains of the dead either on or in association with a reflective mica surface, the soul of the deceased would somehow enter the otherworld—through the doorway of the mica mirror.

OFFERINGS

Have you ever given a small gift or a present to your spouse, or your boss, or some other socially important person? Of course, you have; we all have. And, if we will admit it, the hope or even expectation is that the recipient of our little present will, in turn, see fit to bestow on us some token of friendship, goodwill, or material wealth.

Human beings have been conducting their social business with each other like this for thousands of years. For some strange reason, though, we seem to think that this same approach will also work with the gods. Hence, we make sacrifices and offerings of food, money, and even other creatures to the gods in the hope that they will grant our wishes.

The Hopewell, too, made offerings in the form of tremendous caches of precious materials and manufactured goods. Most of the well-known Hopewell effigy pipes, for example, were found in two major caches, one at Mound City and the other at Tremper. In the case of the Mound City pipes, close to 200 pipes were found in a cache located in Mound 8 (Squier and Davis 1848:152). At Tremper, 136 pipes were found in a cache located in the central burial mound (Mills 1916:285). Appropriately enough, most of the pipes from both Mound City and Tremper had been broken into pieces and burned, thus suggesting that they were ritually "killed" in order to release their spirits to the otherworld.

Other large Hopewell caches that have been discovered include a tremendous cache of more than eight thousand flint disks found in Mound 2 at the Hopewell site (Moorehead 1922:96). Each nodule had been roughly shaped into a disk averaging six to nine inches in diameter. At Mound City, William C. Mills (1922:453) discovered a cache in Mound 13 of more than five thousand shell beads, all in a buckskin bag. In this instance, too, the beads had been "killed" by placing the bag on a hard surface and then repeatedly striking the bag with a hammer, "the result being that the greater part of the contents were crushed and broken" (Mills 1922:453).

At the Hopewell site, a cache of more than nineteen thousand perforated pearls was found on Altar 1 in Mound 25 (Willoughby, quoted in Greber and Ruhl 1989:77). And a cache of sixty-six copper celts was also found in this same mound.

In many instances, Hopewell caches are found by themselves. That is, no burials are found in association. Where this is the case, it seems reasonable to conclude that such caches were meant as offerings intended to please and placate the gods or spirits so that the gods or spirits, in turn, would provide such favors as good crops, successful hunts, freedom from illness, good weather, and a variety of other things important to the Hopewell community.

Operationally, it makes sense to leave such offerings in places that are easily accessible to the gods—places where the gods or spirits can cross over from the otherworld into this world and, conversely, where the spirit essence of the offerings can cross over from this world to the next. If this logic was employed by the Hopewell, then, because the cache offerings just discussed were all found within the enclosures, it follows that the Hopewell considered the geometric enclosures to be places where the boundaries of this world and the otherworld over-lapped, and where the transition could most easily be made between this world and the next.

ALTERED STATES OF CONSCIOUSNESS

For the Hopewell, death was a one-way ticket to the otherworld. It may be that the direction to the otherworld was revealed to the dead by the lunar orientation of the Hopewell charnel houses. And it may be that the Hopewell believed the deceased soul ascended to the other-world on a wisp of smoke or through the reversed dimensions of a mica mirror. But, in either case, the journey to the otherworld by death was final.

Still, another way of passage to the otherworld—one that was not so final—also appears to have been known to the Hopewell. This sec-ond way of passage was through altered states of consciousness brought about by several methods, including rhythmic driving and the use of psychotropic, or mind-altering, drugs.

SHAMANS AND SHAPE-SHIFTERS

Imagine, if you will, the scene more than a thousand years ago, as dozens or even hundreds of Hopewell people gathered at a place like Newark on some dimly lit night—a night, perhaps, when the moon fi-nally reached its most northerly or southerly point in the sky, thus heralding the closest proximity of this world and the next. Slowly at first, but then with ever increasing rhythm, the percussion rattles forced a driving beat as the light from nearby fires flickered and cast fleeting shadows over the people. Excitement mounted as the dancers stomped and whirled and chanted to the old songs, further driving the rhythmic firing of nerve synapses, bringing the dancers closer and closer to the otherworld.

Then, out of the shadows, he appeared—the Great Bear Spirit. Standing bigger than any human warrior ever known and more dangerous than any monster imagined, the Great Bear danced and whirled, around and around. Every so often, he would charge and take a swipe with long tearing claws at a dancer who happened too close. But what was really frightening was that there, in his right hand, the Great Bear held a severed human head.

Who, or what, was this dark form that danced with a human head? Was it really a bear, or was it a human dressed like a bear? Or was it in fact, a shaman who put on the skin of a bear and, in so doing, became the bear? Here, among the dancing moon shadows and flickering night fires, it was hard to tell. Here, primitive forces ruled. Here, in the dark of the night, anything was possible.

Fiction? Just a story I made up? Probably not, for the archaeological evidence tells us that the Hopewell had little copper rattles, filled with pebbles, that were probably used as percussion instruments. Such rattles have been found with burials at Mound City. And the archaeological evidence tells us that there were Hopewell shamans who could assume the guise of a bear, or a deer, and perhaps other animals.

The Wray figurine (Dragoo and Wray 1964), for example, shows a Hopewell shaman dressed in a bearskin and holding a decapitated human head. Notably, the Wray figurine was found within the Newark Earthworks. At Mound City, Mills (1922:452) discovered a bear effigy headdress, made out of copper, in Mound 13. And he found, also in this same mound, another copper headdress, this one fashioned in the shape of a set of deer antlers (Mills 1922:454). Two more copper deer antler headdresses were found by Warren K. Moorehead (1922:108) at the Hopewell site.

Tales of magical transformation brought about by the wearing of a mask, or the fur or skin of some animal, or by eating or drinking some magic potion are found throughout the stories and legends of Native Americans (see, for example, Marriott and Rachlin 1968). Eyewitness accounts of such transformations also are found. In describing the powers of Ojibway shamans, for example, a certain Reverend Jones observed: "They are believed . . . to turn themselves into bears, wolves, foxes, owls, bats, and snakes. Such metamorphoses they pretend to accomplish by putting on the skins of these animals, at the same time crying and howling in imitation of the creature they wish to represent" (Hoffman 1891:237). In such cases, as explained by archaeologist E. O. James, "When a ritual expert arrayed himself in the skin and antlers of a stag, or in the feathers of a bird, he did so in the belief that for the time being, and for the prescribed purpose, he was what he represented himself to be" (James 1957:233).

The Wray figurine and the bear and deer and other animal headdresses found in the Hopewell mounds all suggest that the Hopewell were engaged in some sort of man-animal transformations. By definition, such transformations imply passage from this world into alternate realities—or the otherworld—where the consciousness of human beings are merged with those of animals. Necessarily, then, the finding of the Wray figurine and the bear and deer headdresses within the geometric enclosures again tell us that the enclosures were associated with passage from this world to the otherworld.

MAGIC MUSHROOMS

So far, I have proposed that the Hopewell journeyed to the otherworld through death, as well as through altered states of consciousness assisted by the wearing of animal masks and headdresses, percussion driving, and most likely, rhythmic chanting, dancing, and singing. Clearly such methods are effective. Just think of all the altered minds in attendance at any hard rock concert or high-energy nightclub. Still, there are even more effective ways to alter one's view of reality. Psychotropic or hallucinogenic drugs, for example, will quickly take one to worlds beyond imagination.

Interestingly enough, it appears that the Hopewell may have been familiar with at least one very powerful hallucinogen. That hallucinogen is known as *Amanita muscaria*. I am jumping ahead in my story, however. So let me start at the beginning.

Hallucinogenic substances occur naturally in a wide variety of plant and mushroom species. The effects of these substances include visions of imaginary beings, altered perceptions of time, distortions in the size and shape of objects, sensations and visions of flight, and other well-known psychedelic effects. As we might expect, such experiences often have the effect of reinforcing beliefs in the reality of the supernatural. Indeed, hallucinogenic drugs have long been used to journey to the otherworld.

Relevant to the discussion here is that some of the earliest evidence for the use of hallucinogens is found among the Aryan invaders of India some thirty-five hundred years ago. In a brilliant piece of detective work, ethnopharmacologist R. Gordon Wasson (1968) persuasively argued that these ancient people used a hallucinogenic mushroom known as *Amanita muscaria*, or fly agaric, to achieve ecstatic states that are recorded in the *Rig Veda*. In the eighteenth century, European explorers found this very same mushroom again being used for religious purposes by the Koryak, Yakut, Chukchee, Ostyak, and other peoples of Siberia.

As to the effects of the mushroom, Walderman Jochelson, who lived among the Koryak from 1902 to 1905, described the experience as follows:

> if the Agaric should say to a man, "You will melt away soon," then the man would see his legs, arms and body melt away, and he would say, "Oh why have I eaten of the Agaric? Now I am gone!" Or should the Agaric say, "Go to The-One-on-High," . . . the latter would put him on the palm of his hand and twist him like a thread, so that his bones would crack, and the entire world would twirl around. "Oh, I am dead!" that man would say, "Why have I eaten the Agaric?" But when he came to, he would eat it again, because sometimes it is pleasant and cheerful. Besides, the Agaric would tell every man . . . what ailed him when he was sick, or explain a dream to him, or show him the upper world, or the un-

derground world, or foretell what would happen to him. (quoted in Morgan 1995:106)

In North America, *Amanita muscaria* is found across most of the continent. In eastern North America, for example, it ranges from Minnesota to Labrador and down to Florida and Louisiana (Smith 1963:177).

In Ohio, *A. muscaria* favors open woods of poplar, oak, and pine (Graham 1944:163). Generally, *A. muscaria* is the most commonly occurring variety of the *Amanita* genus.

The history of *Amanita* is fascinating. But where all of this becomes really intriguing is in the discovery that the Hopewell, too, may have known about the effects of the *Amanita*. This assertion is based on the finding of *Amanita* effigies within the Hopewell enclosures.

More specifically, an effigy wand in the shape of an *Amanita* mushroom was discovered by Ohio Historical Society archaeologist William C. Mills in Mound 7, at Mound City. Mills described the object this way:

> In Fig. 71 is shown a remarkable effigy of a mushroom, evidently intended to represent the so called death-cup, or deadly amanita. . . . It had been placed upon a large sheet of mica, and over it were heaped the cremated remains comprising the burial. The length of the effigy is 13 ½ inches. The specimen is made of wood, covered with thin copper. (Mills 1922:547)

The mushroom effigy that was discovered by Mills is shown here in figure 7.1. Similar effigies, however, may have also been found by Warren K. Moorehead at the Hopewell site. According to Moorehead: "We found in the Hopewell altars some small mushroom-shaped objects of copper; and several, which were larger and with longer stems, were discovered by Mills at Mound City. Mills concludes that they portray the deadly Amanita, and we concur with him in this theory" (Moorehead 1922:174). As far as I can tell, only the whereabouts of the Mound 7, Mound City effigy wand is known today, so not much can be said about the other effigies that Moorehead makes reference to. Like Mills and Moorehead, though, I am of the opinion that the Mound City effigy does, in fact, represent an *Amanita* mushroom.

Fig. 7.1. Mushroom effigy wand recovered from Mound 7 at Mound City. The mushroom effigy had been placed on a large sheet of mica and then covered with cremated remains. The copper-covered wood effigy is 13½ inches in length. *From Mills 1922: fig. 71.*

As a group, the *Amanitas* are easy to recognize, even by a nonexpert. Reference to any good guidebook will provide ample details. However, some of the more important identifying criteria include shape of the cap, smoothness of the edge of the cap, shape of the stem, presence or absence of a ring or annulus, location of the annulus, and color of the mushroom, especially the cap (Pearson 1987).

Using these criteria, we find that the cap of the Mound City mushroom effigy matches the shape of actual *Amanita* caps. So, too, the relatively smooth edges of the effigy cap correspond to the smooth edges of real *Amanita* caps. Also, the Mound City mushroom has an untapered stem, which is characteristic of the *Amanitas*. The Mound City effigy also has a ring, or annulus, present on its stem, which is typical to most of the *Amanitas* including *A. muscaria*. Last, the location of the ring on the Mound City effigy is fairly high up on the stem, a further characteristic of the *Amanitas*. Quite simply, the Mound City effigy looks like an *Amanita*.

The most pressing question, of course, is what species of *Amanita* is represented by the Mound City effigy. Is it the famed *Amanita muscaria*?

As pointed out above, and as a good identification guide will again corroborate, one of the best ways to distinguish between the *Amanitas* is by the color of the mushroom's cap. More to the point, *A. muscaria* varies in color from golden yellow to orange, while other *Amanitas* are of different colors. *A. pantheria*, for example, has a gray-brown to dingy yellow cap. *A. phalloides* has a pale, yellowish-green cap. *A. umbria* has a brown cap. *A. verna* and *A. virosa* have white caps, and so on. Notably, though, the yellow color of the copper-covered Mound City effigy matches the golden yellow to orange color of the *A. muscaria*. Given this particular resemblance, as well as the other identifying criteria already mentioned, it seems entirely possible that the Mound City effigy was meant to represent an *Amanita muscaria* mushroom.

The eating of an *Amanita muscaria* mushroom would have facilitated a trip to the otherworld. However, even if the Mound City effigy depicts some other species of *Amanita*, a trip to the otherworld was still in store for the mushroom eater, because virtually all of the *Amanitas* are either hallucinogenic, or poisonous, or both.

What makes all of this relevant is that, because they were found within the enclosures, the *Amanita* mushroom effigies again tell us that the enclosures were indeed associated with passage from this world to the next.

SMOKING PIPES

Evidence that the Hopewell used mind-altering substances is not limited to the mushroom effigy wands. In fact, the best evidence in this regard is also the most prolific, and that is in the form of the many platform and effigy smoking pipes found within the Hopewell enclosures. As mentioned earlier, close to 200 such pipes were discovered within the Mound City enclosure, while another 140 or so were found within the Tremper enclosure. Dozens more have been found in many burial mounds.

The effigy pipes tell us that the Hopewell were expert craftsmen. Even more importantly, though, the pipes tell us that the Hopewell were smoking something, thus altering their consciousness. Simply stated, people smoke in order to change their brain chemistry.

Unfortunately, we do not know for certain what the Hopewell were smoking in their pipes, because even the residues that would normally be found in a pipe bowl have, in the case of the Hopewell pipes, long since faded away.

On the other hand, there is some very tentative evidence that *Nicotiana rustica*, a very strong variety of tobacco, was being cultivated in the Midwest as early as A.D. 100 (Riley, Edging, and Rossen 1990:529). The evidence to date is only from one site. But what if the Hopewell were smoking *Nicotiana rustica*? Just what are the effects of this native tobacco? For one thing, *Nicotiana rustica* is far more powerful than the variety of tobacco known as *Nicotiana tabacum* that we are familiar with today in the form of packaged cigarettes. The nicotine content of *N. rustica*, for example, can be as much as five times higher than the levels found in *N. tabacum* (Robicsek 1978:46). In fact, *N. rustica* was used by the Natchez Indians to stupefy their victims prior to ritual strangulation, thus demonstrating, in a most unfortunate way, the powerful effects of this plant. Indeed, *N. rustica* is so powerful that today, in the United States, this variety of tobacco is only used in the manufacture of insecticides (Robicsek 1978:46).

For most Native Americans, though, tobacco was used as a means of communication with the otherworld. Typical of this use is the following explanation of how tobacco was used by the Iroquois: "The Iroquois believed that tobacco was given to them as the means of communication with the spiritual world. By burning it they could send up their petitions with its ascending incense to the Great Spirit" (Morgan 1851:164). Again, we cannot state with certainty that the Hopewell were smoking *Nicotiana rustica* in their pipes. However, the sudden proliferation of smoking pipes in Hopewell times, together with the finding that *Nicotiana rustica* was being cultivated by the Indians of the Midwest as early as A.D. 100, strongly suggests that tobacco, in some form or mixture, was being used by the Hopewell. If this is the case, then the mind-altering effects of this powerful drug clearly would have facilitated journeys to the otherworld. Moreover, the finding of these pipes within the geometric enclosures again tells us that passage from this world to the next—through altered states of consciousness, as well as by death—was one of the uses associated with the geometric enclosures.

As explained in the next section, however, passage from this world to the next was not the only purpose for which the geometric enclosures were used.

DEATH, REBIRTH, AND WORLD RENEWAL

The ultimate question that each of us will eventually face is, what happens when we die? Do we cease to exist as an individual consciousness made up of unique thoughts, feelings, and memories? Or do we somehow continue for all time? What will it be—eternal nothingness, or everlasting heaven and hell?

For most people, the prospect of eternal nothingness and dissolution of the ego is beyond imagination and too frightening to contemplate. Perhaps for this reason, the idea of an immortal soul that somehow survives the death of the body has persisted and even flourished for thousands of years. Most often, the idea of an immortal soul finds further elaboration in theories of rebirth, resurrection, and reincarnation. In other words, death is viewed as a temporary state which is followed by a new beginning. For a splendid example of this thought process, we need look only as far as the nearest Catholic church, where the doctrine of the resurrection is preached to Sunday school toddlers.

On a deeper level, though, I suppose we have good reason to believe in the possibility of eternal life, or rebirth, or resurrection, given that, throughout nature and all around us, we are a frequent witness to the process of rebirth. A new moon is followed by the full moon. Winter is followed by spring. Cold is followed by warmth. And the barren snow-covered fields are followed by blossomings of plant life. In fact, microbiologist Darryl Reanney has proposed that the idea of religious rebirth results from the imprinting of natural phenomenon on our brains: "human experience was (and is) dark (night) always followed by light (day). . . . The chemical and electrical patterns of our brains reflect and reinforce this oscillatory character of nature. Hence, inevitably, death has become identified with sleep, to be followed (as our most basic experience 'proves'), by awakening" (Reanney 1991:108–109). In other words, "resurrection and reincarnation have been successful in gaining adherents because they correspond to the way our brains work. In an important sense, the rebirth of the self is a memory, not a prediction—by the time we die, our mind clocks will have recorded, on average, about 27,000 successive rebirths" (Reanney 1991:108).

Evidence that the Hopewell were cognizant of the idea of rebirth finds expression in several forms. One example is provided by the orientation of the square enclosures as discussed in chapter 4. As the reader will recall, several of the square enclosures—such as Hopewell, Hopeton, Mound City, Anderson, and Dunlap—are oriented to the summer or winter solstices. By definition, such alignments mark the end of one season and the beginning of the next, thus implying some sort of recognition of the idea of death and rebirth as expressed in the cycles of the sun and progression of the seasons.

Further, as discussed in chapter 6, the idea that the geometric earthworks were used for ceremonies relating to death and rebirth seems expressed by the occurrence of burials within many of the circular enclosures and their association with layered, waterborne soils, and the Earth Diver myth.

WORLD RENEWAL CEREMONIES AND THE BUSK

Where people have some concept of religious rebirth, such ideas often find physical expression in ceremonies of creation or world renewal. The native peoples of North America are no exception. And so we find many well-documented instances of world renewal ceremonies among the Indians of North America.

One of the best known of the world renewal ceremonies, for example, is the Plains Indian Sun Dance, which at one time was performed by more than twenty different tribes. Its rituals were intended "for the renewal of the tribe's cosmos and welfare" (Nabokov and Easton 1989:168). More specifically, "The theme of the Sun Dance of the Cheyenne was the re-creation of the world in successive phases during which the void and infertile earth became filled in turn by water . . . and finally, the Cheyenne" (Guidoni 1978:63).

Similarly, the Delawares' world renewal ceremony was meant to "celebrate the unity of all creation and the renewal of the earth. This ceremony, they said, ensured that the cycle of seasons would be maintained. . . . The rite reenacted creation and emphasized beginnings: the beginning of a new year and the beginning of a new earth" (Rockwell 1991:165). Notably, the Delaware ceremony took place in a large rectangular enclosure known as the "big house." As pointed out earlier, this lodge symbolically recreated, in its structure, the shape of the universe.

Among the Tewa (Ortiz 1969), there was an intricate series of nine ceremonies, each of which was performed at a different time of the year. Each particular ceremony, such as the "bringing the buds to life" ceremony, was intended to help the seasonal cycle of nature progress to its next phase.

For our purposes, the most relevant of the world renewal ceremonies were those of the Southeastern Indians. And for those Indians—which include the Creek, Seminole, Natchez, Yuchi, and Chickasaw—the Busk, or Green Corn Ceremony, was the most important ceremony of the year. As explained below, there are certain parallels between features of the Busk and the Hopewell enclosures.

To begin with, the Busk marked the beginning of the new year. At this time, ceremonial and individual dwellings were swept clean for the new year. The sacred fire was rekindled, noble deeds were publicly recognized, and a series of dances was held in honor of certain bird and animal species that were either clan totems or otherwise important to the tribe. Mostly, though, the Busk was concerned with plant fertility, its primary purpose to celebrate the ripening of the corn. Only then could the corn be eaten.

A useful description of the central Busk ceremony is provided by Howard: "four perfect ears of corn are fed to the fire . . . to be consumed by the flames. The ceremony is a classic example of the first fruits rite, the connotation being that the first ears of the new maize crop are reserved for the Supreme being as a thanks offering" (Howard 1968:83). Notably, the Busk was performed within the square ground enclosures discussed in chapter 6.

Of course, the Hopewell did not rely on corn for their main sustenance. Nevertheless, it was the Adena-Hopewell who initiated agriculture in eastern North America with such crops as maygrass, goosefoot, knotweed, and sunflower. Basically seed plants that we now think of as weeds, these plants were domesticated, cultivated, and used as food by the Adena-Hopewell. We can surmise that as time went on—from early Adena times up through Hopewell times—these plants became progressively more important to these early peoples' survival. Given this increasing reliance on such food plants, what I am proposing is that a series of ceremonies, like the Busk, were performed within the Hopewell geometric enclosures for precisely the same reasons that similar ceremonies were performed in similar geometrically shaped areas hundreds of years later by the Indians of the Southeast—that is, to give thanks for the previous year's food, to improve the chances for a successful harvest in the coming year, and to offer prayers to both plant and animal spirits.

FURTHER CORRESPONDENCES WITH THE BUSK

In chapter 6, we looked at some of the correspondences between the Hopewell enclosures and the square grounds within which the Busk, or Green Corn Ceremonies, were held. Correspondences were found in geometry, orientation, and symbolism. In particular, it was noted that both the Hopewell and Busk ceremonial areas are shaped as squares, both are oriented to the sky, and both were associated with sky symbols.

Further correspondences, however, are also apparent. For example, it happens that the timing of the Busk was determined by the positions of either the stars or the moon (Williamson 1992:64). In the timing of the Busk by the moon, in particular, we can see a correspondence with the Hopewells' association and alignment of their ceremonial enclosures to the cyclic events of the sun and moon.

Turning to another correspondence, it happens that one of the most important features of the Busk was the "going to water" ritual. In this ritual, Busk participants spiritually purified and renewed themselves by bathing in a nearby river (Witthoft 1949:35, 37). This ritual bathing took place at several junctures in the Busk ceremony.

Of special interest here is that a number of Hopewell enclosures have walled avenues or passageways that lead directly to nearby rivers or streams. Such avenues are found, for example, at Newark, Hopeton, Marietta, Seal, Dunlap, Portsmouth, and Turner. If my analogy holds, then perhaps these avenues were in some way connected with the purifying, as well as life-giving and rejuvenating, effects associated with water by Indians throughout the Americas (see Hultkrantz 1979:62). In other words, maybe the walled Hopewell avenues were used for processions to the water, for purification and renewal rituals, just as was done during the Busk. Notably, the sacred nature of the walled passageways is vastly increased when they are also in alignment with the sun, as is the case at Marietta and Hopeton.

In any event, given the above, I have to agree with Howard, who proposed that "Many of the elements [of the Busk], in fact, probably stem from Hopewellian or other pre-Mississippian cultures. As such, [the Busk] . . . probably represents one of the oldest ceremonial traditions in the New World" (Howard 1968:88). If what Howard and I are proposing is the case, then the Hopewell enclosures provide further evidence for a continuity of belief and symbolism extending from historic and Mississippian times back into the Middle Woodland.

Let us also keep in mind that, if the circular enclosures were meant to symbolize the Earth Diver myth, then they, too, are expressive of world renewal. The central theme of the Earth Diver myth, after all, is the creation of the world. By adding yet another layer of earth to a centrally located burial mound within a circular enclosure, or by performing a sacred dance within the enclosure, the Earth Diver myth is reenacted, the earth is magically increased in size, and the world is thus recreated and renewed.

FURTHER EVIDENCE

In addition to the evidence presented thus far, there are a few more reasons for thinking that the enclosures were used for world renewal ceremonies.

Within some of the Hopewell enclosures, for example, several peculiar artifacts have been found that are best described as copper cutouts. Figures 7.2 and 7.3 show several of these cutouts, although others have been found that are of different designs. In any event, I think many people will agree that the designs shown in figures 7.2 and 7.3 strongly resemble plant forms (also see Quimby 1943) that include flowers, germinating seeds, and flower petals.

These particular plant symbols, if that is what they are, were found within the Hopewell and Turner geometric enclosures. My own opinion is that the discovery of these plant images within the enclosures further supports the idea that the geometric earthworks were associated with world renewal and, in particular, with the renewal of plant resources.

The evidence is not limited, however, to mere images of plant forms. Physical evidence such as charred plant remains is also found within the enclosures in such contexts as to suggest ceremonial activities. As noted in an earlier chapter, for example, Squier and Davis (1848:181) point out that thin layers of charred organic matter are found in many of the mounds located within the enclosures. Indeed, Squier and Davis (1848:181) further note that "It has been suggested that sacrifices or offerings of vegetables or 'the first fruits' of the year were sometimes made, of which these traces alone remain."

Perhaps the best evidence though, comes from the Capitoleum Mound, located within the Marietta Large Square. Specifically, recent excavations at the Capitoleum Mound uncovered the remains of various plant materials which were examined by archaeologist Dee Anne Wymer (1993). What Wymer found was that no less than fifteen different kinds of wood were deposited and burned on several superimposed, prepared mound floors. As Wymer (1993:19) points out, Hopewell habitation sites typically average far less diversity in the number of species represented. Even more intriguing, however, is that these different varieties of wood were apparently collected from very different environments, some of which are not typical to the immediate area. As Wymer (1993:20) explains, the implication is "that a wide variety of species from a wide variety of environments had been deliberately collected and utilized during as yet unspecified ceremonial activities. . . ."

Fig. 7.2. Floral motif copper cutouts from the central altar of Mound 3, Turner site. Among the floral motifs represented are sprouting seeds and flower petals. *From Willoughby and Hooten 1922:plate 11.*

Fig. 7.3. *Top,* floral motif copper cutout from the Hopewell site. *From Moorehead 1922:plate 65.* Bottom, floral motif copper cutout from the Turner site. *From Willoughby and Hooten 1922:plate 10.*

To me, Wymer's findings represent the best evidence that world renewal ceremonies, associated with the renewal of floral resources, were held within the geometric enclosures.

Indeed, as darkness falls and a brisk winter wind swirls and sweeps all around, one can imagine the laughing and excited faces as dozens of Hopewell people brought to some ancient ceremony at the Capitoleum Mound the greatest variety of floral species possible, to be presented as offerings in the hope that all plant life would be renewed. How appropriate, too, that this ceremony would take place at the Capitoleum Mound, which is aligned to the winter solstice, for as discussed above, it is the winter solstice that marks the beginning of the sun's return, bringing with it renewed warmth, longer days, and new life.

A FINAL THOUGHT

It would take another book to thoroughly explore the idea, but I think a pretty good argument can be made that, as the Adena people began to cultivate various plant foods sometime before 500 B.C., they simultaneously built and used their sacred circle earthworks for plant and world renewal ceremonies. No doubt, matters of human magic and plant fertility were closely intertwined in those early days, with a strong belief that domesticated plant foods could best flourish with the help of ritual magic. In this scenario, the Adena circles would have been associated with the Earth Diver myth. Perhaps a circle might have been used for a decade or two, or maybe even a generation.

When, for whatever reason, this first sacred circle's useful ceremonial life ended, yet another circle would be constructed and the tradition of the world renewal ceremony would be continued within that second circle. In some instances, this practice eventually resulted in groups of earthen circles that were located very near to each other, such as those found near the Plains, in Athens County, Ohio, and in the Kanawha Valley, near Charleston, West Virginia.

As time went on, and as horticultural efforts became more sophisticated, with a greater variety of plant foods being cultivated by the Hopewell, the earthworks within which the plant renewal and world renewal ceremonies were conducted likewise became more complex and bigger. Earthworks such as Newark and Marietta represent the zenith of such efforts.

For reasons that archaeologists do not yet fully understand, the Hopewell eventually stopped building the large geometric earthworks. World renewal ceremonies continued. However, as we have seen, they took place in smaller geometrically shaped areas like the square grounds.

As for the Hopewell earthworks themselves, with the end of the Hopewell, the great tradition of geometric earthwork building in Ohio stopped. No longer were the sacred circles and squares maintained. No longer did the people use their power. And with time, as memories faded, so did the geometric creations, as wind and rain and human beings from another age eventually reduced the great symbols to mere reflections of their former glory.

Chapter 8

CONCLUSION

The Ways of the Old
    are Forever Gone,
Only in Our Dreams
    can they Live.
                —Ronnie C. Bradley, Cherokee

On July 20, 1969, at 10:56 P.M. eastern standard time, human beings from the planet earth set foot on the moon. For many of us who
witnessed this event on television, our journey to another celestial body
was humankind's greatest achievement so far.

Yet, from another perspective, it almost seems destined to have
happened, for there seems to be a driving force from deep within that
compels all living matter—from the simple, one-celled amoeba to complex human beings—to search out and probe the farthest reaches of our
boundaries. So maybe it was bound to happen: after billions of years,
organic matter would finally figure out a way to move itself off the face
of this planet and on to the surface of another world.

In essence, the impulse that resulted in our putting a man on the
moon is not really any different from the drive that motivates all life
forms. Living matter seeks to expand and explore—for food, for genetic
material, and for territory. Moreover, I think that, within the limits of

their own individual capabilities and sensory systems, all forms of living matter seek to interpret and make sense of the world around them. Which brings us back to the Hopewell.

When I look to the Hopewell earthworks, I do not see the broken and tumbled-down relics of some strange and alien thought process; rather, I see another iteration of the thoughts and impulses that have guided humankind since the beginning.

Like their counterparts the world over, the Hopewell sought order and meaning in the world around them. And, like their counterparts the world over, they found it through their discoveries in astronomy, geometry, measuring, and counting. Moreover, they seem to have found meaning in the underlying symbolic and metaphorical relationships between these mathematically based endeavors of the mind and the biological rhythms of life and death.

As we have seen, the discoveries that the Hopewell made in astronomy, geometry, measuring, and counting are reflected and incorporated in their earthworks. These earthworks, or earthen creations, in turn, helped integrate the Hopewell into their universe.

Looking back to some of the more important points that led to these conclusions, let us recall that, in chapter 1, a number of examples were provided showing that the earthworks are often located in transitional areas poised between different realms, both real and maybe not so real. In chapter 2, I demonstrated how various components of individual earthworks are geometrically interrelated, and I showed how a number of fundamental geometrical relationships that have been rediscovered time and again the world over are likewise expressed in the Hopewell earthworks. In chapter 3, two dozen examples were presented showing how the large Hopewell measure of 1,053 feet is incorporated in the earthworks. And it was shown how posthole separation distances may indicate the use of smaller units of length—namely, the units of 2.106 and 1.053 feet. In chapter 4, I presented evidence showing how many of the earthworks are balanced, by way of their celestial alignments, between night and day, and between the yearly cycles of winter and summer. Indeed, it appears that at least nine earthworks, including two still extant rectangular-shaped mounds at Marietta, are oriented to the sun. Recall too, that photographic evidence of the winter solstice sunset alignment of the Sacra Via was also presented. In chapter 5, I proposed that a number of Hopewell charnel houses are aligned to the moon. In chapter 6, the idea that the earthworks were meant as cosmic symbols of the earth and sky was pursued. And finally, in chapter 7, I explored the idea that the Hopewell enclosures are at the threshold locations of human experience—poised not only between seasonal cycles of the sun and moon, but also between life and death, existence and nonexistence, normal consciousness and altered states.

In retrospect, I think it would be fair to say that I was able to show that the geometric Hopewell earthworks were located in special places, that the Hopewell were very accomplished in geometry, and that they used a large unit of measure equal to 1,053 feet. Admittedly, many of the examples regarding the geometry and large unit of measure used old maps, which may be less accurate than I would like. But, as pointed out before, that is what we have to work with. And let us keep in mind that many other of my examples of the Hopewell's expertise in geometry and units of measure utilized maps that are known to be very accurate, such as those provided by Thomas.

As to the evidence for the smaller units of measurement—that is, the 2.106 and 1.053-foot units of length and their proposed relationship to the length of the human arm—I would like to have offered more evidence. However, sufficient instances of these smaller units of length were presented to at least make a persuasive, if not definitive, argument for their existence.

With regard to Hopewell archaeoastronomy, I think I was able to show beyond a reasonable doubt that the Hopewell aligned many of their earthworks to the sun and moon. Some might argue that my conclusions relied too heavily on analyses of small or even fuzzy images on old aerial photos; however, the solstice-aligned features at Marietta are still extant and easily accessible for corroborative research by other investigators. Moreover, the photographic evidence showing the Sacra Via winter solstice alignment seems beyond dispute.

As for the symbolism of the earthworks, I would like to have presented more evidence for my ideas that burial mounds symbolize mountains, circles represent the earth, and squares symbolize the sky. But no matter how voluminous the evidence, we may have to admit that, ultimately, without some written record, we may never be able absolutely to prove what any particular geometric symbol meant to its user. Obviously, this is a problem common to most studies that attempt to reconstruct prehistoric worldviews. There is no easy solution. Sometimes, hypotheses or theories are simply not amenable to empirical testing. Nevertheless, I am satisfied that a good start has been made; and, although we may not be able absolutely to prove the propositions set forth in chapter 6, there is a very good likelihood that we are on the right track.

As for the final chapter and the question of the purpose of the earthworks, we are faced with the problem of how strong a correlation we should draw between the artifacts we find in or around an earthwork and the purpose of that earthwork. Here, as in chapter 6, we walk a fine line between speculation and reasonable conclusions based on test implications. In this regard, all I can do is let the evidence speak for itself and let the reader draw his or her own conclusions, which, in turn, will be dependent upon one's individual comfort levels with hypothetical propositions.

No matter what conclusions we may reach, however, it seems clear that, if we are ever to approach any sort of understanding of what the geometric earthworks meant to the Hopewell, we need to take a holistic approach. Figure 8.1 illustrates my point. In figure 8.1, A can only take its total meaning from its relationships to B, C, D, and E. So, too, B can only take its total meaning from its relationships to A, C, D, and E. And so on. In the same way, a Hopewell earthwork takes its meaning from how the whole figure is a function of its location, its geometric shape, its size, its orientation, and its symbolic meaning and use. In the case of the Hopewell earthworks, truly it can be said that the whole is greater than the sum of its parts.

My last point reflects a rather personal point of view. But, in my

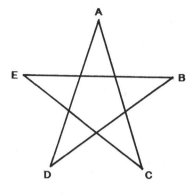

Fig. 8.1. In this figure, point A takes its meaning from its relationships to points B, C, D, and E. Likewise point B takes its total meaning from its relationships to A, C, D, and E. *Drawing by the author.*

belief, there is no intrinsic wisdom to be found in the crushed and broken fragments of bone that were once the Hopewell people. Nor is there anything uplifting to be found in the broken shards of a culture bulldozed into oblivion. As someone once said, "Time is the fire we all burn in." Ultimately, the nobility of the ancient ones can only be found in how they lived.

As to the question of how they lived, it appears that the Hopewell recognized a relationship between the celestial order of things —including the geometric shape of the universe, the movements of the sun and moon, and the biological rhythms of their lives—as marked by the rites and ceremonies celebrated within the geometric earthworks. It is very difficult to flesh out the details of this belief system. However, as anthropologist Flora S. Clancey (1994) has pointed out, the very idea of a relationship between the celestial order of things and individual consciousness seems to imply a belief that there is a greater meaning to existence beyond our own individual lives, and a hope that some sort of enfolding connection can be made between ourselves and this greater cosmic flow.

This is a positive thought. And I would like to think that maybe the Hopewell found, through their earthen creations, a way to make that connection, a way to make an enfolding connection between their individual lives and the awesome and mysterious powers that shaped their universe.

Appendix

THE SERPENT MOUND

Nestled deep in the hills of southern Ohio, high up on a lonely ridge, is a monster serpent. Known as the Serpent Mound, this prehistoric earthwork is one of the world's largest effigy mounds (see figure A.1).

It is not certain who built the Serpent Mound. Early archaeologists (Greenman 1934; Webb and Snow 1945) suggested that the effigy was built by the Adena people sometime between 800 B.C. and A.D. 100. However, Robert N. Converse (1979:3), editor of the *Ohio Archaeologist*, has noted that the effigy looks more like Hopewell than Adena. More recent investigators (Fletcher et. al. 1996) have proposed that the effigy was built by Fort Ancient peoples sometime around A.D. 1070±70. Their opinion is based on two radiocarbon dated samples recovered from within the serpent's body.

My purpose here is not to argue the date of the Serpent Mound. However, it may be that the charcoal samples recovered by Fletcher and Cameron's team were inadvertently recovered from layers of earth that were added to the earthwork in the late 1800s. These layers of earth were added to the effigy by Frederick W. Putnam of the Peabody Museum in an effort to restore the Serpent Mound to its original height. What Putnam did was to scrape up earth from the surrounding area and heap this earth onto the body of the effigy. We know from archaeologist James B. Griffin's (1943) work at the site that, in addition

Fig. A.I. Aerial view of the Serpent Mound. *Photo by the author.*

to Adena people, Fort Ancient people also occupied the Serpent Mound ridge. Given this, it seems possible that in spite of the attention given to this problem by Fletcher and his team, the charcoal fragments that yielded the late Fort Ancient dates may still have come from earth that had been scraped up and deposited on the effigy by Putnam.

In my opinion, the effigy is of Hopewell origin. This opinion is based on several observations. First, the structure exhibits a geometric complexity that is more typical of Hopewell than either Adena or Fort Ancient. Second, as I will show, there is clear evidence that the Serpent Mound builders used lesser multiples of the 1,053-foot unit of length commonly used by the Hopewell. Third, as I will also demonstrate, the serpent effigy incorporates various astronomical alignments, including alignments to the moon's mid-point as well as maximum and minimum rising and setting points. These lunar alignments appear to be exclusive to the Hopewell.

However, because of the uncertainty as to the effigy's date and origin, my Serpent Mound findings are included herein as an appendix, rather than incorporated into the main body of the text which deals with generally accepted Hopewell earthworks.

PUTNAM'S RESTORATION

The first published map of the Serpent Mound was made by Squier and Davis (1848), based on a survey they made in 1846. In the years following their visit, however, the ridge that the serpent rests upon was cleared for cultivation, planted with crops for a brief time, and grazed by cattle.

In 1883, Frederick W. Putnam of the Peabody Museum visited the Serpent Mound and soon thereafter began restoration work. Putnam was conservative in his efforts and limited his excavations of the effigy to the edges of both sides along the length of the earthwork and several trenches cut perpendicularly through the effigy. As Putnam (1892:181) explained, he merely threw back, onto the original embankments, the earth that had "washed down" from the mound. Importantly, Putnam (1890:875) also noted that "the several plowings had not disturbed the underlying clay of which the embankments were constructed."

By excavating along the edges of the effigy, Putnam was able to distinguish between the undisturbed, compact yellow clay stratum of the mound and the looser, dark topsoil that had washed down. As Fletcher (1996:113) and his team explain, Putnam "noted the presence of an underlying layer of mixed clay and ashes—apparently used by the builders to lay out the shape of the embankment—and used that outline as a guide." In this way, Putnam was able to establish the original configuration of the effigy with a great deal of accuracy.

Putnam's restoration efforts with regard to the effigy were not as extensive as might be imagined, and the outline of the effigy as it appears today most likely is an accurate reflection of its appearance when

Fig. A.2. View of the Serpent Mound looking southeast from the neck area in 1883 before restoration. F. W. Putnam is shown in the foreground wearing a top hat. *Photo courtesy of the Cincinnati Historical Society.*

Fig. A.3. View of the Serpent Mound as it appears today looking southeast from the neck area. *Photo by the author.*

first discovered. This conclusion is supported by comparison of the photos shown in figures A.2 and A.3. As figure A.2 shows, the original embankments were still 2 to 3 feet in height and clearly evident before restoration, even after having been plowed down and damaged by weather and erosion. Moreover, comparison of maps of the effigy made before and after restoration also supports the conclusion that what we see today is an accurate reflection of the effigy's appearance when first discovered (see for example, Hardman and Hardman 1987: fig.12).

THE SERPENT MOUND MAP

My own investigations of the Serpent Mound began sometime around 1985; in 1987, I completed a physical survey of the earthwork. A detailed explanation of the methods I used is presented elsewhere (Romain 1987). In brief, what I did first was establish a baseline across the effigy that was oriented to true north. True north was located by making several sets of Polaris observations. For independent corroboration, I also hired a team of professional surveyors to make their own observations (Thomas E. Purtell, P.S., and Eric N. Lutz, S.I.T., of McCarty Engineering, Hillsboro, Ohio). Their Polaris measurements agreed with mine to within 1 minute and 2 minutes of arc, and from these three sets of measurements we were able to establish a true north-south baseline that is accurate to within ±1 minute of arc. On the accompanying figures, this baseline extends from point X to point Y1. Point X is a two and one-half inch diameter brass monument marker that was previously set in concrete by Terry Cameron and Robert Fletcher. Point Y1 is a rebar stake that was set by myself and Serpent Mound area manager William E. Gustin.

The next step in surveying the Serpent Mound was to set small survey stake flags along both edges of the earthwork and along the crest of the embankments. The edge of the earthwork is easy to recognize due to the steepness of the embankments (see figure A.4). I personally set all 265 survey flags and would estimate that these coordinate points define the edges and crest of the embankments to within ±6 inches.

Fig. A.4. View of the Serpent Mound tail area showing the placement of survey flags, February 7, 1987. *Photo by the author.*

Once the survey flags were in place, a Topcon GTS-2B theodolite was set up at point X and a radial traverse survey was carried out using standard surveying techniques. The Topcon GTS-2B uses a built-in laser for distance measuring. For this survey, I was the instrument operator, William E. Gustin was the data recorder, and local surveying student Ty R. Pell was the rodman. The rod was set up at each survey flag coordinate point, and with the theodolite instrument oriented to true north, distance and angle measurements were made from the theodolite to each coordinate point.

The final step was to plot each of the 265 recorded coordinate points onto a 24 x 36 inch sheet of Mylar at a scale of 1 inch to 20 feet. This was done by John E. Dailey, P.S. of Wheeler and Melena, Inc., Cleveland, Ohio, using a Holquin TDS 22/4 software program run on a Wang 2200VP computer. Data output was to a Wang 2232A flatbed plotter having a plotting accuracy to ±0.01 inches. I then connected with

hand-drawn lines plotted coordinate points. Figures A.5–A.10 are reduced versions of the map that resulted.

THE HOPEWELL UNIT OF MEASURE

When I first surveyed the Serpent Mound, I had no idea that it
might incorporate the 1,053-foot unit of length. Early on, I identified
a length of 126.4 feet that seemed repeated throughout the effigy
(Romain 1988). But it was more than a decade later when I discovered
that the effigy incorporates lesser multiples of the 1,053-foot unit. This
section summarizes my most recent findings.

In previous chapters, it was shown how the 1,053-foot unit of
length is manifested in at least 24 different Hopewell earthworks. In
some of these earthworks, it was also found that lesser multiples were
used. Lesser multiples are derived by dividing the 1,053-foot unit by 2,
and then further dividing the resulting number by 2 again, and so on, ad
infinitum. Thus lesser multiples of the 1,053-foot unit include:

$$1,053 / 2 = 526.5$$
$$526.5 / 2 = 263.25$$
$$263.25 / 2 = 131.63$$
$$131.63 / 2 = 65.82$$
$$65.82 / 2 = 32.91$$
$$32.91 / 2 = 16.46$$
$$16.46 / 2 = 8.23.$$

This all becomes interesting with the discovery that these lesser
multiples are found in the lengths of the sides of several triangles that
define the location of various central points on the Serpent Mound.

For example, with reference to figure A.5, what we find is a triangle defined by points A-B-C. Point A is a small pile of fire-cracked rocks
located in the approximate center of the oval embankment. This pile of
rocks, by the way, was noticed in 1846 by Squier and Davis when they
visited the earthwork. Point B is the tip of the serpent's tail, and point C
is the apex of one of the serpent's convolutions. Notably, the length of
line A-B is very close to the following combination of lesser multiples of
the 1,053-foot unit of length: 263.3 feet + 131.6 feet + 65.8 feet. That is to

say, by measuring the length A-B on a 24 x 36 inch version of the map, it is found that the distance between points A and B is 459.7 feet. The length of 459.7 feet is to within 1 foot of the total of the lesser multiples of 263.3 feet + 131.6 feet + 65.8 feet.

Next, we see how the distance between points B and C is very close to equal to the 1,053-foot lesser multiple of 263.3 feet. As measured on the 24 x 36 inch map, the distance between points B and C is 262.3 feet. The lesser multiple of 1,053 feet is 263.3 feet. Hence, line B-C is equal to the Hopewell lesser multiple of 263.3 feet to within 1 foot.

Finally, with reference again to figure A.5, we see how the length of line C-A is almost equal to the sum of the following lesser multiples: 131.6 feet + 65.8 feet + 32.9 feet + 16.5 feet + 8.2 feet. As table A.1 shows, the difference between the ideal length of C-A as calculated by totaling the lesser units and the actual length of C-A as measured on the map is 3 feet. Thus the difference between the ideal length and the actual length is about 1 percent.

The triangle formed by points A-B-C is only one of several such triangles that when combined together serve to locate each and every central point on the Serpent Mound. Figures A.5–A.9 show these triangles along with the lesser multiples that make-up each triangle's side. Also, figure A.7 shows how the north-south length of the Serpent Mound is very close to the 526.6-foot lesser multiple; while figure A.8 shows two additional lines, A-F and L-M, that are equal or near equal to other lesser multiples. Table A.1 summarizes the data just discussed and provides the exact differences between the ideal totals of the lesser multiples and the actual lengths as measured on the 24 x 36 inch maps.

Looking at table A.1, the lengths of lines O-P, B-C, D-E, G-H, K-E, A-F, and L-M are of particular significance. In all seven instances, these lines are equal or near equal to lesser multiples of the 1,053-foot unit— without further combinations with other lesser multiples. With the exception of line L-M, these lines are all to within 1 percent of being equal to the 1,053-foot unit lesser multiples of 526.6 feet, 263.3 feet, or 131.6 feet. My view is that these lines are direct evidence for use of the lesser multiples of the 1,053-foot unit. Moreover, these particular lines counter

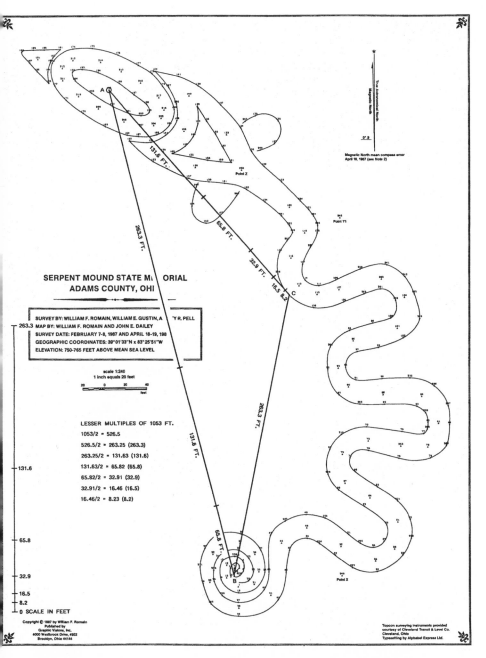

Fig. A.5. Serpent Mound map showing triangle A-B-C, which is made-up of lines that incorporate lesser multiples of the 1,053-foot unit of length. *Drawing by the author.*

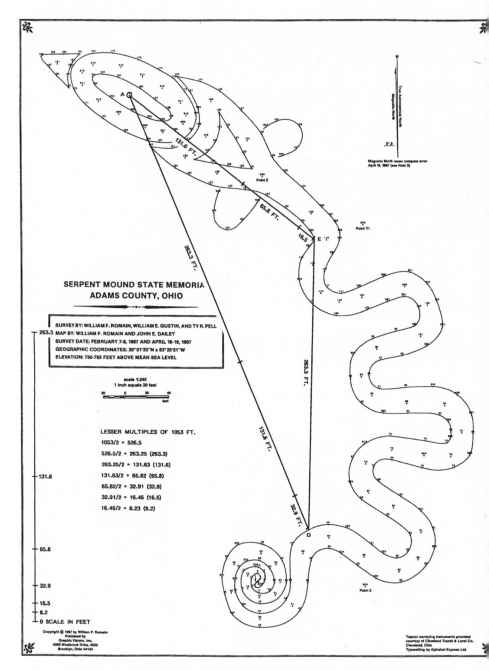

Fig. A.6. Serpent Mound map showing triangle A-D-E, which is made-up of lines that incorporate lesser multiples of the 1,053-foot unit of length. *Drawing by the author.*

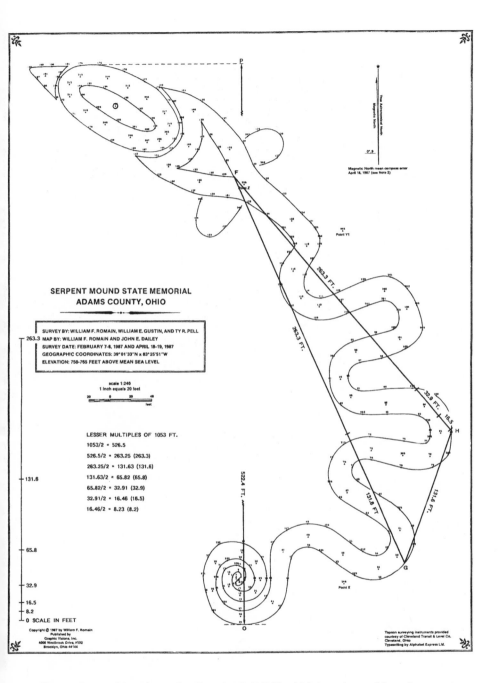

Fig. A.7. Serpent Mound map showing triangle F-G-H, which is made-up of lines that incorporate lesser multiples of the 1,053-foot unit of length. Also note how the over-all length of the effigy, shown by line O-P, is almost equal to the 526.6 lesser multiple of the 1,053-foot unit of length. *Drawing by the author.*

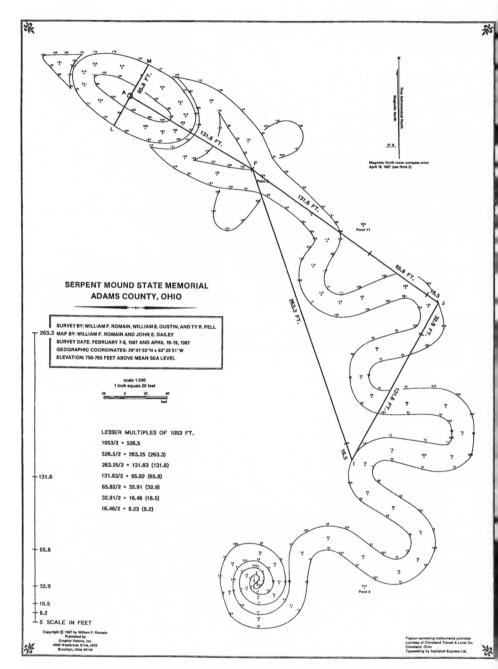

Fig. A.8. Serpent Mound map showing triangle F-I-J, which is made-up of lines that incorporate lesser multiples of the 1,053-foot unit length. Note too, how lines F-A and L-M are lesser multiples of the 1,053-foot unit. *Drawing by the author.*

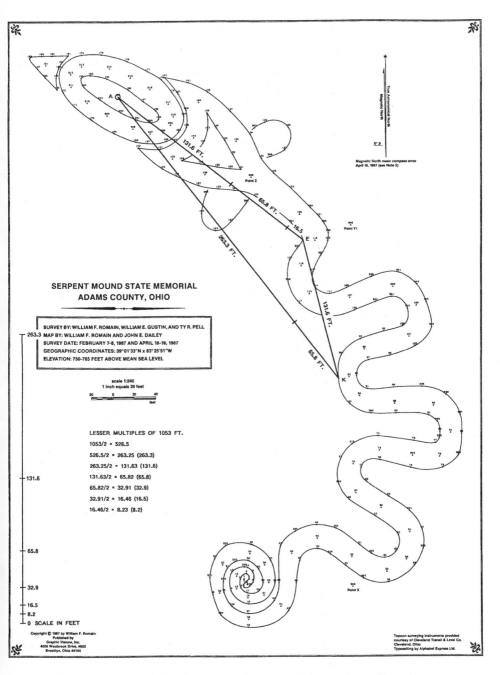

Fig. A.9. Serpent Mound map showing triangle A-K-E, which is made-up of lines that incorporate lesser multiples of the 1,053-foot unit of length. *Drawing by the author.*

Table A.I. Lesser multiples of the 1,053-foot unit found in the Serpent Mound (all distances are in feet)

Line	Lesser Multiples	Ideal Length	Actual Length	Difference
A-B	263.3 + 131.6 + 65.8	460.7	459.7	0.2%
B-C	263.3	263.3	262.3	0.4%
C-A	131.6 + 65.8 + 32.9 + 16.5 + 8.2	255.0	258.0	1.2%
A-D	263.3 + 131.6 + 32.9	427.8	429.8	0.5%
D-E	263.3	263.3	262.3	0.4%
E-A	131.6 + 65.8 + 16.5	213.9	215.9	0.9%
F-G	263.3 + 131.6	394.9	396.9	0.5%
G-H	131.6	131.6	130.6	0.8%
H-F	263.3 + 32.9 + 16.5	312.7	314.7	0.6%
F-I	263.3 + 16.5	279.8	279.8	0.0%
I-J	131.6 + 32.9	164.5	164.5	0.0%
J-F	131.6 + 65.8 + 16.5	213.9	216.9	1.4%
A-K	263.3 + 65.8	329.1	329.1	0.0%
K-E	131.6	131.6	132.6	0.8%
E-A	131.6 + 65.8 + 16.5	213.9	215.9	0.9%
A-F	131.6	131.6	131.6	0.0%
L-M	65.8	65.8	67.8	2.9%
O-P	526.6	526.6	522.4	0.8%

the potential argument that the length of any line can be defined by a lesser length that is subdivided and those subdivisions then added for a total that will be to within plus or minus a given distance.

In summary, in this section a total of 18 instances were shown wherein lesser multiples of the 1,053-foot unit of length, either by themselves or in combination with other lesser multiples, are found in the design of the Serpent Mound. Of these 18 instances, the map-measured lengths of 15 lines are to within 1 percent of the ideal lengths. The average accuracy is to within 0.7 percent, meaning that, on average, a length of 100 feet was laid out by the Serpent Mound builders to an accuracy of within plus or minus about 5 inches. Use of these lesser multiples, however, is only part of the remarkable engineering evident in the Serpent Mound. As I will show, the Serpent Mound builders also aligned central features of the effigy to significant celestial events.

CELESTIAL ALIGNMENTS

As pointed out in earlier chapters, we are not able to test for the existence of astronomical alignments at many Hopewell earthworks because of their poor state of preservation. This is not the case, however, with the Serpent Mound. At the Serpent Mound, there are several alignments that appear unequivocal. These alignments include alignment of the serpent to true north, and an alignment through the oval embankment to the summer solstice sunset. Less definitive, but nevertheless intriguing, are several lunar alignments through the serpent's body convolutions. We begin with the true north alignment.

One of the results of my 1987 survey was the finding that the serpent is aligned to true north to within ±10 minutes of arc. As shown in figure A.10, this north-south alignment extends from the very tip of the serpent's tail, to the central apex of the triangular space of the serpent's head. The significance of this alignment is that true north is a direction that can only be established by reference to astronomical phenomena. There is no other way.

The Serpent Mound north-south alignment gives us some potential insight into the belief systems of the Mound Builders. That is, if the Serpent Mound builders recognized true north, then most likely they also recognized its directional opposite, south, as well as the half-way divisions of east and west. If this is the case, then in both the Serpent Mound, and at the Seal Earthwork, we have suggestive evidence for a mental division of the cosmos into its four cardinal directions. Together with the tripartite division of the cosmos into upperworld, earth, and underworld levels, these mental constructs are fundamental to Native American cosmology.

In any event, the second alignment is through the oval embankment to the summer solstice sunset. This sightline does not define the major axis of the oval embankment, but rather extends from the central apex of the triangular space of the serpent's head, through the small pile of fire-cracked rocks at the center of the oval. In figure A.10, the

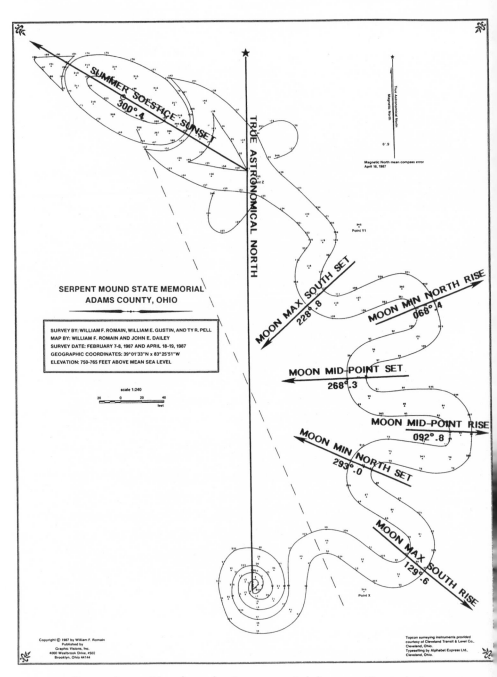

Fig. A.10. Serpent Mound map showing astronomical alignments. *Drawing by the author.*

line I have drawn shows the azimuth of the summer solstice sunset as calculated using Aveni's (1972) tables, with a measured horizon elevation of 1°.0, lower limb tangency, 39° north latitude, and date of A.D. 250. (An earlier published set of solar and lunar azimuths [Romain 1991b] used a date of 250 B.C.)

As mentioned in chapter 4, calculated azimuths are informative, but when it comes to proof, the best evidence of any proposed alignment will always be an actual photograph. So on June 21, 1990, I captured on film the summer solstice sun as it set in alignment with the earthwork. Figure A.11 shows this alignment. (In Hopewell times, the sun would have set about one-half of one sun diameter farther north.)

Once again, however, I have to note that a photograph alone, fails to adequately convey the warmth, and excitement, and sense of wonder that overtakes the witness to such an event, as the sun and earth slowly move into perfect alignment with each other. The sight is awesome.

Next, we will look at the lunar alignments that extend through the serpent's body convolutions. In all cases, the lunar alignments shown in figure A.10 were calculated from Aveni's tables, using measured horizon elevations, a date of A.D. 250, 39° north latitude, and lower limb tangency. Horizon elevation measurements were taken in early 1987, using a Topcon TL-60 theodolite and were made to distant tree top levels. Measurements were made from the approximate location indicated by the tail end of each sightline shown in figure A.10.

Before presenting the data, I should clarify that I do not think the serpent's body convolutions were used as sighting devices. Rather, the alignments of the convolutions were more likely important for their symbolic implications, in that they linked the serpent to the moon. I will return to this idea below.

The first lunar azimuth to be considered is the moon's maximum south set. Given a measured horizon elevation of 1°.8, date of A.D. 250, 39° north latitude, and lower limb tangency, it is found from Aveni's tables that the moon's maximum south set azimuth was at 228°.8. As shown in figure A.10, when plotted onto the Serpent Mound map, this lunar azimuth neatly bisects the serpent's first body convolution.

Fig. A.II. Summer solstice sunset at the Serpent Mound, June 21, 1990. *Photo by the author, in company with Serpent Mound Area Manager William E. Gustin.*

The next lunar azimuth is the moon's minimum north rise. Given a measured horizon elevation of 2°.0, Aveni's tables tell us that the moon's minimum north rise was at 68°.4. As can be seen, this lunar azimuth neatly bisects the serpent's second body convolution.

The reader will be familiar with the terms moon maximum south set, moon minimum north rise and so on, from chapter 5. In figure A.10, however, two new terms are introduced. They are "moon mid-point set" and "moon mid-point rise." Hively and Horn (1982:S17) found that the diagonal of the Newark Square is aligned to these lunar events, and they provide the following explanation of this phenomenon: "As the rising point of the Moon moves from south to north during the monthly cycle, there is a unique azimuth for which the Moon can be observed to rise and set on the same day in opposite directions along the same line. Due to the Moon's rapid apparent motion this azimuth is not 90° as it is for the Sun at the equinoxes; rather, for the Moon it is 92°.0."

Given the latitude of the Serpent Mound and measured horizon elevations, the azimuths for the moon's mid-point rise and set differ slightly from the azimuth and reciprocal azimuth discussed by Hively and Horn. As shown by figure A.10, using a measured horizon elevation of 1°.0 and 39° north latitude yields a lunar mid-point setting azimuth of 268°.3. This azimuth does not bisect the serpent's third body convolution quite as accurately as one might expect. However, the correspondence is not totally unreasonable when considered in the context of the other alignments.

The next azimuth is the moon's mid-point rise. Using a measured horizon elevation of 2°.0 the calculated azimuth for this event is 92°.8. As can be seen, when this azimuth is plotted onto the map, it accurately bisects the serpent's fourth body convolution.

The fifth lunar azimuth is the moon's minimum north set. Given a measured horizon elevation of 0°.5, it is found from Aveni's tables that the azimuth for this event was 293°.0. Notably, the azimuth of 293°.0 very closely bisects the serpent's fifth body convolution.

The sixth lunar alignment is to the moon's maximum south rising point. As figure A.10 shows, Aveni's tables tell us that given a measured horizon elevation of 0°.5, the azimuth for this event was 129°.6. Plotting this azimuth onto the Serpent Mound map we see that this azimuth does not bisect the sixth convolution perfectly. However, the match is very close.

To date, I have not been able to figure out what, if any, celestial event the seventh convolution points to. I have checked for possible solar, lunar, and planetary alignments, but without success. Of course, there is nothing to say that the seventh convolution necessarily has to point to a celestial event. And, for what it is worth, I note that the seventh convolution points directly to the center of the oval embankment. Perhaps this alignment to the oval embankment carries some significance in and of itself.

In summary, these data show that eight astronomical alignments are found in the Serpent Mound. The most accurate alignment is to true north, while the next most certain alignment is through the oval embankment to the summer solstice sunset. Six lunar alignments were also found. When considered in context of the information to be presented below, I think the rationale for the alignments will become apparent.

SERPENT MOUND SYMBOLISM

In an early article (Romain 1988), I proposed that the Serpent Mound might represent a solar eclipse. Many North American Indian legends tell of eclipses being caused by a giant serpent or other animal who swallows the sun. Still, it is impossible to say with certainty what the effigy means, simply because we have no direct evidence of what the serpent and oval symbols meant to the Serpent Mound builders.

What we do know, however, is that many Native American peoples believe that since the beginning, there has been an on-going struggle between the forces of the upperworld and the underworld. In Native American mythology, the upperworld is represented by the sun and the Thunderbird beings, whereas the underworld is represented by either the Great Horned Serpent or Underwater Panther. As might be expected, the upperworld creatures are usually benefactors of humankind, whereas the underworld creatures bring death and destruction. (For a further discussion of these beliefs see Hudson 1976:120–183.)

My thought is that maybe the Serpent Mound represents the struggle between the Great Horned Serpent of the underworld and the sun, with the sun represented by the oval embankment. In this scenario, we can imagine that a flat circular symbol of the sun has been rotated in space around its major axis, so that an oval results. Likewise, the serpent's head has also been rotated so that a profile view results. True to legend, the underworld serpent is shown trying to bite or swallow the upperworld sun.

As to why this mythological conflict might be important enough for the Mound Builders to go to the trouble of building the Serpent Mound, we can speculate that the serpent effigy symbolized the dark forces which would include the moon, night, winter, darkness, and death; while the oval represented the sun, daytime, summer, light, and life. Notably, the summer solstice sunset alignment suggests a balance between these two opposing cosmic forces. In this scenario, we can further speculate that perhaps the Mound Builders celebrated world renewal ceremonies at the site, in order to help strengthen the powers of the upperworld in the continuing struggle against the forces of the underworld. In this way, the Serpent Mound builders would have been able to exercise some control over the forces that ruled their universe and affected their lives. The world renewal ceremonies at the Serpent Mound might have been similar to those possibly practiced at the Capitoleum Mound and similar to the earlier mentioned "bringing the buds to life" ceremony practiced by later peoples of the Southeast.

If my interpretation holds, then what we see in the Serpent Mound is yet another iteration of a theme that has fascinated humanity since the beginning—that is, the eternal conflict between the opposite forces of light and dark, good and evil, life and death.

ACKNOWLEDGMENTS

And so we come to the end of our journey. It has been said that half the fun of any trip is getting there. And, certainly, this has been true for me. While researching and writing this book, I met dozens of fascinating people and had many interesting adventures. Now it is my pleasure to thank those who helped me along the way.

First, I would like to acknowledge my debt to the distinguished experts who reviewed my efforts. Not all agreed with what I had to say. And I did not always follow their good advice. Nevertheless, I value each person's counsel and owe a tremendous debt of thanks to Don Cochran, Robert Connolly, Brad Lepper, and Paul Pacheco.

To my mentors at the University of Akron Press, warmest thanks are extended to Michael Carley, Elton Glaser, Beth Pratt, Jana Russ and Julia Gammon for their patient and thorough editing and support. And, sincere thanks are extended to Kachergis Book Design for their tremendous work.

Next, I would like to thank the many kind people who provided information, data, permissions and morale support. Especially helpful were Jerrel C. Anderson, Jack Blosser, James A. Brown, William Burke, Terry C. Cameron, Robert Converse, Wes Cowan, Sylvia A. Cullen, John E. Dailey, Andy Davenport, Jim Duwe, Julia Engle, Robert V. Fletcher, Terry L. Frazier, William Gibson, Hazel Gustin, William E. Gustin, Ross Hamilton, Kate Hancock, Michael C. Hansen, John K. Hartsock, Thomas Hillger, George Horton, John T. Hubbell, Rebecca Jones, Robert Karoleski, Roger G. Kennedy, Cynthia Keller, Wayne Kline, Edwin C. Krupp, Suzanne B. Langlois, Tom Lubin, Diane Mace,

Patricia Mason, James and Ruth McNutt, Paula Miller, Doug Pauley, Robert Pavlovic, Herbert L. Petersen, Robert Petersen, Ty R. Pell, Stephen P. Reidel, Nancy Riley, Robert Riordan, Lee Rothenberg, Bret Ruby, William T. Schultz, Ruth Schumaker, Ted Sushka, William Tiell, Ray Wells, Kent Vickery, Jane Vollmer, and Dee Anne Wymer.

Last but not least, I would like to thank my mother, Frances Spania Rothenberg, and my wife, Evie Romain, for their encouragement and faith in me. They were always my biggest supporters.

To all, I offer the following poem (adapted after Roberts and Amidon 1991):

> May the Earth and Sky
> and the Wind and Water
> always speak to your spirit.

REFERENCES

Anderson, Jerrel C. 1980. A Recent Discovery—The Anderson Earthwork. *Ohio Archaeologist* 30(1):31–35.

Atwater, Caleb. 1820. Description of the Antiquities Discovered in the State of Ohio and Other Western States. *Archaeologia Americana* 1:105–267.

Aveni, Anthony. 1992. Somebody Else's Cosmology. In *Mysteries of Life and the Universe*, edited by William H. Shore. New York: Harcourt, Brace, Jovanovich.

———. 1972. Astronomical Tables Intended for Use in Astroarchaeological Studies. *American Antiquity* 37(4):531–40.

Baby, Raymond S., Bert C. Drennen III, and Suzanne M. Langlois. 1975. Excavation of Section M1 and M2, Mound City Group National Monument. Report to the National Park Service (PX473030119). Report on file, Ohio Historical Society, Columbus.

Baby, Raymond S., and Suzanne M. Langlois. 1984. Analysis of the Human Skeletal Remains from Fairchance Mound. *West Virginia Archaeologist* 36(1):52–58.

———. 1979. Seip Mound State Memorial: Nonmortuary Aspects of Hopewell. In *Hopewell Archaeology: The Chillicothe Conference*, edited by David S. Brose and N'omi Greber. Kent, Ohio: Kent State University Press.

———. 1977. Excavation of Section 01 and 02, Mounds 8 and 9, Mound City Group National Monument. Report to the National Park Service (PX600040811). Report on file, Ohio Historical Society, Columbus.

Baby, Raymond S., Martha A. Potter, and Stephen C. Koleszar. 1971. Excavation of Sections I and J. Mound City Group National Monument. (Contract NER950-195 and 353-27). Report on file, Ohio Historical Society, Columbus.

Bass, William M. 1971. *Human Osteology: A Laboratory and Field Manual of the Human Skeleton*. Columbus, Mo.: Missouri Archaeological Society.

Beauchamp, William M. 1922. *Iroquois Folk Lore, Gathered from the Six Nations of New York*. Empire State Historical Publication 31. New York: Kennikat Press.

Bernbaum, Edwin. 1990. *Sacred Mountains of the World*. San Francisco: Sierra Club Books.

Blackwell, William. 1984. *Geometry in Architecture*. New York: John Wiley and Sons.

Bowditch, Nathaniel. [1802] 1966. *American Practical Navigator: An Epitome of Navigation*. Reprinted and appended as U.S. Naval Oceanographic Office, H.O. Publication No. 9. Washington, D.C.: U.S. Government Printing Office.

Brown, James A. 1982. Mound City and the Vacant Ceremonial Center. Paper prepared for the 47th Annual Meeting of the Society for American Archaeology.

————. 1979. Charnel Houses and Mortuary Crypts: Disposal of the Dead in the Middle Woodland Period. In *Hopewell Archaeology: The Chillicothe Conference*, edited by David S. Brose and N'omi Greber. Kent, Ohio: Kent State University Press.

Brown, James A., and Raymond S. Baby. 1966. Mound City Revisited. Manuscript on file, Department of Archaeology, Ohio Historical Society, Columbus.

Buikstra, Jane E. 1976. *Hopewell in the Lower Illinois Valley: A Regional Approach to the Study of Human Biological Variability and Prehistoric Behavior*. Northwestern University Archaeological Program. Scientific Papers No. 2.

Byers, A. Martin. 1996. Social Structure and the Pragmatic Meaning of Material Culture: Ohio Hopewell As An Ecclesiastic-Communal Cult. In *A View From the Core: A Synthesis of Ohio Hopewell Archaeology*, edited by Paul J. Pacheco. Columbus: The Ohio Archaeological Council.

Campbell, Joseph. 1988. *Historical Atlas of World Mythology*, vol. 1, part 2. *Mythologies of the Great Hunt*. New York: Harper and Row.

Capra, Fritjof. 1991. *The Tao of Physics: An Exploration of the Parallels Between Modern Physics and Eastern Mysticism*. Boston: Shambala.

Clancey, Flora S. 1994. *Pyramids*. Montreal, Canada: St. Remy Press; Washington, D.C.: Smithsonian Books.

Cochran, Donald R. 1992. Adena and Hopewell Cosmology: New Evidence from East Central Indiana. In *Native American Cultures in Indiana*, edited by Ronald Hicks. Muncie, Ind.: Minnetrista Cultural Center and Ball State University.

Coffer, William. 1978. *Spirits of the Sacred Mountains: Creation Stories of the American Indian*. New York: Van Nostrand Reinhold.

Connelley, William E. 1899. Notes on the Folk-lore of the Wyandots. *Journal of American Folklore* 12:116–25.

Connolly, Robert P. 1997. The Evidence for Habitation at the Fort Ancient Earthworks, Warren County, Ohio. In *Ohio Hopewell Community Organization*, edited by William S. Dancey and Paul J. Pacheco. Kent, Ohio: Kent State University Press.

———. 1996. Middle Woodland Hilltop Enclosures: The Built Environment, Construction and Function. Ph.D. diss., University of Illinois at Urbana-Champaign, Urbana, Illinois.

Converse, Robert N. 1979. Editor's Page. *Ohio Archaeologist* 29(2):3.

Conway, Thor. 1992. The Conjurer's Lodge: Celestial Narratives from Algonkian Shamans. In *Earth and Sky: Visions of the Cosmos in Native American Folklore*, edited by Ray A. Williamson and Claire R. Farrer. Albuquerque: University of New Mexico Press.

Count, Earl W. 1952. The Earth-Diver and the Rival Twins: A Clue to Time Correlation in North-Eurasiatic and North American Mythology. In *Indian Tribes of Aboriginal America*, edited by Sol Tax. Chicago: University of Chicago Press.

Cowan, C. Wesley. 1996. Social Implications of Ohio Hopewell Art. In *A View From the Core: A Synthesis of Ohio Hopewell Archaeology*, edited by Paul J. Pacheco. Columbus: The Ohio Archaeological Council.

Cross, William P., and Ronald I. Mayo. 1969. *Floods in Ohio: Magnitude and Frequency. A Supplement to Bulletin 32*. Ohio Department of Natural Resources, Division of Water, Bulletin No. 43. Columbus.

Cross, William P., and Earl W. Webber. 1959. *Floods in Ohio: Magnitude and Frequency*. Ohio Department of Natural Resources, Division of Water, Bulletin No. 32. Columbus.

Dancey, William S. 1992. Village Origins in Central Ohio: The Results and Implications of Recent Middle and Late Woodland Research. In *Cultural Variability in Context. Woodland Settlements of the Mid-Ohio Valley*, edited by Mark F. Seeman. Mid-Continental Journal of Archaeology Special Paper No. 7. Kent, Ohio: Kent State University Press.

D'Aquili, Eugene G., Charles D. Laughlin Jr., and John McManus. 1979. *The Spectrum of Ritual. A Biogenetic Structural Analysis*. New York: Columbia University Press.

Denny, J. Peter. 1986. Cultural Ecology of Mathematics: Ojibway and Inuit

Hunters. In *Native American Mathematics*, edited by Michael P. Closs. Austin: University of Texas Press.

Dragoo, Donald W., and Charles Wray. 1964. Hopewellian Figurine Rediscovered. *American Antiquity* 30:195–99.

Drennen, Bert C. III. 1974. Excavation of Section L, Mound 15, Mound City Group National Monument. (Purchase order PX473030120.) Report on file, Ohio Historical Society, Columbus.

———. 1972. Mound City Group National Monument. Examination and Restoration of Embankment. (Contract 5950120756.) Report on file, Ohio Historical Society, Columbus.

Eiseley, Loren C. 1970. *The Invisible Pyramid*. New York: Charles Scribner's Sons.

Erdoes, Richard, and Alfonso Ortiz, eds. 1984. *American Indian Myths and Legends*. New York: Pantheon Books.

Essenpreis, Patricia S., and David J. Duszynski. 1989. Possible Astronomical Alignments at the Fort Ancient Monument. Paper presented at the Society for American Archaeology Annual Meeting.

Farrer, Claire R., and Bernard Second. 1981. Living the Sky: Aspects of Mescalero Apache Ethnoastronomy. In *Archaeoastronomy in the Americas*, edited by Ray A. Williamson. Los Altos, California: Ballena Press.

Fletcher, Robert V., Terry L. Cameron, Bradley T. Lepper, Dee Anne Wymer, and William Pickard. 1996. Serpent Mound: A Fort Ancient Icon? *Midcontinental Journal of Archaeology* 21(1):105–43.

Ford, James A. 1969. *A Comparison of Formative Cultures in the Americas*. Washington, D.C.: Smithsonian Institution Press.

Gaunt, Bonnie. 1979. *Stonehenge: A Closer Look*. Ann Arbor, Mich.: Braun-Brumfield.

Genoves, Santiago. 1967. Proportionality of the Long Bones and Their Relation to Stature Among Mesoamericans. *American Journal of Physical Anthropology* 26:67–77.

Goodman, Ken. 1973. A Hopewell Burial Trait. *Ohio Archaeologist* 23(1):24–25.

Graham, Verne Ovid. 1944. *Mushrooms of the Great Lakes Region*. Chicago: Chicago Academy of Sciences and Chicago Natural History Museum.

Greber, N'omi B. 1996. A Commentary on the Contexts and Contrasts of Large to Small Ohio Hopewell Deposits. In *A View From the Core: A Synthesis of Ohio Hopewell Archaeology*, edited by Paul J. Pacheco. Columbus: The Ohio Archaeological Council.

———. 1983. *Recent Excavations at the Edwin Harness Mound, Liberty Works, Ross County, Ohio*. Mid-Continental Journal of Archaeology Special Paper No. 5. Kent, Ohio: Kent State University Press.

———. 1979. A Comparative Study of the Site Morphology and Burial Patterns at Edwin Harness Mound and Seip Mounds 1 and 2. In *Hopewell Archaeology: The Chillicothe Conference*, edited by David S. Brose and N'omi B. Greber. Kent, Ohio: Kent State University Press.

Greber, N'omi B., and Katherine C. Ruhl. 1989. *The Hopewell Site: A Contemporary Analysis Based on the Work of Charles C. Willoughby*. Boulder, Colo.: Westview Press.

Greenman, Emerson F. 1934. *Guide to Serpent Mound*. Columbus: Ohio Historical Society.

———. 1928. Field Notes on the Excavation of the Eagle Mound. Manuscript on file, Department of Archaeology, Ohio Historical Society, Columbus.

Griffin, James B. 1943. *The Fort Ancient Aspect: Its Cultural and Chronological Position in Mississippi Valley Archaeology*. Ann Arbor: University of Michigan Press.

Grim, John A. 1983. *Shaman: Patterns of The Siberian and Ojibway Healing*. Norman: University of Oklahoma Press.

Guidoni, Enrico. 1978. *Primitive Architecture*. New York: Harry N. Abrams.

Hall, Robert L. 1979. In Search of the Ideology of the Adena-Hopewell Climax. In *Hopewell Archaeology: The Chillicothe Conference*, edited by David S. Brose and N'omi B. Greber. Kent, Ohio: Kent State University Press.

Hanson, Lee H. Jr. 1966. Excavation of Section B, The East Gateway at Mound City Group National Monument. Report on file, National Park Service, Hopewell Culture National Historic Park, Chillicothe, Ohio.

———. 1965. Excavation of Section B, The East Gateway at Mound City Group National Monument. Report on file, National Park Service, Hopewell Culture National Historic Park, Chillicothe, Ohio.

Hardman, Clark Jr., and Marjorie H. Hardman. 1987. An Analysis of the Maps of the Great Serpent Mound. *Ohio Archaeologist* 37(2):18–25.

Hemmings, E. Thomas. 1984. Fairchance Mound and Village: An Early Middle Woodland Settlement in the Upper Ohio Valley. *West Virginia Archaeologist* 36(1):3–68.

Hewitt, John Napolean Brinton. 1918. Seneca Fiction, Legends, and Myths. In Thirty-second Annual Report of the Bureau of American Ethnology. Washington, D.C.

Hirschfelder, Arlene, and Paulette Molin. 1992. *The Encyclopedia of Native American Religions*. New York: Facts on File.

History of Washington County. 1881. n.p.:H. Z. Williams and Brothers, Publishers. Reprint, n.p.: Washington County Chapter O.G.S., 1989.

Hively, Ray, and Robert Horn. 1984. Hopewellian Geometry and Astronomy at

High Bank. *Archaeoastronomy* 7:S85–S100. (Supplement to Vol. 15, *Journal for the History of Astronomy*.)

———. 1982. Geometry and Astronomy in Prehistoric Ohio. *Archaeoastronomy* 4:S1–S20. (Supplement to Vol. 13, *Journal for the History of Astronomy*.)

Hoffman, Walter J. 1891. The Midewiwin or "Grand Medicine Society" of the Ojibwa. In *7th Annual Report of the Bureau of American Ethnology for the Years 1885–1886*. Washington, D.C.

Holmes, William H. 1883. Art in the Shell of the Ancient Americans. In *Second Annual Report of the Bureau of American Ethnology*. Washington, D.C.

Howard, James H. 1968. *The Southeastern Ceremonial Complex and Its Interpretation*. Missouri Archaeological Society, Memoir No. 6, University of Missouri, Columbia.

Hudson, Charles. 1976. *The Southeastern Indians*. Knoxville: University of Tennessee Press.

Hultzkrantz, Ake. 1979. *The Religions of the American Indians*. Translated by Monica Setterwall. Berkeley: University of California Press.

———. 1953. *Conceptions of the Soul Among North American Indians*. Museum of Sweden, Monograph Series, No. 1, Stockholm.

James, E. O. 1957. *Prehistoric Religion: A Study in Prehistoric Archaeology*. London: Thames and Hudson.

Kennedy, Roger G. 1994. *Hidden Cities: The Discovery and Loss of Ancient North American Civilization*. New York: The Free Press.

Kongas, Eli Kaija. 1960. The Earth-Diver (Th.A812). *Ethnohistory* 7(2):151–80.

Kosko, Bart. 1993. *Fuzzy Thinking: The New Science of Fuzzy Logic*. New York: Hyperion.

Laughlin, Charles D., Jr., and Eugene G. D'Aquili. 1974. *Biogenetic Structuralism*. New York: Columbia University Press.

Lepper, Bradley T. 1995. Tracking Ohio's Great Hopewell Road. *Archaeology* 48(6):52–56.

Lilly, Eli. 1937. *Prehistoric Antiquities of Indiana*. Indianapolis: Indiana Historical Society.

Long, Mark. 1981. The Forgotten McKittrick Earthworks. *Ohio Archaeologist* 31(2):4–7.

MacLean, John P. 1903. Ancient Works at Marietta, Ohio. *Ohio Archaeological and Historical Quarterly* 12:37–66.

Magrath, Willis H. 1940. The Temple of the Effigy. *Scientific American* 163:76–78.

Mandelbrot, Benoit. 1977. *The Fractal Geometry of Nature*. New York: W. H. Freeman.

Marriott, Alice, and Carol K. Rachlin. 1968. *American Indian Mythology*. New York: Thomas Y. Crowell.

Marshall, James A. 1987. An Atlas of American Indian Geometry. *Ohio Archaeologist* 37(2):36–49.

———. 1980. Geometry of the Hopewell Earthworks. *Ohio Archaeologist* 30(2):8–12.

Maslowski, Robert F., and Mark F. Seeman. 1992. Woodland Archaeology in the Mid-Ohio Valley: Setting Parameters for Ohio Main Stem/Tributary Comparisons. In *Cultural Variability in Context: Woodland Settlements of the Mid-Ohio Valley*, edited by Mark F. Seeman. Mid-Continental Journal of Archaeology Special Paper No. 7. Kent, Ohio: Kent State University Press.

Michell, John. 1988. *The Dimensions of Paradise*. New York: Harper and Row.

Mills, William C. 1922. Exploration of the Mound City Group. *Ohio Archaeological and Historical Quarterly* 31:423–584.

———. 1916. Exploration of the Tremper Mound. *Ohio Archaeological and Historical Quarterly* 25:262–398.

———. 1909. Exploration of the Seip Mound. *Ohio Archaeological and Historical Quarterly* 18:269–321.

Mooney, James. 1900. Myths of the Cherokee. In *19th Annual Report of the Bureau of American Ethnology for the Years 1897–1898, Pt. 1*. Washington, D.C.

Moorehead, Warren K. 1922. The Hopewell Mound Group of Ohio. *Field Museum of Natural History Anthropological Series* 6(5):73–184.

Morgan, Adrian. 1995. *Toads and Toadstools. The Natural History, Folklore, and Cultural Oddities of a Strange Association*. Berkeley: Celestial Arts.

Morgan, Lewis H. 1851. *League of the Ho-de-no-sau-nee or Iroquois*. New York: M. H. Newman.

Morgan, Richard G. 1941. A Hopewell Sculptured Head. *Ohio State Archaeological and Historical Quarterly* 50:384–87.

Murphy, James L. 1977. Authorship of Squier and Davis' Map of the Marietta Earthworks: A Belated Correction. *Ohio Archaeologist* 27(3):20–21.

Nabokov, Peter, and Robert Easton. 1989. *Native American Architecture*. New York: Oxford University Press.

National Park Service. 1979. An Evaluation of the Feasibility of Adding Hopeton Earthworks to Mound City Group National Monument. Washington, D.C.: U.S. Government Printing Office.

O'Brien, Patricia J., and Hanne D. Christiansen. 1986. An Ancient Maya Measurement System. *American Antiquity* 51(1):136–51.

Ohio Department of Natural Resources. 1962. *An Inventory of Ohio Soils: Ross County*. Ohio Department of Natural Resources, Division of Lands and Soil, Progress Report No. 22, Columbus.

Ohio Department of Natural Resources. 1959. *Preliminary Report of Floods in Ohio, January 1959*. Ohio Department of Natural Resources, Division of Water, Columbus.

Ortiz, Alfonso. 1969. *The Tewa World: Space, Time, Being, and Becoming in a Pueblo Society*. Chicago: University of Chicago Press.

Otto, Martha Potter, ed. 1980. Excavation of Mounds 11, 12, and 16, Mound City Group National Monument, Chillicothe, Ohio. Report to the National Park Service (5950L10180 and 5950L10209). Report on file, Ohio Historical Society, Columbus.

Pacheco, Paul J. 1996. Ohio Hopewell Regional Settlement Patterns. In *A View From the Core: A Synthesis of Ohio Hopewell Archaeology*, edited by Paul J. Pacheco. Columbus, Ohio: The Ohio Archaeological Council.

Parmalee, Paul W., and Gregory Perino. 1971. A Prehistoric Archaeological Record of the Roseate Spoonbill in Illinois. *Central States Archaeological Journal* 18:80–85.

Pearson, Lorentz C. 1987. *The Mushroom Manual*. Happy Camp, Calif.: Naturegraph Publishers.

Pedoe, Dan. 1976. *Geometry and the Visual Arts*. New York: Dover Publications.

Peet, Stephen D. 1891. The Religion of the Mound-Builders. *American Antiquarian* 13(6):307–30.

Pennick, Nigel. 1989. *Games of the Gods: The Origins of Board Games in Magic and Divination*. New York: Samuel Weiser.

———. 1980. *Sacred Geometry: Symbolism and Purpose in Religious Structures*. New York: Harper and Row.

Penny, David W. 1985. Continuities of Imagery and Symbolism in the Art of the Woodlands. In *Ancient Art of the American Woodland Indians*, edited by David S. Brose, James A. Brown, and David W. Penny. New York: Harry N. Abrams.

Petro, James H., William H. Shumate, and Marion F. Tabb. 1967. *Soil Survey of Ross County, Ohio*. U.S. Department of Agriculture, Soil Conservation Service. Washington, D.C.: Government Printing Office.

Prufer, Olaf H., and Orrin C. Shane III. 1970. *Blain Village and the Fort Ancient Tradition in Ohio*. Kent, Ohio: Kent State University Press.

Putnam, Frederick W. 1892. Abstract of Lecture upon the Ancient Earthworks of Ohio delivered by Prof. F. W. Putnam before the Western Reserve Historical Society, October 25, 1887. Reported by Prof. G. Frederick Wright. Western Reserve Historical Society, tract no. 76:178–84.

———. 1890. The Serpent Mound of Ohio. *Century Illustrated Magazine* 39:871–88.

Quimby, George I. 1943. A Subjective Interpretation of Some Design Similarities Between Hopewell and Northern Algonkian. *American Anthropologist* 45(4):630–33.

Reanney, Darryl. 1991. *After Death: A New Future for Human Consciousness.* New York: William Morrow.

Reed, George. 1974. *Naked I Astronomy.* n.p.: Alfred Publishing.

Riley, Thomas J., Richard Edging, and Jack Rossen. 1990. Cultigens in Prehistoric Eastern North America. *Current Anthropology* 31(5):525–41.

Roberts, Elizabeth, and Elias Amidon, eds. 1991. *Earth Prayers from Around the World: 365 Prayers, Poems, and Invocations for Honoring the Earth.* New York: Harper Collins.

Robicsek, Francis. 1978. *The Smoking Gods: Tobacco in Maya Art, History, and Religion.* Norman: University of Oklahoma.

Rockwell, David. 1991. *Giving Voice to Bear: North American Indian Rituals, Myths, and Images of the Bear.* Niwat, Colo.: Roberts Rinehart.

Romain, William F. 1993. Hopewell Ceremonial Centers and Geomantic Influences. *Ohio Archaeologist* 43(1):35–44.

———. 1992. Hopewellian Concepts in Geometry. *Ohio Archaeologist* 42(2):35–50.

———. 1991a. Evidence for a Basic Hopewell Unit of Measure. *Ohio Archaeologist* 41(4):28–37.

———. 1991b. Symbolic Associations at the Serpent Mound. *Ohio Archaeologist* 41(3):29–38.

———. 1988. Geometry at the Serpent Mound. *Ohio Archaeologist* 38(1):50–54.

———. 1987. The Serpent Mound Map. *Ohio Archaeologist* 37(4):38–42.

Salisbury, James and Charles. 1862. Accurate Surveys and Descriptions of the Ancient Earthworks at Newark, Ohio. Transcribed from the original by B. T. Lepper and B. T. Simmons. Manuscript on file, American Antiquarian Society, Worcester, Massachusetts.

Savage-Rumbaugh, Susan, and Roger Lewin. 1994. *Kanzi: The Ape at the Brink of the Human Mind.* New York: John Wiley and Sons.

Seeman, Mark F. 1995. When Words Are Not Enough: Hopewell Interregionalism and the Use of Material Symbols at the GE Mound. In *Native American Interactions: Multiscalar Analyses and Interpretations in the Eastern Wood-*

lands, edited by Michael S. Nassaney and Kenneth E. Sassaman. Knoxville: University of Tennessee Press.

———. 1988. Ohio Hopewell Trophy-Skull Artifacts as Evidence for Competition in Middle Woodland Societies Circa 50 B.C.–A.D. 350. *American Antiquity* 53:565–77.

———. 1979. Feasting with the Dead: Ohio Hopewell Charnel House Ritual as a Context for Redistribution. In *Hopewell Archaeology: The Chillicothe Conference*, edited by David S. Brose and N'omi B. Greber. Kent, Ohio: Kent State University Press.

Shane, Orrin C. III. 1971. The Scioto Hopewell. In *Adena: The Seeking of an Identity*, edited by B. K. Swartz Jr. Muncie, Ind.: Ball State University.

Sherrod, P. Clay, and Martha Ann Rolingson. 1987. *Surveyors of the Ancient Mississippi Valley: Modules and Alignments in Prehistoric Mound Sites*. Arkansas Archaeological Survey Research Series No. 28. Fayetteville, Ar.: Arkansas Archaeological Survey.

Shetrone, Henry C. 1930. *The Mound-Builders*. New York: Appleton-Century.

Shlain, Leonard. 1991. *Art and Physics: Parallel Visions in Space, Time, and Light*. New York: William Morrow.

Skinner, Alanson. 1924. *The Mascoutens or Prairie Potawatomi Indians. Part I*. Bulletin of the Public Museum of the City of Milwaukee 6:1.

Smith, Alexander H. 1963. *The Mushroom Hunter's Field Guide*. Ann Arbor: University of Michigan Press.

Smith, Bruce D. 1992. *Rivers of Change: Essays on Early Agriculture in Eastern North America*. Washington, D.C.: Smithsonian Institution Press.

Smucker, I. 1881. Mound Builder's Works Near Newark, Ohio. *American Antiquarian* 3(4):261–70.

Squier, Ephraim G., and Edwin H. Davis. 1848. *Ancient Monuments of the Mississippi Valley*. Smithsonian Contributions to Knowledge. Volume 1. Washington, D.C.: Smithsonian Institution.

Suzuki, David, and Peter Knudtson. 1992. *Wisdom of the Elders: Honoring Sacred Native Visions*. New York: Bantam Books.

Swanton, John R. 1946. *Indians of the Southeastern United States*. Bureau of American Ethnology, Bulletin 137. Washington, D.C.

———. 1931. *Modern Square Grounds of the Creek Indians*. Smithsonian Miscellaneous Collections 85(8):1–46.

———. 1911. *Indian Tribes of the Lower Mississippi Valley and Adjacent Coast of the Gulf of Mexico*. Bureau of American Ethnology, Bulletin 43. Washington, D.C.

Taylor, Charles E., and Richard Spurr (compilers). 1973. *Aerial Photographs in the National Archives*. Special List No. 25. National Archives and Records Service, General Services Administration, Washington, D.C.

Thomas, Cyrus. 1894. *Report on the Mound Explorations of the Bureau of Ethnology for the Years 1890–1891*. In Twelfth Annual Report of the Bureau of American Ethnology. Washington, D.C.

Tomak, Curtis H. 1990. *The Mount Vernon Site: A Hopewell Ceremonial/Burial Site in Posey County, Indiana*. Indiana Department of Transportation, Division of Program Development, Indianapolis.

Tompkins, Peter. 1971. *Secrets of the Great Pyramid*. New York: Harper and Row.

Ubelaker, Douglas, H. 1978. *Human Skeletal Remains: Excavation, Analysis, Interpretation*. Chicago: Aldine.

United States Department of Agriculture. 1983. ASCS Aerial Photography. Information leaflet. U.S. Department of Agriculture, Agricultural Stabilization and Conservation Service, Salt Lake City.

United States Geological Survey. 1991. Values of Magnetic Declination. (Tables.) U.S. Geological Survey, Branch of Global Seismology and Geomagnetism, Denver.

Waring, A. J. Jr., and Preston Holder. 1945. A Prehistoric Ceremonial Complex in the Southeastern United States. *American Anthropologist*, n.s., 47 (1):1–34.

Wasson, R. Gordon. 1968. *Soma: Divine Mushroom of Immortality*. New York: Harcourt, Brace, Jovanich.

Webb, William S., and Raymond Baby. 1957. *The Adena People No. 2*. Columbus, Ohio: The Ohio Historical Society.

Webb. William S., and Charles E. Snow. 1945. *The Adena People. Publications of the Department of Anthropology and Archaeology*, vol. 6. Lexington: University of Kentucky.

Whitman, Janice Keister. 1977. Kohl Mound, A Hopewellian Mound in Tuscarawas County. *Ohio Archaeologist* 27(3):4–8.

Whittlesey, Charles. 1884. Metrical Standard of the Mound Builders, Deduced by the Method of Even Divisors. *Proceedings of the American Association for the Advancement of Science for the Year 1883* 32:422–25.

Wilcox, Frank. [1933] 1970. *Ohio Indian Trails*. Reprint, Kent, Ohio: Kent State University Press.

Williams, D. H. 1900. *A History of Jackson County, Ohio*. Vol. 1. *The Scioto Salt Springs*. Jackson, Ohio: N.p.

Williamson, Ray A. 1992. The Celestial Skiff: An Alabama Myth of the Stars. In

Earth and Sky: Visions of the Cosmos in Native American Folklore, edited by Ray A. Williamson and Claire R. Farrer. Albuquerque: University of New Mexico Press.

——. 1984. *Living the Sky: The Cosmos of the American Indian*. Boston: Houghton Mifflin.

Willoughby, Charles C. 1932. Notes on the History and Symbolism of the Muskhogeans and the People of Etowah. In *Etowah Papers I: Exploration of the Etowah Site in Georgia*, edited by Warren K. Moorehead. Andover, Mass.: Phillips Academy; New Haven, Conn.: Yale University Press.

——. 1919. The Serpent Mound of Adams County, Ohio. *American Anthropologist* 21(2):153–63.

——. 1897. An Analysis of the Decorations Upon Pottery from the Mississippi Valley. *Journal of American Folklore* 10(36):9–20.

Willoughby, Charles C., and Ernest A. Hooten. 1922. *The Turner Group of Earthworks, Hamilton County, Ohio*. Papers of the Peabody Museum, No. 8(3). Cambridge: Harvard University.

Witthoft, John. 1949. *Green Corn Ceremonialism in the Eastern Woodlands*. Occasional Contributions from the Museum of Anthropology, University of Michigan, No. 13.

Wood, John E. 1978. *Sun, Moon, and Standing Stones*. Oxford, UK: Oxford University Press.

Wymer, Dee Anne. 1993. The Ohio Hopewell Econiche: Human-Land Interaction in the Core Area. Paper presented at the Ohio Archaeological Council's Second Annual Conference, Chillicothe, Ohio.

INDEX

ABOUT THE AUTHOR

William F. Romain holds a Master of Arts degree in anthropology from Kent State University. He has published more than two dozen articles on Ohio prehistory. Recently, he was awarded the Archaeological Society of Ohio's Robert Converse Award for outstanding contributions to Ohio archeology. Romain is a member of the Society of Professional Archeologists and MENSA and a fellow of the Explorer's Club. He lives in Olmsted Township, Ohio with his wife, Evie.

ABOUT THE BOOK

Mysteries of the Hopewell: Astronomers, Geometers, and Magicians of the Eastern Woodlands was designed and typeset by Kachergis Book Design of Pittsboro, North Carolina. The typeface, Monotype Dante, was designed by Giovanni Mardersteig who made his typographic reputation with the magnificent books he designed and printed on the hand press at his Officina Bodoni before the Second World War.

Mysteries of the Hopewell: Astronomers, Geometers, and Magicians of the Eastern Woodlands was printed on sixty-pound Glatfelter Supple Opaque Recycled Natural and bound by Thomson-Shore, Inc., of Dexter, Michigan.